INTRODUCTION TO
FLOWCHARTING
AND
COMPUTER PROGRAMMING
LOGIC

ANAHEIM PUBLISHING COMPANY
Specialist in Data Processing Textbooks

INTRODUCTION TO DATA PROCESSING

Introduction to Computers and Data Processing, Shelly & Cashman
Our Computerized Society, Logsdon & Logsdon
Introduction To Flowcharting and Computer Programming Logic, Shelly & Cashman

BASIC

Introduction To BASIC Programming, Shelly & Cashman
Programming In BASIC, Logsdon
Programming In BASIC With Applications, Logsdon

STRUCTURED COBOL

Introduction To Computer Programming Structured COBOL, Shelly & Cashman
Advanced Structured COBOL Program Design and File Processing, Shelly & Cashman

COBOL

Introduction To Computer Programming ANSI COBOL, Shelly & Cashman
ANSI COBOL Workbook, Testing & Debugging Techniques & Exercises, Shelly & Cashman
Advanced ANSI COBOL Disk/Tape Programming Efficiencies, Shelly & Cashman

RPG II

Computer Programming RPG II, Shelly & Cashman

RPG

Introduction To Computer Programming RPG, Shelly & Cashman

SYSTEMS ANALYSIS AND DESIGN

Business Systems Analysis and Design, Shelly & Cashman

ASSEMBLER LANGUAGE

Introduction To Computer Programming IBM System/360 Assembler Language, Shelly & Cashman
IBM System/360 Assembler Language Workbook, Shelly & Cashman
IBM System/360 Assembler Language Disk/Tape Advanced Concepts, Shelly & Cashman

FORTRAN

Introduction To Computer Programming Basic FORTRAN IV-A Practical Approach, Keys

PL/I

Introduction To Computer Programming System/360 PL/I, Shelly & Cashman

JOB CONTROL - OPERATING SYSTEMS

DOS Utilities Sort/Merge Multiprogramming, Shelly & Cashman
OS Job Control Language, Shelly & Cashman
DOS Job Control for Assembler Language Programmers, Shelly & Cashman
DOS Job Control for COBOL Programmers, Shelly & Cashman

FLOWCHARTING

Introduction To Flowcharting and Computer Programming Logic, Shelly & Cashman

INTRODUCTION TO FLOWCHARTING AND COMPUTER PROGRAMMING LOGIC

By:

Gary B. Shelly
Educational Consultant
Instructor, Long Beach City College

&

Thomas J. Cashman, CDP, B.A., M.A.
Long Beach City College
Long Beach, California

ANAHEIM PUBLISHING COMPANY
2632 Saturn, St., Brea, CA 92621
(714) 993-3700

Tenth Printing
June 1981

Printed in the United States of America

ISBN 0 - 88236 - 345 - X

Library of Congress Catalog Card Number: 72 - 95674

© Copyright 1972 Anaheim Publishing Company

10 9 8 7 6 5 4 3

PREFACE

In the past, one of the difficulties in training programming students has been in developing the ability to apply the knowledge of the specific characteristics of a computer language and the coding "mechanics" to the logical solution of a given problem. Typically students have become proficient in the use of the instructions comprising the programming language yet they have not had training in the area where most programming difficulties occur, the logic of programming!

This text is designed to provide instruction in the basic logic and flowcharting of business applications programming. By applying the concepts presented in this text students should be able to efficiently analyze and flowchart the logic of typical business programming problems no matter how complex.

Beginning with an introduction to the computerized processing of a business application and the role of the programmer in designing business application programs, the text continues with the following subject matter: Basic Input/Output, Crossfooting and Final Totals, Comparing, Control Codes in Input Records, Report Headings, Sub-routines and Programmed Switches, Control Breaks, Sequential File Updating, Table Search including both Sequential and Binary Search Techniques, and In-Core Sorting.

Each of these topics is illustrated through the use of an actual business application problem. The input to the computer and the desired output are illustrated so that the student is aware of the exact processing which is to be accomplished. In addition to a detailed analysis of flowcharting logic, the processing within the computer is also illustrated in a step-by-step sequence so that the processing which will occur is easily seen. There is no assumption that the student will be able to visualize what is happening. Each step and the resultant contents of main storage and the output produced is shown in detail. In addition to the logic which is illustrated, the student is introduced to the correct techniques of flowcharting a program—the proper symbols to be used, the methods of illustrating program logic and the use of flowcharting worksheets.

At the conclusion of each chapter, there are two student flowcharting assignments. The first assignment is similar to the problem solved in each chapter and should serve to reinforce the concepts and methods contained in the problems illustrated in the text. The second flowcharting assignment presents a more complex extension of the logic contained in each chapter and should serve as an important learning problem for the student. He will be required to apply the concepts studied to a problem which differs enough to require a very thorough understanding of the logic of programming.

This textbook may be used as the primary textbook in a course in computer programming logic or as a supplementary textbook in data processing or related courses which are designed to develop an understanding and appreciation of computer problem solving methods. Because of the design of the textbook, moving from basic data processing concepts such as input/output operations and systematically to more complex problems such as file updating, the book may be used effectively as a supplementary textbook in programming language courses. Each of the assignments with the input defined and the output illustrated, provide excellent programming assignments. The logic and programming techniques illustrated are programming language independent and apply to any of the machine oriented or high level languages currently available today.

When the student completes the study of the material contained within the text, he will possess a knowledge of the programming logic required to solve the large majority of business applications problems. By completing the student assignments at the conclusion of the chapters, the student will have had the opportunity to apply his knowledge in meaningful and practical applications.

Gary B. Shelly

Thomas J. Cashman

TABLE OF CONTENTS

CHAPTER 1

INTRODUCTION TO PROBLEM SOLVING

INTRODUCTION

The data processing industry has undergone dramatic changes since it first began in the late 1940's. Much of the drama has centered around the changes and improvements in the computer hardware and the related peripheral equipment, such as card readers, magnetic tape units, disk storage devices and other input/output units which are used with the computer.

As computer hardware has gone through an evolutionary period, so too has the art or science of programming. This includes both the jobs done by programmers and the methods available to the programmer for solving problems. Programming may be broken down into two broad categories: systems programming, and applications programming. The systems programmer is concerned with writing programs that make it easier to operate and program computers. Systems programmers turn out control programs that operate input/output equipment, test programs that detect errors and malfunctions within the computer, utility programs, such as sorts, which are available for the applications programmer to use to solve problems.

Applications programming is utilized in two general areas: scientific or engineering applications and business applications. The scientific applications programmer is normally involved in programs requiring a great deal of complex mathematical work. In many cases, scientific applications programmers are also mathematicians or engineers who are using the computer to solve problems with which they are directly concerned.

The business applications programmer writes programs to solve problems relating to the business transactions of a company. Such applications as payroll, billing, and inventory control are the areas of concern to a business applications programmer. Business programming is normally not performed by an accountant or sales manager or production manager. The job of programming most business applications is normally assigned to an individual working in the data processing department. Thus, the "business programmer" writes a wide variety of programs for the various business applications within the company.

Regardless of the type of programming which is to be accomplished, however, there are some common procedures which must be followed whenever a program is to be written. These include problem analysis, flowcharting, coding, testing and debugging, and documentation. Although subject to some flexibility, the diagram below illustrates the approximate time spent by a programmer on each of these areas when programming an application.

EXAMPLE

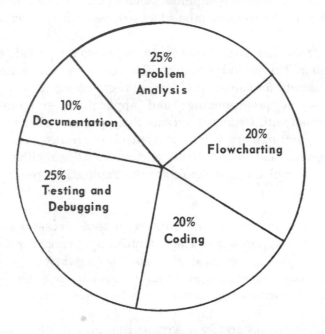

Figure 1-1 Average Time Spent on a Task by an Applications Programmer

Note from the illustration above that, contrary to popular belief, a programmer does not spend all of his time "writing" programs, that is, coding a program in a programming language. A great deal of the programmer's time is spent in analyzing a problem and determining a method of solution. The various job duties of the programmer as described in Figure 1-1 are explained on the following pages.

1. **Problem Analysis** - The normal sequence of a project which is to be implemented on a computer is for a systems analyst to design the overall system, which is composed of one or more programs. The system analyst gathers the information which is necessary to comprise the system from the eventual user of the system, from management, and from past experience which would indicate the type of processing which should be included in the system. He then places this information in a form which may be communicated to the programmer. Typically, the manner of presentation will include record formats, that is, the format of the input and output records which are to be processed by the program, printer spacing charts which are used to illustrate the format of a printed report, and some type of written narrative which will describe in detail the processing which is to take place within the system and within each program included in the system.

For example, the Design phase of a "typical" system could involve the following steps:

a. The Marketing Director in consultation with the Systems Analyst has determined that two reports are required by the management of the company to assist in analyzing current sales. These reports include a sales analysis report listing the items that have been sold each day, and a sales analysis report listing the daily sales by each salesman. These reports are currently being prepared manually and it has been determined that they could be prepared efficiently utilizing the computer at a saving of many hours of clerical effort. Figure 1-2 illustrates the reports.

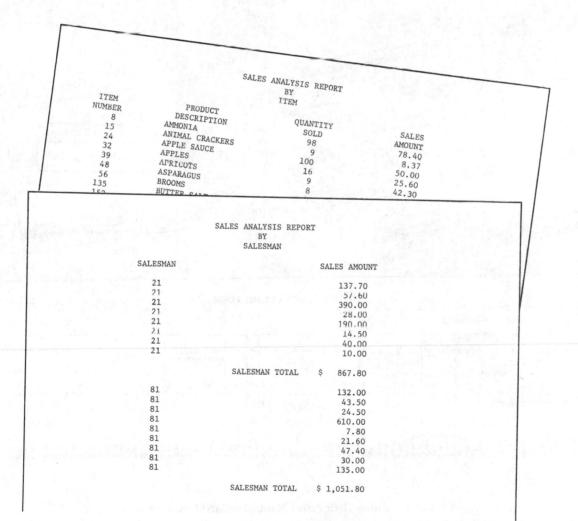

Figure 1-2 Sales Report

b. After determining the reports that are needed, the systems analyst must then review the original sales orders which are used as the basis for preparing the reports. Selected information on these documents must be converted to punched cards for processing by the computer. The Multiple-Card Layout Form provides a convenient method of planning the format of the punched card. The sequence and the size of the fields which are to be punched are normally recorded on a Multiple-Card Layout Form by drawing a vertical line between the card columns separating the various fields on a card, and labeling these fields with the proper headings. The information from this form will provide the basis for the actual design of the punched card. Figure 1-3 illustrates a Sales Order and a Multiple-Card Layout Form. Note the fields which are recorded on the card. There will be one card punched for each of the items listed on the order.

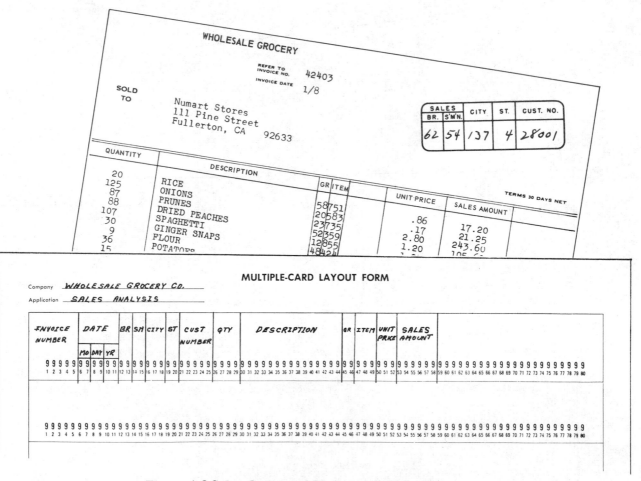

Figure 1-3 Sales Order and Multiple-Card Layout Form

c. After the card has been designed, the format of the reports, as they are to be prepared by the computer, must be designed. A Printer Spacing Chart is commonly used. Figure 1-4 illustrates a Printer Spacing Chart for the Sales Analysis Report listing the items that have been sold.

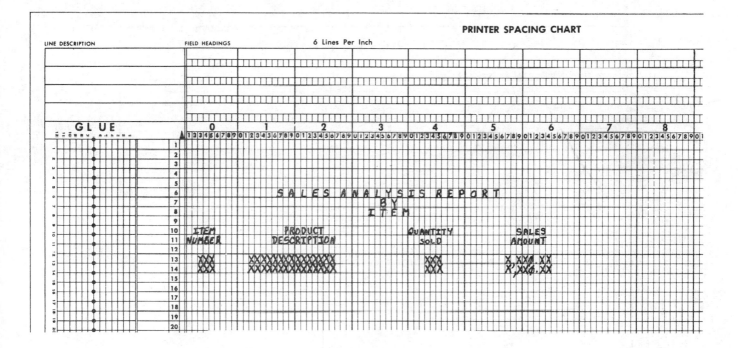

Figure 1-4 Printer Spacing Chart

To lay out a report on the Printer Spacing Chart the programmer selects the print positions for the headings and fields to be printed on the report and makes a notation in the selected positions. The numbers across the top of the spacing chart represent the actual print positions used by the computer printer. The numbers down the left are line numbers. There are six horizontal lines to an inch. Heading or constant information to be printed is written on the printer spacing chart in the same form as it is to be printed on the report. Variable information is represented by placing an "X" in the appropriate position on the spacing chart. It should be noted that the position in a field where zero suppression ends is indicated by a zero rather than an "X" and punctuation is shown as it would appear in edited amounts.

When the programmer writes the program to process the data to produce the report the definition of the input and printed output will normally be in the form of a Multiple-Card Layout Form and a Printer Spacing Chart. Thus, through the use of these forms, the analyst informs the programmer of the formats of the records to be processed by the program.

In addition to the forms which are normally used by the systems analyst, a "system flowchart" is usually included in the specifications presented to the programmer. The System Flowchart indicates the "flow" of data in the system, that is, the sequence of events which is to occur within the system to process the data.

The procedure for preparing the reports in the example system involves converting the information on the Sales Orders into punched cards, sorting the cards by the Item Number field and processing the cards on the computer to prepare the sales analysis report by item. The next step requires that the cards be resorted by Salesman Number and then processing the cards on the computer again to prepare the second report. Figure 1-5 illustrates the System Flowchart. Note that special symbols are utilized to represent specific types of operations.

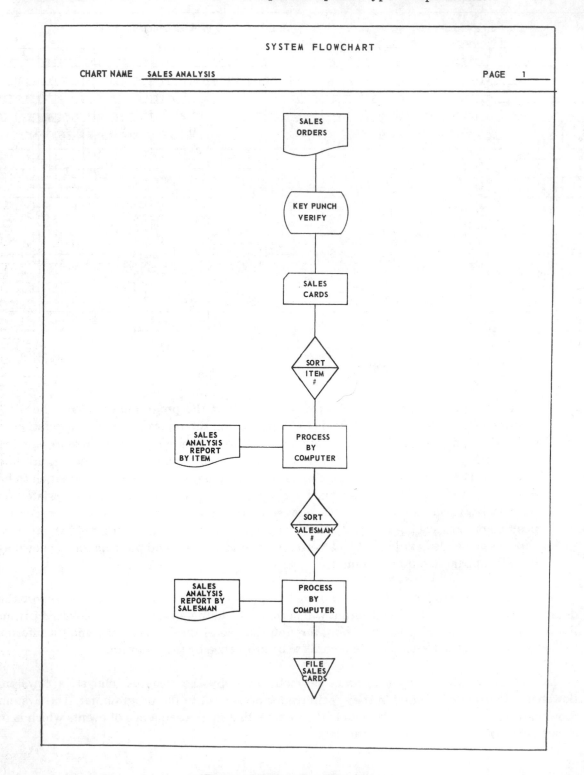

Figure 1-5 Systems Flowchart

In addition to the Multiple-Card Layout Form, the Printer Spacing Chart, and the System Flowchart, the systems analyst will normally provide the programmer with additional written instructions explaining any special processing that is to occur. When the programmer receives this package of specifications from the systems analyst, he must study and understand every aspect of processing which is to occur within the system. For example, the programmer must understand how to handle error cards such as cards containing blanks in the sales amount field; the programmer must know if all item numbers are to be considered valid; the programmer must know the maximum size of all calculations that can develop, etc.

It is absolutely mandatory that the programmer understand all of the processing which is to be performed by the programs which he is to write before attempting to determine the logic and processing which is necessary in order to solve the problem. One of the difficulties encountered in data processing is that the programmer does not understand all of the requirements of a program before beginning the flowchart and coding. Thus, when the program is written, certain aspects of the program are not included. Making corrections to a program and adding routines to process data in a manner not originally planned for is a very time-consuming and difficult task. It has been found that errors in a program are more apt to occur when routines are added and logic is changed after the original program design has been finalized than when all contingencies have been planned for in the original design of the program.

2. **Flowcharting** - When the programmer has determined that he understands all of the processing which is to take place within a program and all questions have been satisfactorily answered, the next step is to determine the logic within the program which is to be used to solve the problem. In most cases, the best way to express this logic is in terms of block diagrams or FLOWCHARTS. A Flowchart is a diagram using pre-defined symbols which represent the logic required to solve a defined problem. Figure 1-6 is an example of a flowchart which could be used to illustrate the logic necessary to read the Sales Order cards and create the Sales Analysis Report listing the items which have been sold.

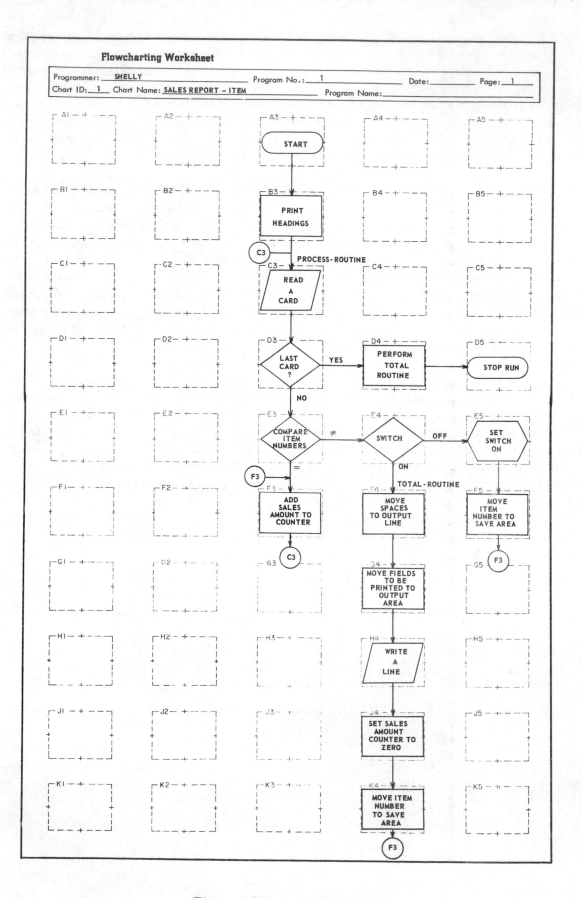

Figure 1-6 Program Flowchart

In the example in Figure 1-6 it can be seen that the flowchart, using specific symbols for each operation, illustrates the detailed logic which must be incorporated into the program to properly process the data. The use of the flowcharting symbols and the logic required to solve many business applications will be illustrated and explained in subsequent chapters.

3. **Coding** - After the logic which is to be incorporated into a program has been symbolically illustrated using a flowchart, the steps in the flowchart are converted into a computer program by the programmer. Commonly used programming languages include COBOL, Assembler Language, RPG, PL/I, and FORTRAN. The following is an illustration of a segment of a COBOL program to prepare the Sales Analysis Report listing the items sold.

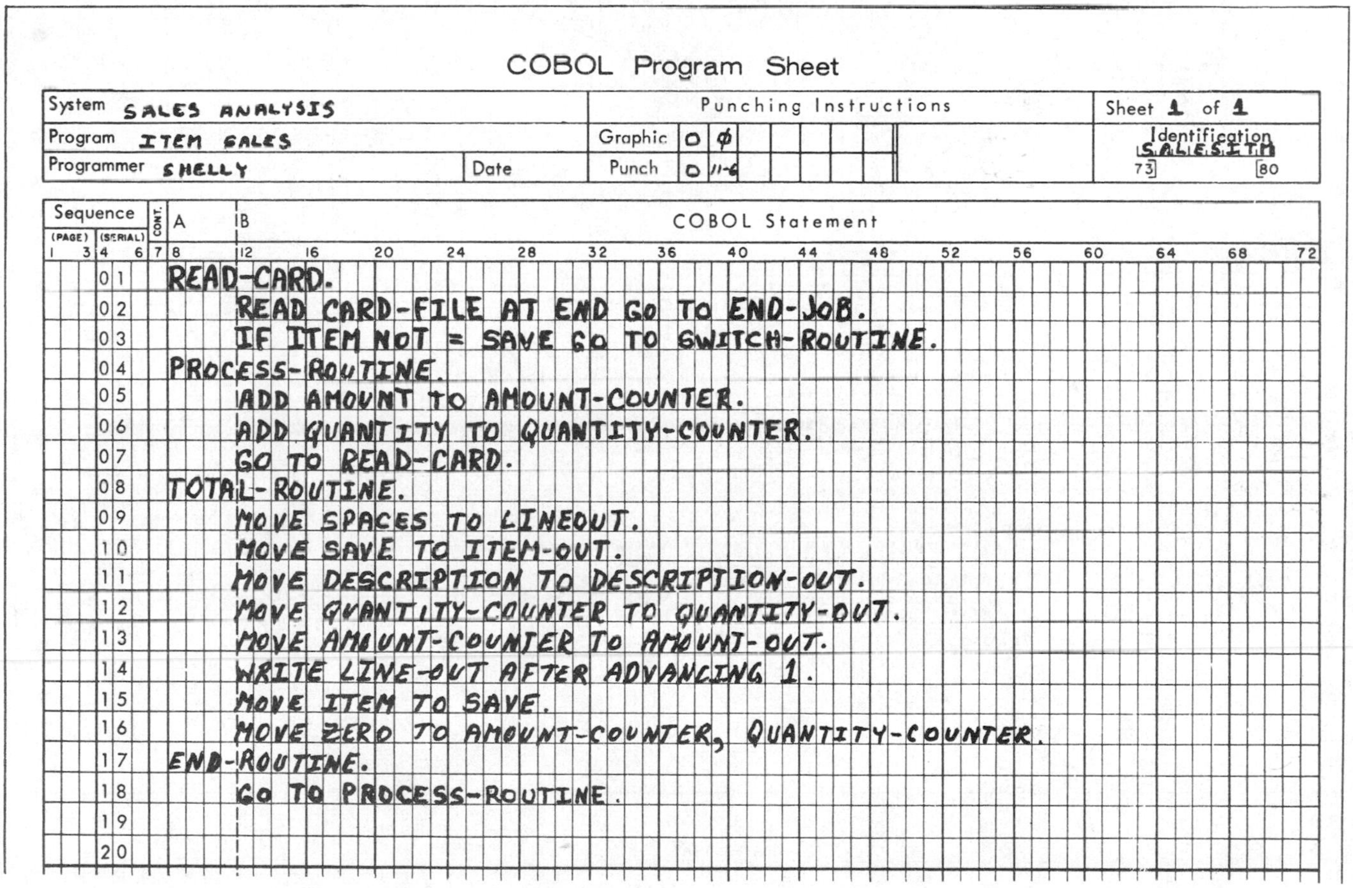

```
COBOL Program Sheet

System  SALES ANALYSIS          Punching Instructions        Sheet 1 of 1
Program ITEM SALES        Graphic  O  Ø                      Identification
Programmer SHELLY    Date  Punch   O  11-6                    SALES.ITM
                                                              73        80

Sequence
(PAGE)(SERIAL)  A   B          COBOL Statement
01   READ-CARD.
02       READ CARD-FILE AT END GO TO END-JOB.
03       IF ITEM NOT = SAVE GO TO SWITCH-ROUTINE.
04   PROCESS-ROUTINE.
05       ADD AMOUNT TO AMOUNT-COUNTER.
06       ADD QUANTITY TO QUANTITY-COUNTER.
07       GO TO READ-CARD.
08   TOTAL-ROUTINE.
09       MOVE SPACES TO LINEOUT.
10       MOVE SAVE TO ITEM-OUT.
11       MOVE DESCRIPTION TO DESCRIPTION-OUT.
12       MOVE QUANTITY-COUNTER TO QUANTITY-OUT.
13       MOVE AMOUNT-COUNTER TO AMOUNT-OUT.
14       WRITE LINE-OUT AFTER ADVANCING 1.
15       MOVE ITEM TO SAVE.
16       MOVE ZERO TO AMOUNT-COUNTER, QUANTITY-COUNTER.
17   END-ROUTINE.
18       GO TO PROCESS-ROUTINE.
19
20
```

Figure 1-7 COBOL

COBOL (COmmon Business Oriented Language) is the programming language on a well-defined form of English and is especially suited for commercial or business applications.

4. **Testing And Debugging** - After a source program has been written, it is normally keypunched into cards so that it may be processed on the computer. After it is keypunched, the program must be assembled or compiled. This process is accomplished on the computer by a program, called a "Compiler," which translates the source statements into machine-language instructions which can then be executed on the computer. When this compilation process is performed, errors are many times found in the coding due to improperly used statements or keypunching errors. These errors must be corrected by the programmer until the program is compiled or assembled with no errors in the source coding. The following illustrates a segment of the COBOL program and related diagnostics.

```
LINE NO. SEQ. NO.          SOURCE STATEMENT

     93          READ-CARD.
     94              READ CARD-FILE AT END GO TO ENDJOB.
     95              IF ITEM NOT = SAVE GO TO SWITCH-ROUTINE.
     96          PROCESS-ROUTINE.
     97              ADD AMOUNT TO AMOUNT-COUNTR.
     98              ADD QUANTITY TO QUANTITY-COUNTER.
     99              GO TO READ-CRD.
    100          TOTAL-ROUTINE.
    101              MOVE SPACES TO LINE-OUT.
    102              MOVE SAVE TO ITEM-OUT.
    103              MOVE DESCRIPTION TO DESCRIPTION-OUT.
    104              MOVE QUANTITY-COUNTER TO QUANTITY-OUT.
    105              MOVE AMOUNT-COUNTER TO AMOUNT-OUT.
    106              WRITE LINE-OUT AFTER ADVANCING 1.
    107              MOVE ITEM TO SAVE.
    108              MOVE ZERO TO AMOUNT-COUNTER, QUANTITY-COUNTER.
    109          END-TOTAL-ROUTINE.
    110              GO TO PROCESS-ROUTINE.
    111          SWITCH-ROUTINE.
    112              IF SWITCH = 'OFF' GO TO SWITCH-ON
    113                  OTHERWISE GO TO TOTAL-ROUTINE.
    114          SWITCH-ON.
    115              MOVE 'ON' TO SWITCH.
    116              MOVE ITEM TO SAVE.
    117              GO TO PROCESS-ROUTINE.
    118          HEADING-ROUTINE.
    119              WRITE LINE-OUT FROM HEAD1 AFTER ADVANCING 0.
    120              WRITE LINE-OUT FROM HEAD2 AFTER ADVANCING 1.
    121              WRITE LINE-OUT FROM HEAD3 AFTER ADVANCING 1.
    122              WRITE LINE-OUT FROM HEAD4 AFTER ADVANCING 2.
    123              WRITE LINE-OUT FROM HEAD5 AFTER ADVANCING 1.
    124          END-JOB.
    125              PERFORM TOTAL-ROUTINE.
    126              CLOSE PRINT-FILE, CARD-FILE
    127              STOP RUN
```

```
                              DIAGNOSTICS

LINE/POS ER CODE   CLAUSE                                    MESSAGE
   94- 5  IJS606I E              PROCEDURE-NAME 'ENDJOB' NOT DEFINED.
   97- 4  IJS401I C ADD          SYNTAX REQUIRES A DATA-NAME. FOUND 'AMOUNT-COUNTR'.
   99- 1  IJS606I E              PROCEDURE-NAME 'READ-CRD' NOT DEFINED.
```

Figure 1-8 COBOL Program with Diagnostics

After a program has been successfully assembled or compiled, it must be tested in order to determine that the logic of the program is correct and the data is being processed properly. Testing a program involves several important steps which must be followed in order to ensure that a program is debugged completely and that it will operate successfully. These steps are explained below.

a. Desk Checking - After a program has been compiled, it should be "desk-checked" prior to being executed on the computer. Desk-checking refers to the process of the programmer "playing computer," that is, examining each source statement within the program as if the computer were processing the statements. By doing this, the programmer can find errors both in the use of statements and in the logic which will be performed by the program. Desk-checking is a very important part of debugging a program because errors can be found which would otherwise not be found until the program were actually processed on the computer.

b. Preparing Test Data - When a program is to be tested, it should be tested with data which was specifically prepared to test the various routines within the program. It should not be tested with data which will be processed by the program after it has been put into production, that is, after it has been debugged and is ready to be run using actual "live" data. The reasons for this is that a small sampling of "live" data, no matter how it is chosen, is not likely to contain all of the situations which may occur in the program. Thus, some routines and some logic paths which are in the program will never be adequately tested. It is these routines which are probably going to fail when the program is in production. Instead, the programmer should design data which can be used to test all aspects of the program so that all routines and processing decisions are tested. The preparation of test data is a difficult and arduous task but a program cannot be adequately tested unless good test data is used.

c. Program Debugging - After the program has been desk-checked and good test data has been prepared, the program may be tested on the computer. The number of test runs which will be required to completely debug a program is normally dependent upon the size and complexity of the program. Regardless of the size and complexity of the program, however, it is important that the program be completely debugged prior to being used in actual production runs. Too often it has been found that programs have not been entirely debugged prior to processing actual data and this leads to many problems both within the data processing department and with the users of the program. Testing a program is a difficult task and only when great care is used in testing will a properly debugged program result. Figure 1-9 illustrates a segment of a COBOL program with the output produced.

```
LINE NO. SEQ. NO.              SOURCE STATEMENT

        93              READ-CARD.
        94                  READ CARD-FILE AT END GO TO END-JOB.
        95                  IF ITEM NOT = SAVE GO TO SWITCH-ROUTINE.
        96              PROCESS-ROUTINE.
        97                  ADD AMOUNT TO AMOUNT-COUNTER.
        98                  ADD QUANTITY TO QUANTITY-COUNTER.
        99                  GO TO READ-CARD.
       100              TOTAL-ROUTINE.
       101                  MOVE SPACES TO LINE-OUT.
       102                  MOVE SAVE TO ITEM-OUT.
       103                  MOVE DESCRIPTION TO DESCRIPTION-OUT.
       104                  MOVE QUANTITY-COUNTER TO QUANTITY-OUT.
       105                  MOVE AMOUNT-COUNTER TO AMOUNT-OUT.
       106                  WRITE LINE-OUT AFTER ADVANCING 1.
       107                  MOVE ITEM TO SAVE.
       108                  MOVE ZERO TO AMOUNT-COUNTER, QUANTITY-COUNTER.
       109              END-TOTAL-ROUTINE.
       110                  GO TO PROCESS-ROUTINE.
       111              SWITCH-ROUTINE.
       112                  IF SWITCH = 'OFF' GO TO SWITCH-ON
       113                      OTHERWISE GO TO TOTAL-ROUTINE.
       114              SWITCH-ON.
       115                  MOVE 'ON' TO SWITCH.
       116                  MOVE ITEM TO SAVE.
       117                  GO TO PROCESS-ROUTINE.
       118              HEADING-ROUTINE.
       119                  WRITE LINE-OUT FROM HEAD1 AFTER ADVANCING 0.
       120                  WRITE LINE-OUT FROM HEAD2 AFTER ADVANCING 1.
       121                  WRITE LINE-OUT FROM HEAD3 AFTER ADVANCING 1.
       122                  WRITE LINE-OUT FROM HEAD4 AFTER ADVANCING 2.
       123                  WRITE LINE-OUT FROM HEAD5 AFTER ADVANCING 1.
       124              END-JOB.
       125                  PERFORM TOTAL-ROUTINE.
       126                  CLOSE PRINT-FILE, CARD-FILE
       127                  STOP RUN
```

```
                    S A L E S   A N A L Y S I S   R E P O R T
                                      B Y
                                   I T E M

     ITEM            PRODUCT              QUANTITY           SALES
    NUMBER         DESCRIPTION              SOLD            AMOUNT
       8         AMMONIA                      98             78.40
      15         ANIMAL CRACKERS               9              8.37
      24         APPLE SAUCE                 100             50.00
      32         APPLES                       16             25.60
      39         APRICOTS                      9             42.30
      48         ASPARAGUS                     8             29.60
      56         BROOMS                       60            336.00
     135         BUTTER SALT                  47            145.70
     152         CELERY                      360             64.80
     161         CEYLON TEA                   70             77.00
     169         CHICKEN SOUP                 10             48.00
     192         CHOW CHOW                    60            226.80
     207         CIDER                        29              9.86
     216         CLAM BROTH                  290            406.00
     233         COCOA                        60              3.00
     257         COFFEE                      486            403.38
     263         CONDENSED MILK              470          1,353.60
     272         CORN                        150            390.00
     289         CRACKERS                     50            120.00
     312         DRIED PEACHES                20             62.00
     359         FLOUR                       183            150.06
     383         GELATINE                     26            210.60
     408         GINGER SNAPS                 30             43.50
     424         HORSE RADISH                 37            129.50
     456         LEMON SODA                   90             37.80
```

Figure 1-9 COBOL Program with Output

5. **Documentation** - Documentation is the process of recording the facts concerning a computer program. Included in the documentation will normally be a program flowchart, a program narrative describing the routines and programming techniques used in the program, the source listing, the formats of the data which is processed by the program, and a sample running of the program including control cards which must be used and any reports which are produced by the program.

The documentation of a program is an often neglected job of the applications programmer. This neglect may be caused by data processing management, which desires the programmer to begin writing new programs, or by the programmer himself, who does not enjoy the rather mundane task of preparing narratives of his program and drawing file layouts, etc. It has been found, however, that proper documentation of a program is absolutely vital to the smooth functioning of a data processing department. In many applications, changes must be made to a program once it has been put into production and many times, the programmer making the changes is not the same person who originally wrote the program. Thus, if the "maintenance programmer," that is, the programmer who is making the changes, does not have sufficient documentation to indicate the processing which is occuring in the program and the methods used in the program, it becomes quite difficult to make changes which will work properly. It is, therefore, incumbent upon the programmer who originally writes a program to supply enough documentation to ensure that any programmer assigned to make changes to the program can do so with a minimum of time spent on the job of determining how the program processes the data.

ADDITIONAL PROGRAMMING LANGUAGES

There are a variety of programming languages that may be utilized effectively by the business applications programmer. The selection and use of one or more of these languages is normally the decision of the data processing manager and based upon considerations such as the type and size of computer available, the types and complexity of the applications to be programmed, and the knowledge and skills of the available personnel. The following pages illustrate programs to prepare a sales commission report in some of the commonly used programming languages.

a. Assembler Language - Assembler is a "machine-oriented" language which is applicable to any programming problem. Coding is done with Symbolic instructions which are translated into machine-language instructions. Assembler language closely resembles the actual machine language and the instruction set which is available on any given computer. The example in Figure 1-10 is an Assembler Language program written for the System/360 computer.

EXAMPLE

```
   LOC  OBJECT CODE     ADDR1 ADDR2  STMT   SOURCE STATEMENT

                                      1           PRINT  NOGEN
   000000                             2 PGM4      START  0
                                      3 SALESFL   DTFCD  DEVICE=2501,                         C
                                                         DEVADDR=SYSIPT,                      C
                                                         TYPEFLE=INPUT,                       C
                                                         IOAREA1=SALESCRD,                    C
                                                         EOFADDR=END
                                     24 PRINT4    DTFPR  DEVICE=1403,                         C
                                                         DEVADDR=SYSLST,                      C
                                                         IOAREA1=LINEOUT,                     C
                                                         BLKSIZE=132
   000068 0530                       45 START     BALR   3,0              BASE REGISTER = 3
   00006A                            46           USING  *,3
                                     47           OPEN   SALESFL,PRINT4   OPEN FILES
                                     56 PROCESS   GET    SALESFL          READ A CARD
   00008A 9240 3102      0016C       61           MVI    LINEOUT,X'40'
   00008E D282 3103 3102 0016D 0016C 62           MVC    LINEOUT+1(131),LINEOUT   CLEAR OUTPUT LINE
   000094 D203 3102 30BB 0016C 00125 63           MVC    SALESOUT(4),SALESNUM     MOVE SALES NUMBER TO OUTPUT LINE
   00009A D218 310B 30BF 00175 00129 64           MVC    NAMEOUT(25),NAME         MOVE NAME TO OUTPUT LINE
   0000A0 D205 3129 30DF 00193 00149 65           MVC    CUROUT(6),CURRENT        MOVE CURRENT-SALES TO OUTPUT
   0000A6 F245 3186 30DF 001F0 00149 66           PACK   PCURRENT(5),CURRENT(6)   PACK CURRENT SALES
   0000AC D209 3129 3193 00193 001FD 67           MVC    CUROUT(10),CURPATRN      MOVE EDIT PATTERN
   0000B2 DE09 3129 3187 00193 001F1 68           ED     CUROUT(10),PCURRENT+1    EDIT CURRENT SALES
   0000B8 925B 312A      00194       69           MVI    CUROUT+1,X'5B'           MOVE $ TO CURRENT SALES
   0000BC D505 30DF 318B 00149 001F5 70           CLC    CURRENT(6),QUOTA         COMPARE TO 1,000.00
   0000C2 4740 308A      000F4       71           BL     TWOPER                   BRANCH IF LESS THAN 1000
   0000C6 FC40 3186 3191 001F0 001FB 72           MP     PCURRENT(5),FIVE         MULTIPLY CURRENT SALES BY 5%
   0000CC 92F5 3138      001A2       73           MVI    PERCENT,C'5'             MAKE PERCENT 5
   0000D0 926C 3139      001A3       74           MVI    PERCENT+1,C'%'
   0000D4 D206 313E 319D 001A8 00207 75 PRINT     MVC    COMMIS(7),COMPAT         MOVE EDIT PATTERN
   0000DA DE06 313E 3187 001A8 001F1 76           ED     COMMIS(7),PCURRENT+1     EDIT COMMISSION
   0000E0 925B 313E      001A8       77           MVI    COMMIS,X'5B'             MOVE $ TO COMMISSION
                                     78           PUT    PRINT4
   0000F0 47F0 3014      0007E       83           B      PROCESS                  BRANCH TO PROCESS
   0000F4 FC40 3186 3192 001F0 001FC 84 TWOPER    MP     PCURRENT(5),TWO          MULTIPLY CURRENT SALES BY 2%
   0000FA 92F2 3138      001A2       85           MVI    PERCENT,C'2'             MAKE PERCENT 2
   0000FE 926C 3139      001A3       86           MVI    PERCENT+1,C'%'
   000102 47F0 306A      000D4       87           B      PRINT                    CONTINUE WITH MAIN STREAM
                                     88 END       CLOSE  SALESFL,PRINT4
                                     97           EOJ
   00011C                          100 SALESCRD  DS     OCL80
   00011C                          101           DS     CL9                       BLANK
   000125                          102 SALESNUM  DS     CL4                       SALESMAN NUMBER INPUT AREA
   000129                          103 NAME      DS     CL25                      NAME INPUT AREA
   000142                          104           DS     CL7                       BLANK
   000149                          105 CURRENT   DS     CL6                       CURRENT SALES INPUT AREA
   00014F                          106           DS     CL29                      BLANK
   00016C                          107 LINEOUT   DS     OCL132                    OUTPUT LINE
   00016C                          108 SALESOUT  DS     CL4                       SALES NUMBER AREA
   000170                          109           DS     CL5                       BLANK
   000175                          110 NAMEOUT   DS     CL25                      NAME OUTPUT AREA
   00018E                          111           DS     CL5                       BLANK
   000193                          112 CUROUT    DS     CL10                      CURRENT SALES OUTPUT AREA
   00019D                          113           DS     CL5                       BLANK
   0001A2                          114 PERCENT   DS     CL1                       PERCENT OUTPUT AREA
   0001A3                          115           DS     CL5                       BLANK
   0001A8                          116 COMMIS    DS     CL7                       COMMISSION OUTPUT AREA
   0001AF                          117           DS     CL65                      BLANK
   0001F0                          118 PCURRENT  DS     CL5
   0001F5 F1F0F0F0F0F0              119 QUOTA     DC     CL6'100000'
   0001FB 5C                       120 FIVE      DC     PL1'5'
   0001FC 2C                       121 TWO       DC     PL1'2'
   0001FD 4020206B2020214B         122 CURPATRN  DC     XL10'4020206B2020214B2020'  EDIT PATTERN FOR CURRENT
   000207 4020202148 2020          123 COMPAT    DC     XL7'402020214B2020'         EDIT PATTERN
   000068                          124           END    START
```

Figure 1-10 Example of System/360 Assembler Language Program

b. PL/I - PL/I provides the programmer with a unified problem-oriented language for efficiently programming either scientific or commercial problems, as well as problems that can best be solved with a combination of scientific and commercial computing techniques. The example in Figure 1-11 is a source listing of a PL/I program.

EXAMPLE

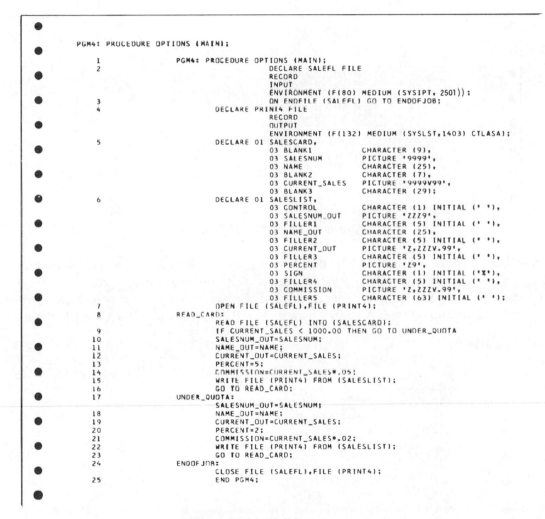

```
      PGM4: PROCEDURE OPTIONS (MAIN);

      1           PGM4: PROCEDURE OPTIONS (MAIN);
      2                  DECLARE SALEFL FILE
                         RECORD
                         INPUT
                         ENVIRONMENT (F(80) MEDIUM (SYSIPT, 2501));
      3                  ON ENDFILE (SALEFL) GO TO ENDOFJOB;
      4           DECLARE PRINT4 FILE
                         RECORD
                         OUTPUT
                         ENVIRONMENT (F(132) MEDIUM (SYSLST,1403) CTLASA);
      5           DECLARE 01 SALESCARD,
                     03 BLANK1         CHARACTER (9),
                     03 SALESNUM       PICTURE '9999',
                     03 NAME           CHARACTER (25),
                     03 BLANK2         CHARACTER (7),
                     03 CURRENT_SALES  PICTURE '9999V99',
                     03 BLANK3         CHARACTER (29);
      6           DECLARE 01 SALESLIST,
                     03 CONTROL        CHARACTER (1) INITIAL (' '),
                     03 SALESNUM_OUT   PICTURE 'ZZZ9',
                     03 FILLER1        CHARACTER (5) INITIAL (' '),
                     03 NAME_OUT       CHARACTER (25),
                     03 FILLER2        CHARACTER (5) INITIAL (' '),
                     03 CURRENT_OUT    PICTURE 'Z,ZZZV.99',
                     03 FILLER3        CHARACTER (5) INITIAL (' '),
                     03 PERCENT        PICTURE 'Z9',
                     03 SIGN           CHARACTER (1) INITIAL ('%'),
                     03 FILLER4        CHARACTER (5) INITIAL (' '),
                     03 COMMISSION     PICTURE 'Z,ZZZV.99',
                     03 FILLER5        CHARACTER (63) INITIAL (' ');
      7                  OPEN FILE (SALEFL),FILE (PRINT4);
      8    READ_CARD:
                         READ FILE (SALEFL) INTO (SALESCARD);
      9                  IF CURRENT_SALES < 1000.00 THEN GO TO UNDER_QUOTA
     10                  SALESNUM_OUT=SALESNUM;
     11                  NAME_OUT=NAME;
     12                  CURRENT_OUT=CURRENT_SALES;
     13                  PERCENT=5;
     14                  COMMISSION=CURRENT_SALES*.05;
     15                  WRITE FILE (PRINT4) FROM (SALESLIST);
     16                  GO TO READ_CARD;
     17    UNDER_QUOTA:
                         SALESNUM_OUT=SALESNUM;
     18                  NAME_OUT=NAME;
     19                  CURRENT_OUT=CURRENT_SALES;
     20                  PERCENT=2;
     21                  COMMISSION=CURRENT_SALES*.02;
     22                  WRITE FILE (PRINT4) FROM (SALESLIST);
     23                  GO TO READ_CARD;
     24    ENDOFJOB:
                         CLOSE FILE (SALEFL),FILE (PRINT4);
     25                  END PGM4;
```

Figure 1-11 PL/I Program

c. FORTRAN - FORTRAN (FORmula TRANslation) is used for both business and scientific applications which are mathematical in nature. The source programs are translated by a FORTRAN compiler into machine-language code. FORTRAN provides many of the routines, such as a square root routine, which are useful in solving mathematical problems. The following is an example of a FORTRAN source program.

EXAMPLE

```
                    DISK OPERATING SYSTEM/360 FORTRAN

      DIMENSION NAME(25)
      DOUBLE PRECISION COMMIS
    1 FORMAT (9X,I4,25A1,7X,F6.2)
    2 FORMAT (1X,I4,5X,25A1,5X,F8.2,5X,'5%',5X,F8.2)
    3 FORMAT (1X,I4,5X,25A1,5X,F8.2,5X,'2%',5X,F8.2)
    4 READ (1,1) KSALMN,NAME,CURREN
      IF (KSALMN - 9999)5,8,8
    5 IF (CURREN - 1000.00)6,7,7
    6 COMMIS = CURREN * .02
      WRITE (3,3) KSALMN,NAME,CURREN,COMMIS
      GO TO 4
    7 COMMIS = CURREN * .05
      WRITE (3,2) KSALMN,NAME,CURREN,COMMIS
      GO TO 4
    8 STOP
      END
```

Figure 1-12 FORTRAN Program

d. RPG - RPG is a high-level language designed specifically for report writing and file maintenance applications. The language facilitates producing programs for a wide variety of reports ranging from a simple listing to a complete report that incorporates calculation and editing. A source listing of an RPG program is illustrated in Figure 1-13.

EXAMPLE

```
001        FSALESFL IP  F  80  80              READO1 SYSIPT
002        FPRINT4  O   F 132 132              PRINTERSYSLST
003        ISALESFL AA  01  01 03
004        I                                         10   130SALESN
005        I                                         14   38 NAME
006        I                                         46   512CURREN
007        C   01      CURREN    COMP 1000.00              020302
008        C   02      CURREN    MULT .05      COMMIS  62
009        C   03      CURREN    MULT .02      COMMIS  62
010        OPRINT4  O  1      01
011        O                            SALESN2  4
012        O                            NAME    34
013        O                            CURREN  47 ' ,  0. '
014        O                  02                 55 '5%'
015        O                  03                 55 '2%'
016        O                            COMMIS  69 ' ,  0. '
```

Figure 1-13 RPG Program

As can be seen from the previous examples, the languages which are available to a programmer allow programs to be written in a variety of ways and each language has advantages and disadvantages for particular applications. The logic which is used with each programming language, however, is basically always the same. When logic is developed to solve a problem, the logic can normally be expressed in any of the programming languages with equally good results. It should be noted, however, that the amount of detail shown within a flowchart may many times depend upon the language used. In an RPG program, for example, the programmer need not be concerned with the problem of placing data in a proper format to operate upon in an arithmetic operation. In Assembler Language, on the other hand, it is imperative that the programmer be aware of the format of the data and the instructions which are used to place the data in the required format. The logic which is illustrated in the flowcharts within this text will, for the most part, not be concerned with the peculiarities of each programming language; instead, they will concentrate on the logic which is required to solve the given problem in any programming language.

SUMMARY

As was noted previously, the job of a programmer is much more diversified than just coding a program in a programming language. The jobs of testing a program and preparing documentation require a significant portion of the programmer's time and effort. As can be seen from the diagram in Figure 1-1, however, the largest portion of a programmer's time is spent in the problem analysis and flowcharting phases of programming. Without a degree of proficiency in these areas, the programmer has little chance of producing effective applications programs. It is, therefore, in the area of problem analysis and flowcharting to which the remaining chapters in this text will be addressed.

CHAPTER 2

BASIC INPUT/OUTPUT

INTRODUCTION

Most data processing applications involve the basic operation of reading some type of data from an input device such as a card reader or a magnetic tape drive, processing the data in main storage, and writing some type of output on an output device such as a printer or a disk drive. The type of processing which occurs on the data which is read is, of course, dependent upon the requirements of the program and may consist of simple operations or very complex operations. The basic operation of read, process, and write, however, remains the same. Thus, before considering the logic which is required for processing data within main storage, it is first necessary to understand the basic input-output process.

In order to illustrate basic input/output operations, a flowchart will be developed for a program which is to read a file of data cards and create a printed report. The cards contain a Name field, an Address field, and a City/State field. The format of the cards are illustrated below.

CARD INPUT

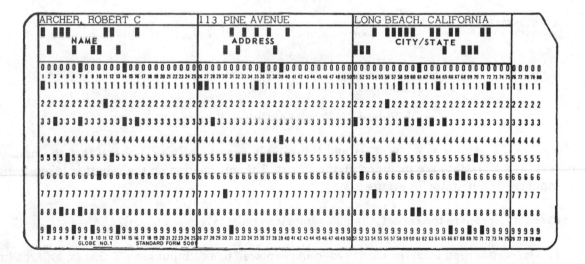

Figure 2-1 Name and Address Card Layout

Note from the diagram above that the Name field in the input card is in card columns 1-25, the Address field is in card columns 26-50, and the City/State field is in card columns 51-75. This card is to be read by the program in order to create a Name and Address Listing.

19

The output from the program is to be the Name and Address Listing which is illustrated below.

OUTPUT REPORT

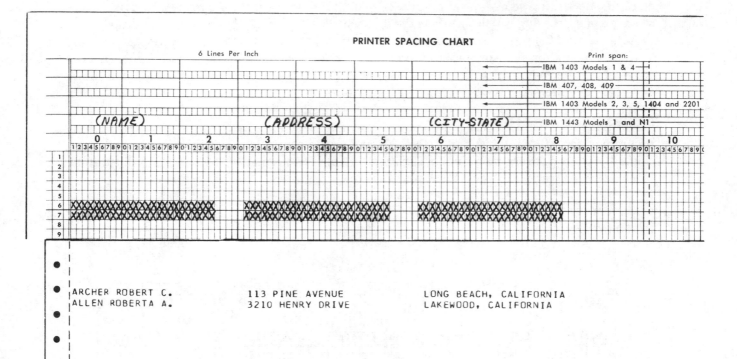

Figure 2-2 Format of Output Report

Note in the printer spacing chart and the sample report illustrated above that the name, address, and city/state are included on the report. The information on the report is taken from the input cards illustrated in Figure 2-1.

In order to prepare the report, the following steps must take place:

1. The card is read from the card reader and is placed in an "input area," that is, an area in main storage which is reserved to store a card after it has been read.

2. The data which is read from the card and stored in the input area is moved to an "output area," that is, an area in main storage which is reserved to store the data which is to be printed on the printer.

INPUT: OUTPUT

N$,A1,A2   N$,A1,A2

  VARIBLE LIST:
    N$ — NAME
    A1 = ST. ADDRESS
    A2 = CITY/STATE

These basic steps which are required to create the Name and Address Listing are illustrated below.

Step 1:   **A card containing a Name, Address, City/State is read into an Input Area in Core Storage.**

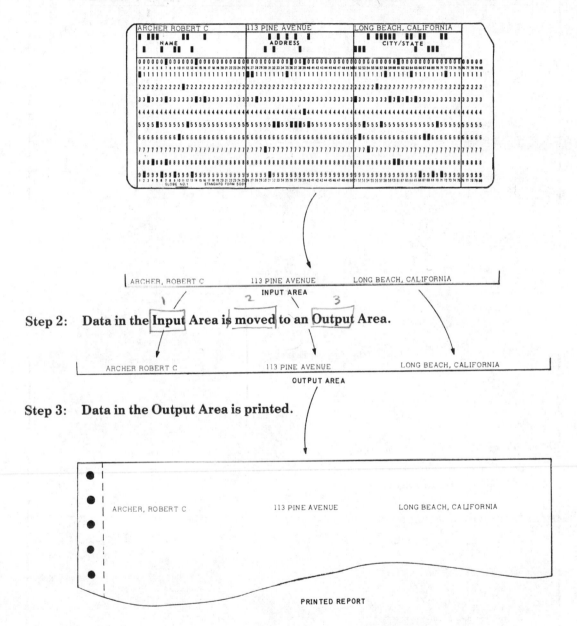

Step 2:   **Data in the Input Area is moved to an Output Area.**

Step 3:   **Data in the Output Area is printed.**

Figure 2-3 Steps in Preparing Report

It can be seen in Figure 2-3 that the data in the card is read into an input area in main storage. The data in the input area is then moved to an output area which is an area reserved for the data which is to be printed on the report. The report is then written.

The programmer normally develops a flowchart to assist in defining the steps which must occur in the solution of a problem. The flowchart for the program to create the Name and Address Report is contained in Figure 2-4.

Program Flowchart

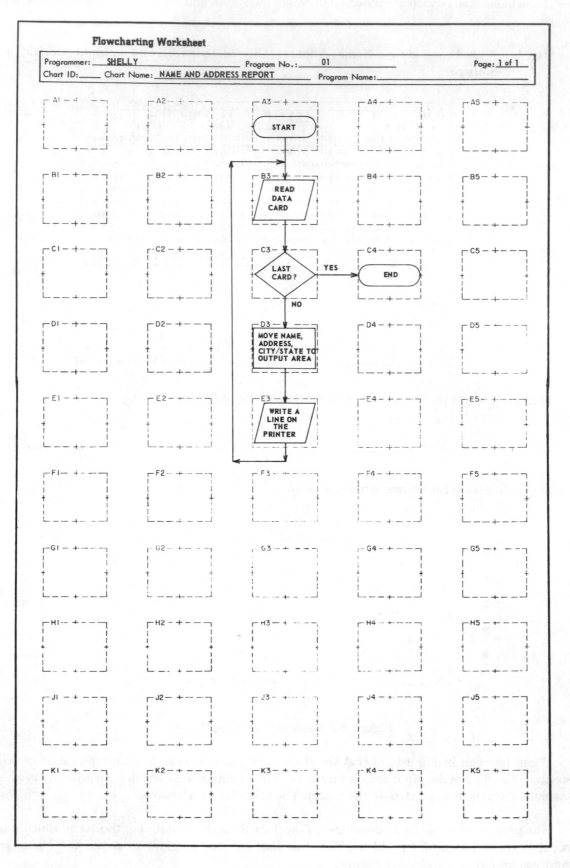

Figure 2-4 Flowchart

In the example in Figure 2-4, it can be seen that a "Flowchart Worksheet" which is specifically designed for flowcharting is used. At the top of the worksheet, space is provided for the flowchart identification. Enough information should be recorded in this space to identify the flowchart and the program to which the flowchart applies. Note in the example that the programmer name, the chart name, and the page number are included.

The body of the flowcharting worksheet contains numbered blocks. These blocks are numbered for ease of reference when flowcharts are drawn on separate areas of the flowchart worksheet. Each of the blocks may contain one flowcharting symbol. This leads to standardized spacing and ease of reading of the flowchart. The shape of each of the symbols has a special meaning. In the sample problem the following symbols are used.

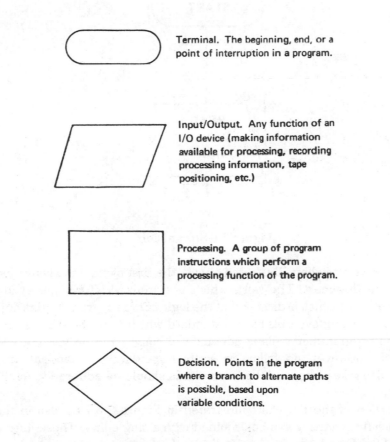

Figure 2-5 Flowchart Symbols

The symbols are drawn using a special "template" which is designed to be used specifically for program flowcharting. This plastic template contains all of the flowcharting symbols which are normally used.

ANALYZING THE FLOWCHART

The flowchart in Figure 2-4 expresses the logical steps which would be used to prepare the Name and Address Listing. Each of these steps is explained in detail below and on the following pages.

Step 1:   The beginning of the flowchart is identified

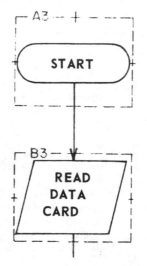

Figure 2-6 Start of Job

In the portion of the flowchart illustrated above, the first symbol is always used to indicate the beginning of the flowchart. The word which is contained within the symbol, start, is a programmer chosen word which indicates that the logic of the program begins at that point. The wording within flowcharting symbols has no standard which must be followed and may be any wording which the programmer feels is adequate to convey the processing which is to take place. The symbols, however, do follow prescribed standards, dependent upon the type of processing which is to take place, and these standards should be adhered to in all flowcharting.

Note in the portion of the flowchart illustrated in Figure 2-6 and also in the flowchart in Figure 2-4 that each flowcharting symbol is joined with a single line. These lines on a flowchart are called FLOWLINES and are used to indicate the sequence of required operations. The "normal" direction of flow within a flowchart is always from top-to-bottom and from left-to-right. When the flow within a flowchart follows the "normal" direction of flow, arrowheads such as illustrated in the example may or my not be used. They may be used at the discretion of the programmer. The examples in this test will all use arrowheads when the normal direction of flow is used.

Whenever the flow runs from bottom-to-top or from right-to-left, arrowheads must always be used. It should be noted that the flowcharting standards dictate that the arrowheads are to be "open" (↓), not "closed" (↓).

Step 3:   A test is made to determine if the last card has been read.

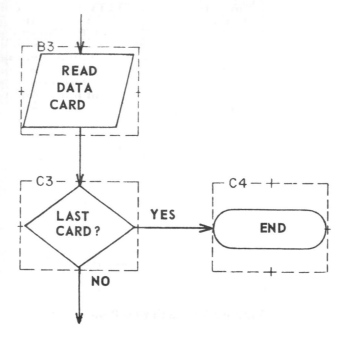

Figure 2-8 Last Card Test

Whenever an input file is read by a program, eventually all of the cards will have been processed. After the last card or record in a file has been read and processed, the program should not attempt to read additional records; therefore, a test must be made in the program to determine if all of the data cards have been read by the program. When all of the cards have been read and processed, the program must perform "end of file" processing. In the sample program when the "last card" is detected processing is terminated.

The method of testing for the last card varies depending upon the programming language used and the type of computer on which the program is processed. In some programming languages, such as COBOL, the end-of-file routine is automatically entered when a special control card is read. In other languages, it may be necessary to test for some value contained in a "trailer" card in order to determine that the last valid data card has been read. In either case, the program must always test to determine that the last card has been processed.

For example, when programming in COBOL with the IBM System/360 a card with a /* in card columns one and two is placed at the end of the cards to be processed to indicate the "last card" condition. When programming with FORTRAN a trailer card containing some high value such as 999's in one of the control fields is frequently used to indicate a "last card" condition. See the example below.

Note: The last card of a file is recognized by placing a card at the end of the file with /* in columns one and two.

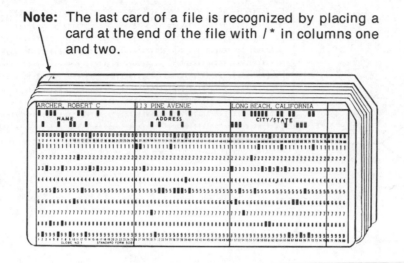

Figure 2-9 Method of Testing for Last Card

In the example in Figure 2-8 it can be seen that a diamond symbol is used when the decision concerning the last card is made. Again, the wording within the symbol is of the programmer's choosing. When a decision is made in a program, two or more paths must be taken dependent upon the results of that decision. The corners of the diamond are used to specify the flow of processing based upon the results of the decision. In Figure 2-8, it can be seen that the question posed by the decision is whether or not the last card was read. The "Yes" path will be taken if the last card was read and the "No" path will be taken if the last card was not read. Note that both of these paths are clearly identified on the flowchart by the words YES and NO being placed at the corners of the diamond to indicate the direction of the path to be taken. Whenever a decision is to be made, the paths to be taken as a result of that decision must be clearly marked on the flowchart. When the question can be answered by a Yes or No, such as in the example above, then YES and NO provide an adequate means of identifying the paths to be taken. In other types of decisions, as will be illustrated in subsequent examples, the paths to be taken may be identified by means other than Yes or No.

END OF FILE TRAILER CARD

FLAG
SENTINEL

Step 4: If the last data card has not been read, the data record is processed by moving the data from the input data area to the output data area.

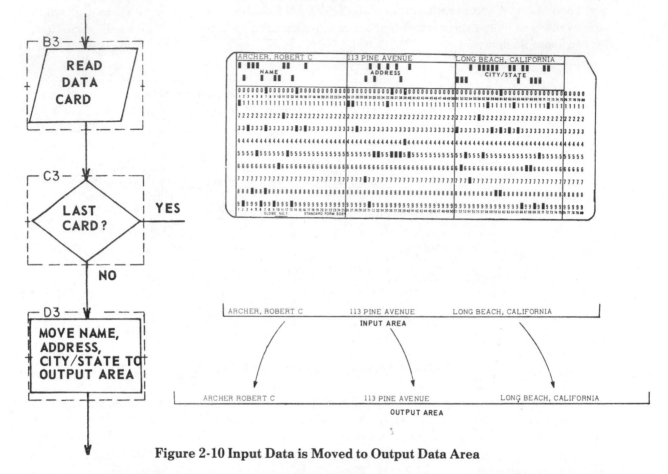

Figure 2-10 Input Data is Moved to Output Data Area

Note from the example in Figure 2-10 that when it is determined that the card read is not the last card, the data in the name field, the address field, and the city/state field is moved from the input area to the output area. After these moves take place, the data in the output area is ready to be written on the printer. Note also in Figure 2-10 that a rectangle is used to indicate the moves are to be performed in the program. Processing in a program refers to operations involving the movement or changing of data within main storage. Thus, moving data from the input data area to the output data area is considered processing. Other examples of processing, such as performing arithmetic operations on data in main storage, will be illustrated in subsequent chapters.

It should be noted that each field that is moved from the input area to the output area is an individual operation, that is, the Name field in the input area is moved to an area reserved for the Name field in the output area, the Address field in an input area is moved to an area reserved for the Address in the output area, etc. Thus, the programmer may move the fields in the input area to any desired position in the output area. It will be noted also that, except for the data moved from the input area, the output area contains blanks. This is normally desirable so that erroneous data is not included on the printed report. The method of placing blanks in an output area varies depending upon the programming language being used. In some programming languages, such as COBOL and Assembler Language, instructions must be included in the source coding to move blanks to the output area prior to moving the data from the input area to the output area. In other languages, such as FORTRAN and RPG, this function is handled automatically by the instructions generated by the compiler.

Step 5:   After the data has been moved to the output data area, it may be written on the printer.

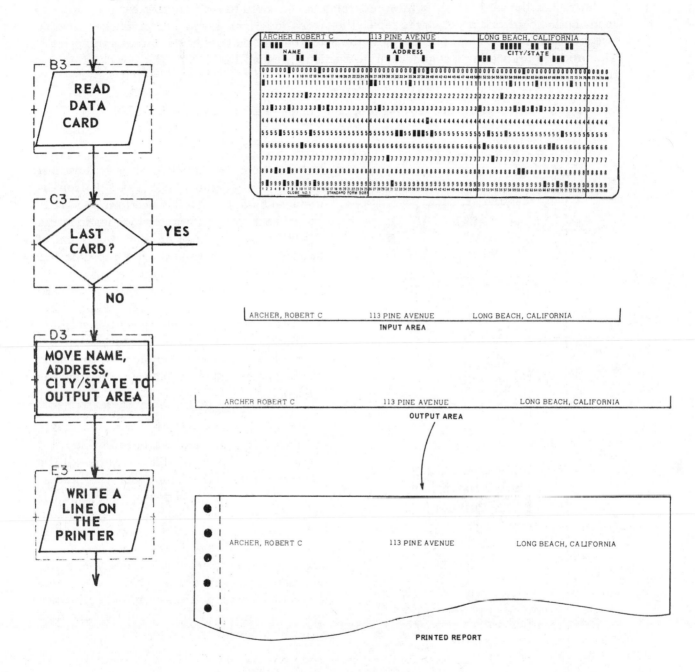

Figure 2-11 Write on Printer

Prallelogram

In Figure 2-11 it can be seen that the ~~trapezoid~~ symbol is used to indicate that a line of data is to be written on the printer. It should be recalled that whenever data is to be transferred either from an input device to main storage or from main storage to an output device, this symbol is used. The choice of wording within the symbols is, again, up to the programmer.

After the line has been written on the printer, the processing for the input data card has been completed, that is, when the line is written, there is no further processing which is to be performed on the card. Thus, in most programs, it is desired to read another card. In order to read another card, it is necessary to repeat the processing which was just accomplished, that is, it is necessary to read another card, move the data from that card to the output area and print it. The process of repeating a sequence of instructions is called LOOPING. The flowchart entries that illustrate a looping process are illustrated below.

Step 6:   After a line is printed, the program "loops" back to read the next card.

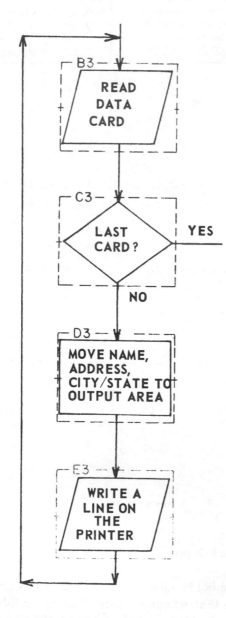

Note from the portion of the flowchart illustrated in Figure 2-12 that a loop is produced by drawing a flowline from the Write symbol back to the flowline which leads to the "Read" symbol. As can be seen, the intent of the loop is to indicate that after the data has been printed on the printer, the next step in the program is to read the next card in the card reader. Within the program, appropriate instructions may be used to cause the program to "branch" to the "Read" instruction so that the next card may be read. In the flowchart, this may be indicated by using the flowlines as indicated.

As noted, by following the path indicated in the flowchart, that is, by returning to read another card, the entire file of cards will be processed within this single loop. The process of looping to repeat a series of instructions is one of the most common programming techniques in use. It allows the program to process different data in the same way for as long as the loop is used. Thus, every card will be read and processed using the same instructions within the program. Different instructions need not be written for each data card which the program is to read.

Figure 2-12 Program Loop

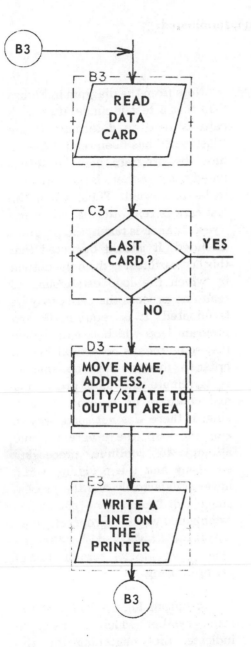

Figure 2-13 Use of Connector Symbols

An alternative method of indicating a loop or branch within a program flowchart is illustrated in Figure 2-13. Note that instead of drawing a flowline back to the "Read" symbol, two Connector Symbols, that is, the small circles, are used. A Connector Symbol is used to indicate transfer of control within a flowchart. The value placed within the connector symbol is the identification of the block to which the transfer of control will take place.

In the example it can be seen that the value B3 is placed in the connector symbol following the Write symbol. This indicates that control is to be passed to the instruction identified by the B3 block on the flowchart worksheet. The B3 block is identified by another connector symbol. This is so the block may be easily identified when looking at the flowchart. Thus, the connector symbols in Figure 2-13 indicate that control is to be passed from the connector symbol following the Write instruction to the connector preceding the Read instruction. This transfer of control is the same as that illustrated in Figure 2-12 with the flowlines.

After all of the cards have been read and processed by printing them on the printer, the program is to be terminated. This is illustrated in Figure 2-14.

Step 7:   After all of the cards are read, the program is terminated.

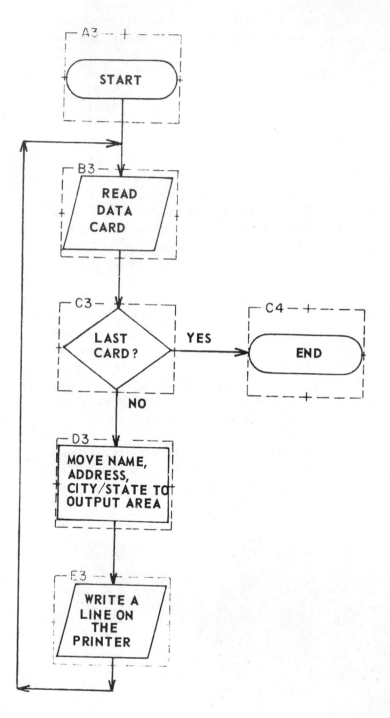

Figure 2-14 END Program

Note from the diagram in Figure 2-14 that a test is made after each card is read to determine if the "last card" has been read. When it has, the program may be terminated because there is no more data to be processed. Thus, when the last card is read, that is, when the "yes" branch is taken, the program is ended. It should be noted that this last card test is the only method by which the loop established to read and process the cards may be terminated. It is required in any program loop which is established that some means be established in order to "break" the loop, that is, to terminate the loop processing and continue on to other processing. If there was not some way to stop the loop, the program would attempt to continue processing endlessly and the program would never satisfactorily end the processing cycle. Thus, whenever a loop is established within a program, some means must always exist within the loop to provide for termination of the processing.

Note from Figure 2-14 that the same symbol which is used to indicate the beginning of the flowchart is used to indicate the end of the flowchart. This "terminal" symbol is always used whenever the program is to stop processing.

As noted previously, the basic process of reading an input record, processing the data, and writing some type of output record is the most basic concept in program logic. The processing involved in this program should be thoroughly understood prior to continuing with more advanced concepts.

CHAPTER 2

FLOWCHARTING ASSIGNMENT 1

INSTRUCTIONS

On a Flowchart Worksheet draw a flowchart to illustrate the logic required to produce a listing of the employees of a company.

INPUT: Employee Name Cards

Input is to consist of Employee Name Cards that contain the Employee Number, Employee Name, and the Department Number to which the employee is assigned. The format of the Employee Name Cards is illustrated below.

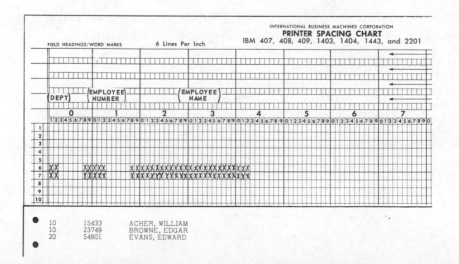

OUTPUT: Employee Listing

Output is to consist of a listing of the employees and is to contain the Department Number, the Employee Number, and the Employee Name. A Printer Spacing Chart and a segment of the report is illustrated below. Note that the Department Number appears first on the report.

Due By Friday

FLOWCHARTING ASSIGNMENT 2

INSTRUCTIONS

On a Flowchart Worksheet draw a flowchart to illustrate the logic to produce two listings of the customers of a company.

INPUT: Customer Name and Address Cards

Input is to consist of Customer Name and Address Cards that contain the Customer Number, Customer Name, and Customer Address. The format of the cards is illustrated below.

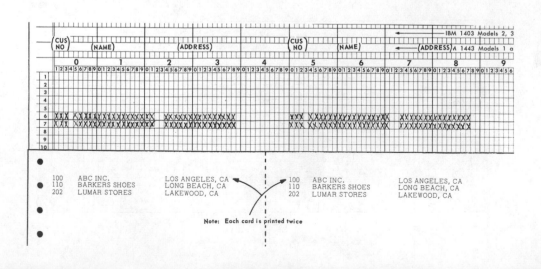

OUTPUT: Customer Listing

Output is to consist of two listings of the Customers. To reduce computer run time it has been decided to print each of the fields on the card twice on the same line. A Printer Spacing Chart and a segment of the report that is to be prepared is illustrated below.

CHAPTER 3

BASIC ARITHMETIC OPERATIONS

ACCUMULATING TOTALS

INTRODUCTION

As noted in Chapter 2, when data is read into main storage, many different types of processing may take place. One of the most common types of processing in business applications involves the adding or subtracting of two or more numbers. This is referred to as crossfooting. In addition, it is many times desirable to accumulate values as the program is processing the data and take a "final total" at the conclusion of the processing of all of the input data.

The sample program in this chapter illustrates the logic required to perform a crossfooting operation and obtain a final total of the calculated amount. The format of the input data cards to be read is illustrated in Figure 3-1.

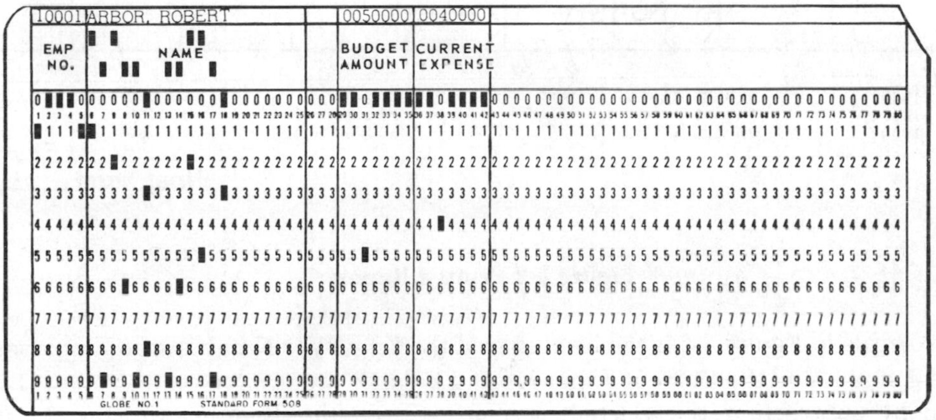

Figure 3-1 Card Format

In the example above it can be seen that the card input contains four fields: the Employee Number field in columns 1-5, the Employee Name field in columns 6-25, the Budget Amount in columns 29-35, and the Current Expenses in columns 36-42.

The report which is to be produced is illustrated in Figure 3-2.

PRINTED REPORT

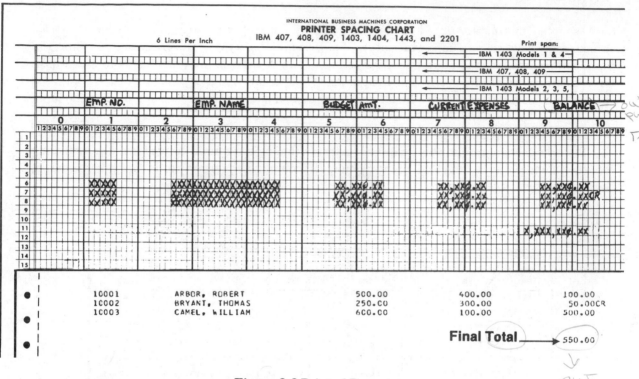

Figure 3-2 Printed Report

In the example in Figure 3-2 it can be seen that the Employee Number, the Employee Name, the Budget Amount and the Current Expenses and Balance are printed on the report. Balance is determined by subtracting the Current Expenses from the Budget Amount. In addition, "Balance" is to be accumulated so that after all of the input data is processed, the final total of the Balance amount is printed. The flowchart for this program is illustrated in Figure 3-3.

Balance = Budget Amount − Current Expenses

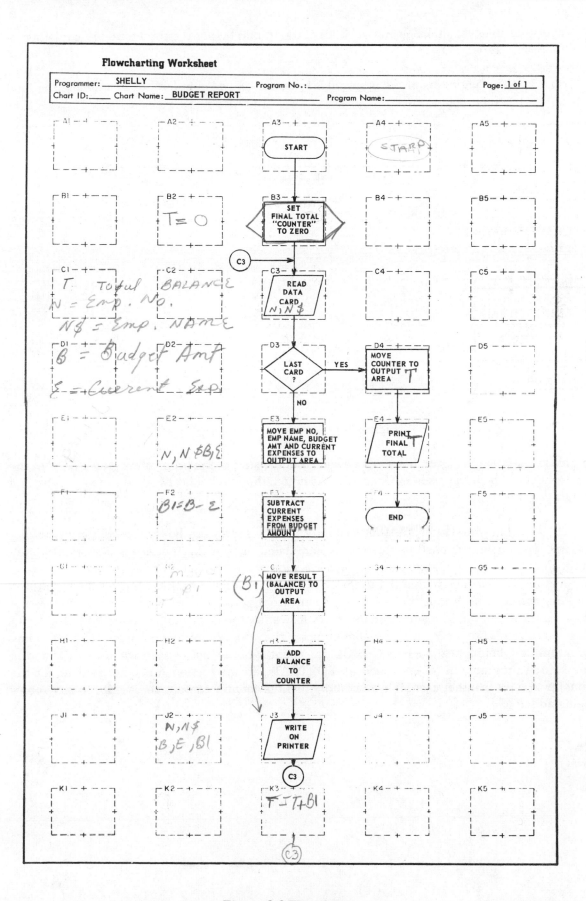

Figure 3-3 Flowchart

The steps involved in preparing the budget report and taking the final total are explained in the following steps.

Step 1: **The beginning of the program is indicated and a "counter" to accumulate the final total is set to zero.**

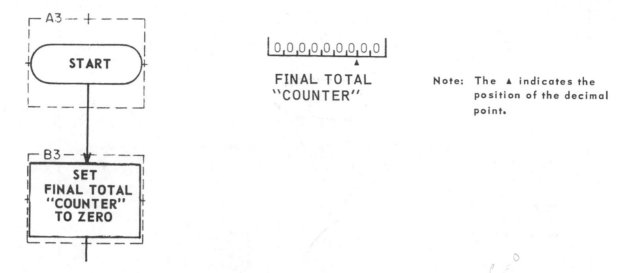

FINAL TOTAL
"COUNTER"

Note: The ▲ indicates the position of the decimal point.

Figure 3-4 Counter is Set to Zero

In the example in Figure 3-4 it can be seen that the start of the program is indicated with the same symbol which was used in Chapter 2. As noted, this symbol is always at the beginning and ending of the program.

The second symbol indicates that a counter is to be set to zero before any other processing begins. The counter is used to store the accumulated total of the Balance which is calculated from all cards read and processed. A counter is merely a term used to refer to an area which is defined in main storage within the program in a manner similar to that used for the input area and the output area. It must be set to zero to ensure that there is not a value already stored in the counter which would result in an incorrect answer for the final total. The method used to set the counter to zero may vary dependent upon the programming language used. In some programming languages, such as COBOL, the counter can be set to zero when it is defined in the source program. In others, such as FORTRAN, an instruction must be used to set the counter to zero. In either case, it is mandatory that the counter contain zeros prior to any values being added to it.

Step 2:   A card containing an Employee Number, Employee Name, Budget Amount, and Current Expenses is read into an Input Area in Core Storage.

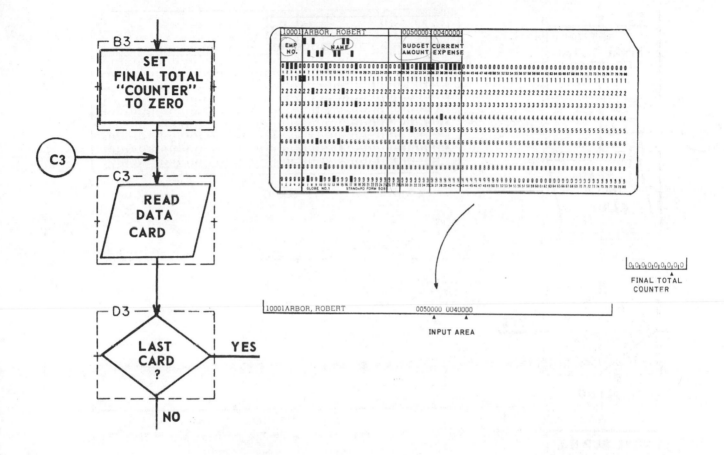

Figure 3-6 Input Card is Read

As in the example in Chapter 2, the input data card is read into an area in main storage which is reserved for it. Also, a test is performed to determine if the last card has been read. It should be recalled that this test must be performed whenever an input file is read so that the reading process will not continue after the last card has been read.

Step 3:   The Employee Number, the Employee Name, the Budget Amount and the Current Expenses which are read from the card are moved to the printer output area.

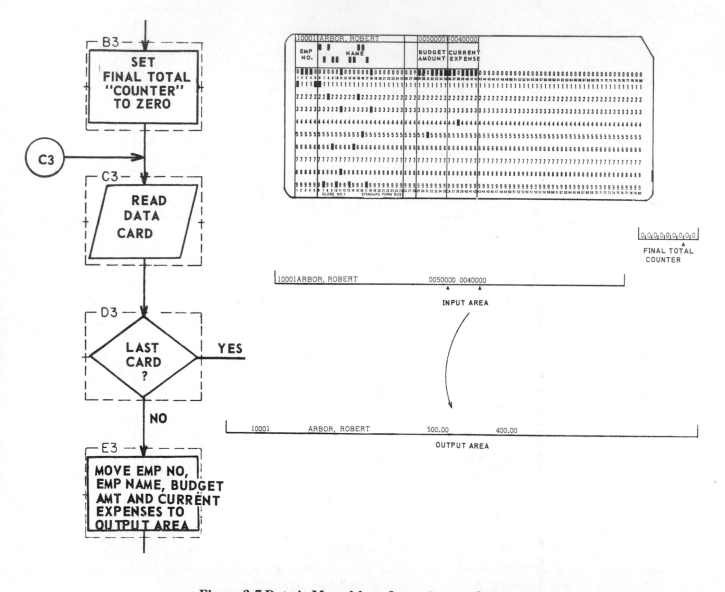

Figure 3-7 Data is Moved from Input Area to Output Area

Note from Figure 3-7 that the data which is stored in the input area is moved to the output area from which it will be printed. As in Chapter 2, the rectangle is used to indicate that some type of processing of data is to take place. Again, the explanation within the rectangle is of the programmer's choosing.

It should be noted also from Figure 3-7 that the Budget Amount and the Current Expenses are stored in the output area in an "edited" format, that is, the leading zeros have been changed to blanks and a decimal point has been inserted at the proper location. This ability to "edit" numeric data is provided by most programming languages and is frequently used on business reports.

Step 4:   The Current Expense field is subtracted from the Budget Amount field to obtain a Balance.

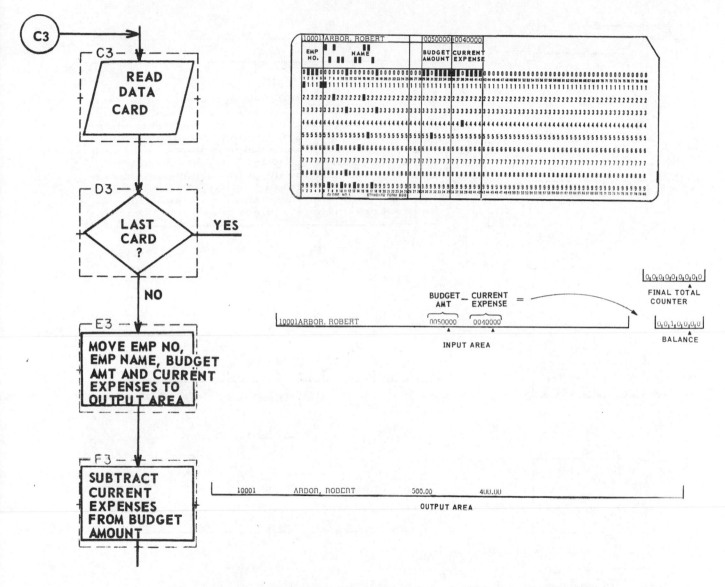

Figure 3-8 Current Expenses are Subtracted from Budget Amount

In the example above it can be seen that the value in the Current Expense field is subtracted from the value in the Budget Amount field and the value is stored in an area called Balance. The Balance field is an area in main storage which is reserved for the answer resulting from the arithmetic operations. It should be noted that some programming languages permit the answer resulting from calculations to be stored directly in the output area. In this example, however, the answer area is a separate area in main storage. Note also from the example in Figure 3-8 that the answer is positive. It is, of course, perfectly valid to have a negative result, that is, if the current expenses are greater than the budget amount, the balance will be a negative number.

Step 5:   The Balance is moved to the output area.

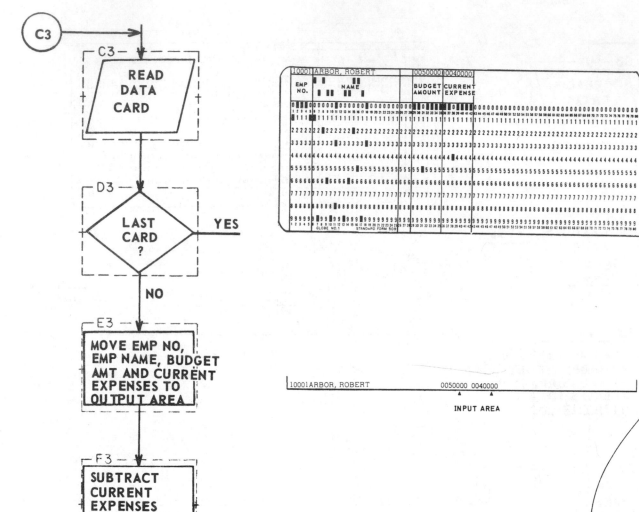

Figure 3-9 Balance is Moved to Output Area

As can be seen from Figure 3-9, the balance which was calculated in Step 4 is moved to the output area to be printed. Note that the Balance, like the Budget Amount and the Current Expense, is "edited" when it is placed in the output area, that is, the leading zeros are replaced with blanks and the decimal point is inserted in the number.

Step 6: The Balance is added to the Final Total Counter.

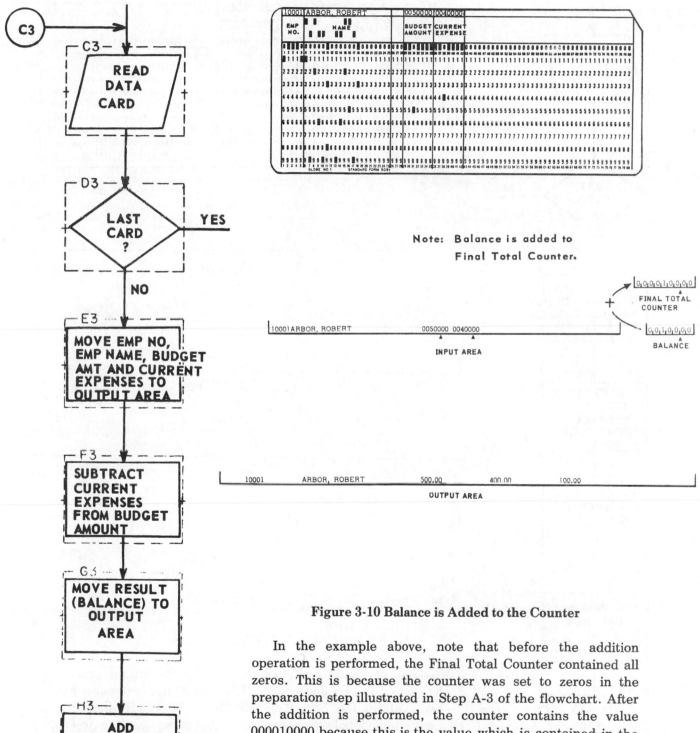

Figure 3-10 Balance is Added to the Counter

In the example above, note that before the addition operation is performed, the Final Total Counter contained all zeros. This is because the counter was set to zeros in the preparation step illustrated in Step A-3 of the flowchart. After the addition is performed, the counter contains the value 000010000 because this is the value which is contained in the Balance field. Thus, after all cards have been processed, the Final Total Counter will contain the accumulated totals from each card.

Step 7:   The output line is printed on the printer and control is returned to the Read instruction to read another card.

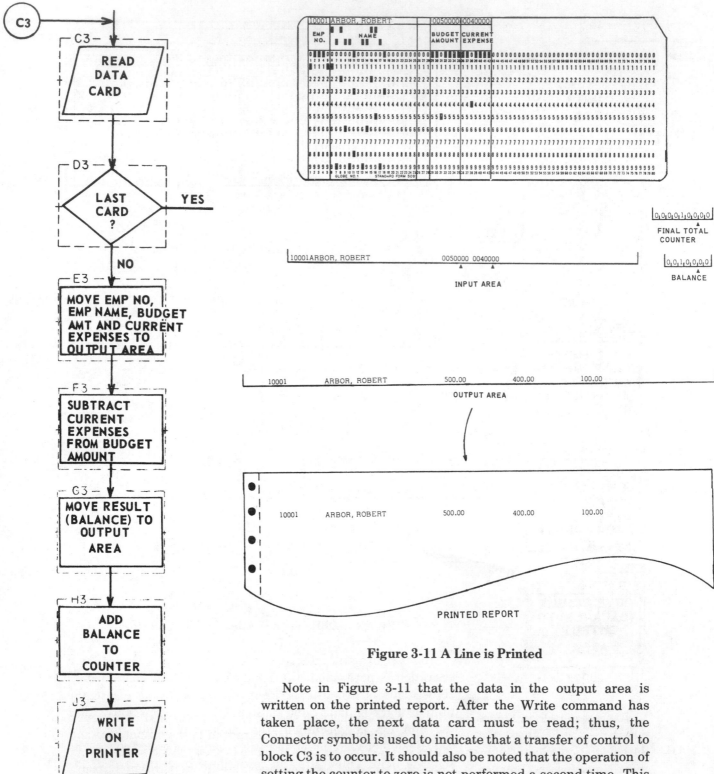

Figure 3-11 A Line is Printed

Note in Figure 3-11 that the data in the output area is written on the printed report. After the Write command has taken place, the next data card must be read; thus, the Connector symbol is used to indicate that a transfer of control to block C3 is to occur. It should also be noted that the operation of setting the counter to zero is not performed a second time. This is because the counter must be set to zeros at the start of the program but after values are added to the counter, they must not be destroyed. The value in the counter is accumulated and printed at the conclusion of processing.

Step 8:   The second card is read and processed.

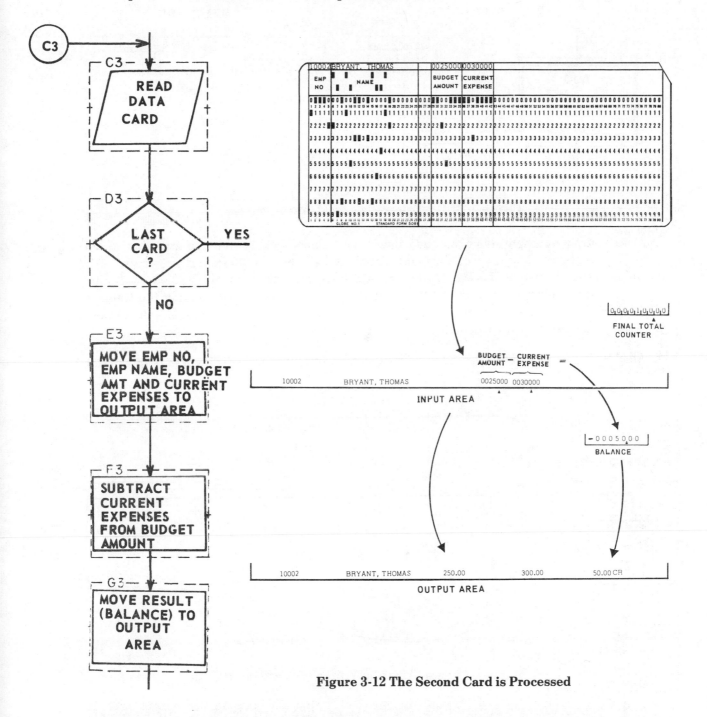

Figure 3-12 The Second Card is Processed

In the example in Figure 3-12 it can be seen that the second card is processed in the same manner as the first card, that is, after the card is read, the data is moved to the output area and the calculation to determine the Balance is performed. The Balance is then moved to the output area. Note that the Balance is a negative number because the value in the Current Expense field is greater than the value in the Budget Amount field. The negative field is indicated on the report by the "CR" (CRedit) which is placed following the Balance. The CR is placed on the report by using the Edit capabilities which are available in most programming languages.

Step 9:   The Balance from the second card is added to the Final Total Counter.

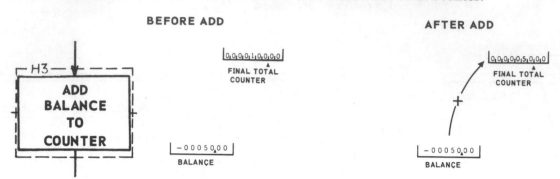

Figure 3-13 The Balance is Added to the Counter

Note from the example above that the value in the Balance field is added to the value stored in the Counter field. Since the Counter field contained the value 100.00 from the first card, and the value in the Balance field is -50.00, the new result stored in the Counter is 50.00. As can be seen, the value which is contained in the Counter field is obtained from adding the Balance fields which are determined from the card input data. Thus, the value in Counter is the total of all of the balances which are calculated from the input data.

Step 10:   The second line is written on the printer and control is transferred to read another card.

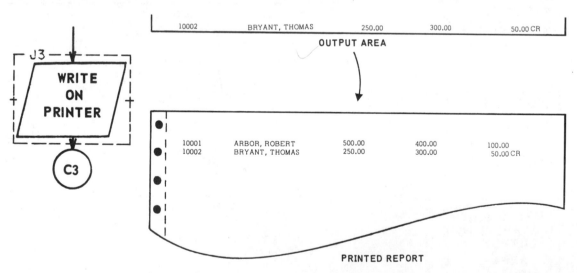

Figure 3-14 Second Line is Written on the Printer

Note from the example in Figure 3-14 that the second line is written on the printed report. The data which was stored in the Output Area in main storage is transmitted to the report in exactly the same format as it was stored in main storage. Note also that after the second line is printed, control is again transferred to block C3 which contains the Read command.

The third card will be read and processed in the same manner as is illustrated for the first two cards. The results of the calculations which are involved in the processing of the third card is illustrated below.

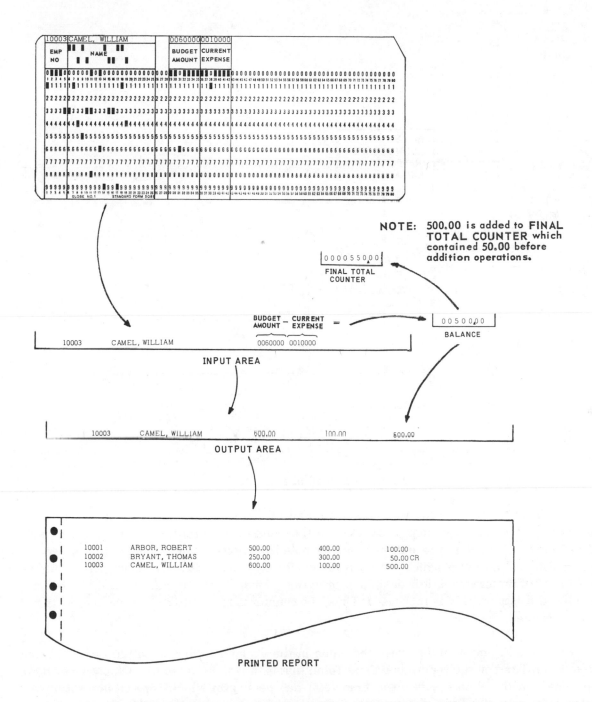

Figure 3-15 Results of Calculations on Third Data Card

Note from the example above that the calculations to determine the balance and also to add the balance to the counter take place as illustrated for the first two cards. The reading of cards, calculating the values, and printing the report will continue for as long as there are cards to be read. When the end of the cards is reached, that is, when the last card is read, the end-of-file routine will be entered.

Step 11:   When the last card is read, the end-of-file routine is entered, the final total counter is moved to the output area and printed.

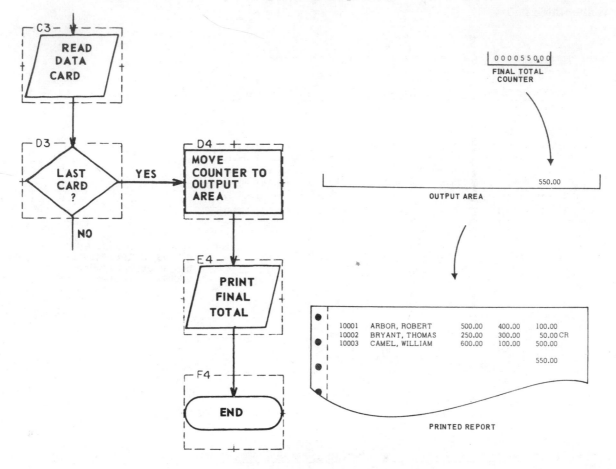

Figure 3-16 End-of-File Routine

Note from Figure 3-16 that when the last data card is read, the "yes" path is taken in the decision symbol. The first step to be taken in the "end-of-file" routine is to move the value stored in the Counter to the output area. As noted previously, the counter area is used to accumulate the balances which were calculated for each data card which was read. At the conclusion of the program, it is desired to print this "Final Total" to indicate the total balance for all of the data which was processed. Thus, the counter is moved to the output area so that it may be printed.

Note from Figure 3-16 that after the value in the Counter is moved to the printer output area, it is printed on the report as a Final Total, that is, it is the total of the balances which are contained on the report. After the final total has been printed, all processing within the program is complete. Thus, the program is terminated and this is indicated in the flowchart by using the terminal processing symbol.

The process of cross-footing and taking a final total is very basic to many business applications and should be well understood.

CHAPTER 3

FLOWCHARTING ASSIGNMENT 1

INSTRUCTIONS

On a Flowchart Worksheet draw a flowchart to illustrate the logic required to produce a Gross Profit Report.

INPUT: Sales Cards

Input is to consist of Sales Cards containing the Item Number, Description, Sales Amount, and Cost Amount. The format of the cards is illustrated below.

ITEM	DESCRIPTION	SALES AMT	COST AMT	

OUTPUT: Gross Profit Report

Output is to consist of a listing of the Item Number, Description, Sales Amount, Cost Amount and Gross Profit. Gross Profit is to be calculated by subtracting the Cost Amount field from the Sales Amount field. Final Totals are to be taken for the Sales Amount field, the Cost Amount field and the Gross Profit. A Printer Spacing Chart and a segment of the report is illustrated below.

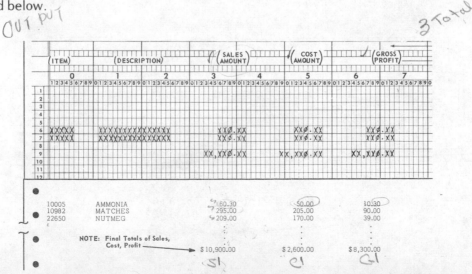

		SALES AMOUNT	COST AMOUNT	GROSS PROFIT
10005	AMMONIA	60.30	50.00	10.30
10982	MATCHES	295.00	205.00	90.00
22650	NUTMEG	209.00	170.00	39.00

NOTE: Final Totals of Sales, Cost, Profit

| | $10,900.00 | $2,600.00 | $8,300.00 |

CHAPTER 3

FLOWCHARTING ASSIGNMENT 2

INSTRUCTIONS

On a Flowchart Worksheet draw a flowchart to illustrate the logic required to produce a Weekly Payroll Report.

INPUT: Employee Payroll Cards

Input is to consist of Employee Payroll Cards containing the Employee Number, Employee Name, Hours Worked, Rate of Pay, and Deductions. The format of the card is illustrated below.

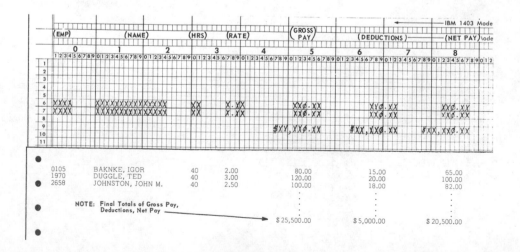

OUTPUT: Net Pay Report

Output is to consist of a Net Pay report listing the Employee Number, the Employee Name, the Hours Worked, Rate of Pay, Gross Pay, Deductions, and Net Pay. Gross Pay is to be calculated by multiplying the Rate of Pay by the Hours Worked. Net Pay is to be calculated by subtracting the Deductions from the calculated Gross Pay to produce the Net Pay. Final Totals are to be taken of Gross Pay, Deductions, and Net Pay.

CHAPTER 4

COMPARING

INTRODUCTION

The ability of the computer to compare numeric or alphanumeric values and perform alternative operations based upon the results of this comparison provides electronic data processing systems with great flexibility in the solution of business and mathematical problems.

Comparisons are normally made on data which is stored in main storage and alternative operations are performed based upon conditions which result from the comparisons. These comparisons may indicate that the data being compared is equal or unequal. In addition, tests may be made to determine if data in one portion of main storage is less than or greater than data stored in another portion of main storage. The examples below illustrate how these comparisons may be made. In the examples an area called Sales Amount is compared to an area called Sales Quota.

Example 1: Numeric data is equal.

| 1 | 7 | 3 | 5 | 4 | = | 1 | 7 | 3 | 5 | 4 |

SALES AMOUNT   SALES QUOTA

Figure 4-1 Example of Equal Numeric Data

Note in the example above that the values contained in the main storage areas called Sales Amount and Sales Quota are equal, that is, both areas contain the value 17354. When the two values above are compared, the computer would indicate that they are equal and the program could then process data based upon the fact that the values are equal.

Example 2: Numeric data is unequal.

| 2 | 8 | 7 | 5 | 4 | ≠ | 4 | 8 | 6 | 3 | 2 |

SALES AMOUNT   SALES QUOTA

Figure 4-2 Example of Unequal Numeric Data

Note in Figure 4-2 that the numeric data stored in Sales Amount and Sales Quota are not equal. Note also the use of the "not equal" sign ($\neq$). This mathematical notation is often used when drawing flowcharts to indicate the relationship of two numbers.

It can be seen also that the data in the area Sales Amount is less than the data contained in the area Sales Quota. This is illustrated in Figure 4-3.

Example 3: Numeric data in one area is less than numeric data in second area.

2 8 7 5 4	<	4 8 6 3 2
SALES AMOUNT		**SALES QUOTA**

Figure 4-3 Example of Less Than Condition

As noted, the value in Sales Amount is less than the value in Sales Quota. Note the use of the less than (<) symbol. This symbol again may be used in flowcharts to indicate the relationship of numeric data.

Example 4: Numeric data in one area is greater than numeric data in a second area.

6 4 0 9 1	>	4 1 2 7 3
SALES AMOUNT		**SALES QUOTA**

Figure 4-4 Example of Greater Than Condition

In the example in Figure 4-5 it can be seen that the numeric data in the field Sales Amount is greater than the numeric data in Sales Quota, as indicated by the greater than symbol (>). Alphabetic data may also be compared. The example below illustrates the comparison of alphabetic data.

Example 5: Comparison of Alphabetic Data.

J O N E S	<	S M I T H
DATA1		**DATA2**

Figure 4-5 Example of Alphabetic Comparison

In the example above it can be seen that the value JONES in the area DATA1 is compared to the value SMITH in the area DATA2. When alphabetic comparisons are made, the "value" of each letter of the alphabet is, in most computers, greater as the alphabet progresses from A—Z. Thus, in the example above, the "J" which begins the name JONES is considered less than the letter "S" which begins the name SMITH. Therefore, the entire field in DATA1 is considered less than the field in DATA2.

It should be noted in all of the examples presented that the comparison proceeded from the left to the right, that is, the left-most characters in the two fields are compared first. If one of these first characters is less than the other, then the entire field is considered less than the other. If the first two characters are equal, then the next characters to the right are compared. This comparison will continue until either an unequal condition occurs or until both fields are found to be equal.

SAMPLE PROBLEM

The problem in this chapter illustrates the logic required to print a Sales Quota Report. The input to the program consists of a file of Employee Sales cards. The format is illustrated below.

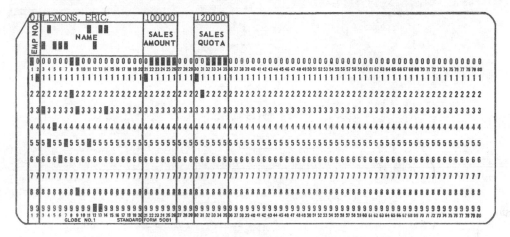

Figure 4-6 Format of Card Input

Note from the general format illustrated in Figure 4-6 that the cards contain an Employee Number in columns 1-2, the Employee Name in columns 3-20, the Sales Amount, that is, the amount of sales by the employee, in columns 21-26, and the Sales Quota for the employee in columns 30-35. The program is to compare the sales amount for the employee with his sales quota and prepare the following report.

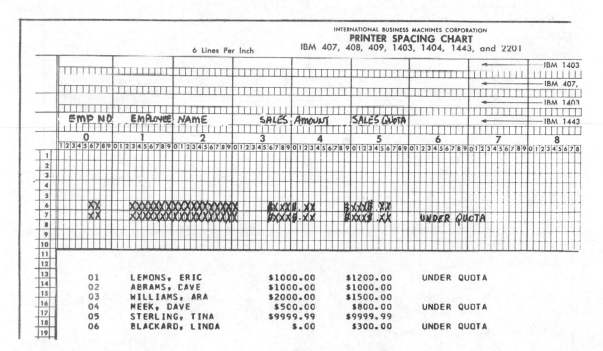

Figure 4-7 Format of Printed Report

As can be seen from Figure 4-7, the report consists of the employee Number, the Employee Name, the Sales Amount, the Sales Quota, and, if the sales are less than the quota, a message which indicates that the salesman is under quota. The flowchart for the program is illustrated in Figure 4-8.

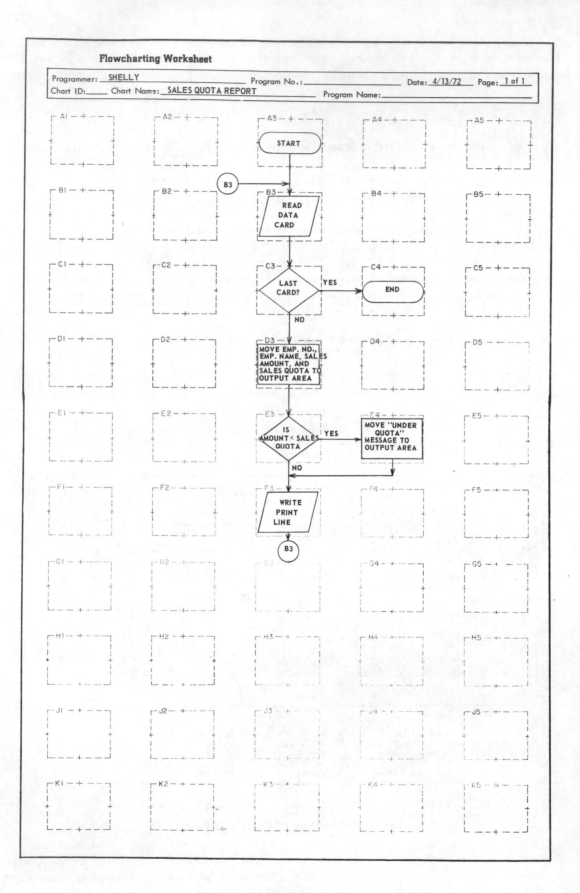

Figure 4-8 Flowchart

The steps involved in creating the Sales Quota Report are explained on the following pages.

Step 1:   The beginning of the program is indicated and a data card is read.

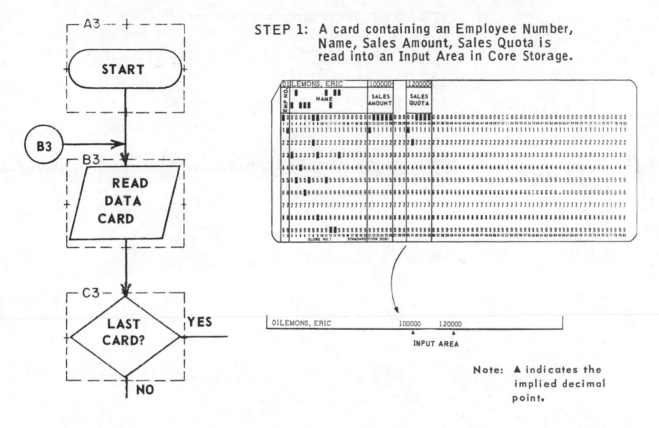

Figure 4-9 The Input Data Card is Read

As in the previous examples, the data card must be read from the card reader and the data within the card is placed in an "input area" which is reserved for it in main storage. The data is always stored in the same format as it is read from the card. The test for the last card must also be performed as in previous examples.

Step 2: The data in the input area is moved to the printer output area.

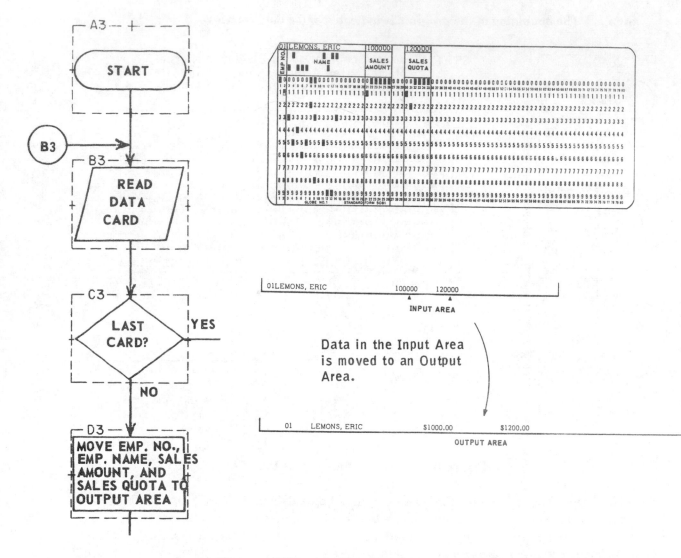

Figure 4-10 Data is Moved to the Output Area

Note in Figure 4-10 that the data which is read from the card and stored in the input area is moved to the output area. Note also that the Sales Amount and the Sales Quota values have been "edited" by inserting decimal points and a dollar sign to indicate that they are dollar values. As with editing performed in Chapter 3, this editing is performed using instructions which are available in most programming languages and this type of editing of numeric fields is quite common on business reports.

Step 3:   The Sales Amount is compared to the Sales Quota.

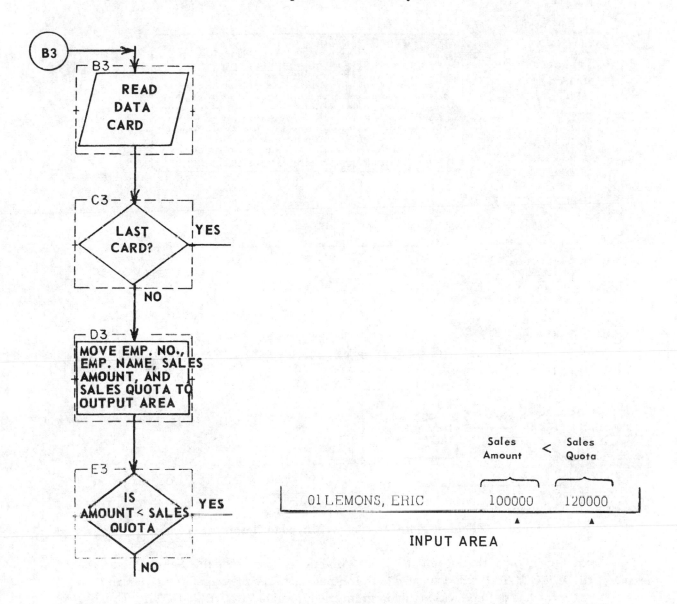

Figure 4-11 Sales Amount and Sales Quota are Compared

Note in Figure 4-11 that the diamond-shaped decision symbol is used in the flowchart to indicate that a comparison is to be made concerning the relative values stored in the Sales Amount field and the Sales Quota field. As noted previously, the comparison is made to determine if the value in the Sales Amount field is less than the value in the Sales Quota field. If it is, a special "Under Quota" message is to be written on the report. If it is not, the message is not to be contained on the report.

The wording which is placed within the decision symbol, as with all flowcharting symbols, is of the programmer's choosing. In the example, the less than symbol (<) is used to indicate the relationship of the values which are to be tested. In the example it can be seen that the value in the Sales Amount field is 1000.00 and the value in the Sales Quota field is 1200.00. Therefore, the answer to the question posed in the decision symbol is Yes, that is, the Sales Amount is less than the Sales Quota. The "Yes" path of the decision is therefore taken.

Step 4:   "Under Quota" message is moved to the output area.

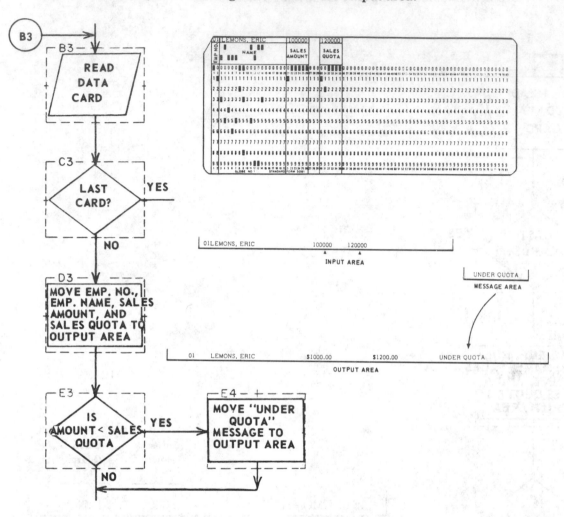

Figure 4-12 Under Quota Message is Moved to Output Area

Note from Figure 4-12 that when the Sales Amount is less than the Sales Quota, the message "UNDER QUOTA" will be moved to the output area. The message is stored in an area of main storage which is defined within the program and the value "UNDER QUOTA" is placed in the area in main storage when the program is compiled or assembled. Note also that the rectangle symbol is used to indicate the movement of data from the message area to the output area.

Step 5: The output line is written on the printer.

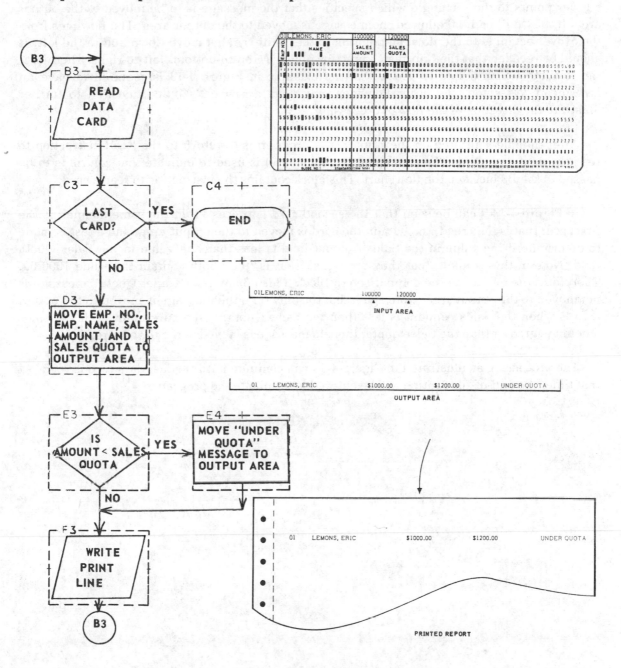

Figure 4-13 Output Line is Written on the Printer

Note from the example in Figure 4-13 that after the Under Quota message has been moved to the output area, the line is written on the printed report. As can be seen, the report will always contain the Employee Number, the Employee Name, the Sales Amount, and the Sales Quota. If the answer to the question "Is the Sales Amount Less than the Sales Quota" is Yes, the Under Quota message is also moved to the output area. If the answer is No, the message is not moved to the output area and the line is printed without the message.

In the example in Figure 4-13, note that the flowline from the Decision Symbol for the "yes" answer points to the rectangle which specifies that the message is to be moved to the output area. If the "no" path is followed, no message is moved to the output area. The flowlines from the Move rectangle to the flowline pointing to the Write symbol move down and to the left. It should be recalled that the "normal" direction of flow is top-to-bottom, left-to-right. Therefore, the flowline which points to the left in the example in Figure 4-13 is required to have an arrowhead. As noted, the other flowlines may have arrowheads if it is desired to further illustrate the direction of the flow of processing.

After the line is printed on the printer, the program is to return to the Read instruction to read the next data card. The connector symbol (circle) is used to indicate that control is to be passed to the B3 block on the flowchart. This block contains the instruction to read a card.

In Figure 4-14 it can be seen that the second card is processed in the same manner as the first card, that is, it is read, the data in the card is moved to the output area, and a test is made to determine if the value in the Sales Amount field is less than the value in the Sales Quota field. Note in the example that they are equal, that is, they both contain the value 1000.00. Therefore, the answer to the comparison in Block E3 is no and the "Under Quota" message is not moved to the output area. Note again that the only time the message is moved to the output area is when the Sales Amount is less than the Sales Quota. If they are equal or if the sales amount is greater than the Sales quota, then no message is moved to the output area.

The processing as illustrated in Figure 4-14 will continue until the last data card is read. At that time, the end-of-file routine will be entered to terminate the program.

Step 6:   A second card is read and processed.

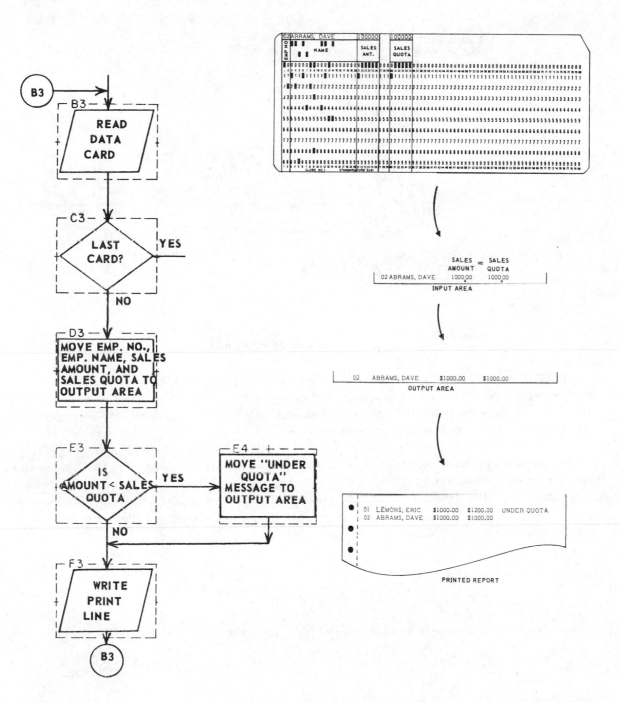

Figure 4-14 Second Card is Processed

Step 7:   The last data card is read.

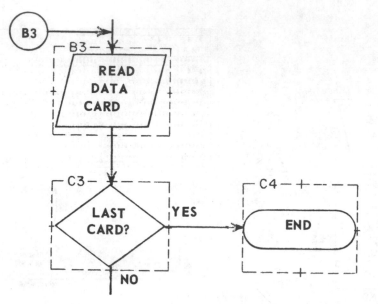

Figure 4-15 Last Card Processing

As in the previous program examples, when the last data card is read, an "end-of-file" routine is entered. In the example above, there is no special processing which must take place after the last card is read such as there was in Chapter 3 when a final total was printed. Therefore, the program is merely terminated.

The problem in this chapter has illustrated the basic concept of comparing two values and taking alternative action dependent upon the results of the comparison. The complexity of a program is normally dependent upon the number of comparisons and processing which is to take place as a result of these comparisons. Subsequent chapters will illustrate the use of comparisons in more complex programming problems.

CHAPTER 4

FLOWCHARTING ASSIGNMENT 1

INSTRUCTIONS

On a Flowchart Worksheet draw a flowchart to illustrate the logic required to produce a Sales Commission Report. For Sales less than $1,000.00 the Salesman receives a 2% commission. For Sales $1,000.00 or more the Salesman receives a 5% commission.

INPUT: Sales Cards

Input is to consist of Sales Cards containing the Salesman Number, Salesman Name, and Sales Amount. The format of the Sales Cards is illustrated below:

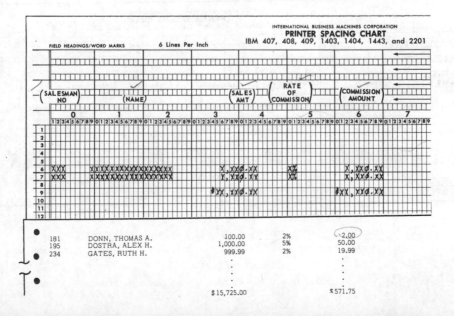

OUTPUT: Sales Commission Report

Output is to consist of a Sales Commission Report. The report is to contain the Salesman Number, Salesman Name, Sales Amount, Commission Rate, and Commission Amount. NOTE: The Commission Rate is not punched on the card, but may be established as a "constant" in storage through the program. For example, if the Sales Amount on the card is $900.00, the Sales Amount field would be multiplied by the constant 2% in storage. If the Sales Amount on the card is $2,000.00, this field would be multiplied by the constant 5% in storage. A final total is to be taken of the Sales Amount field and the calculated Commission Amount.

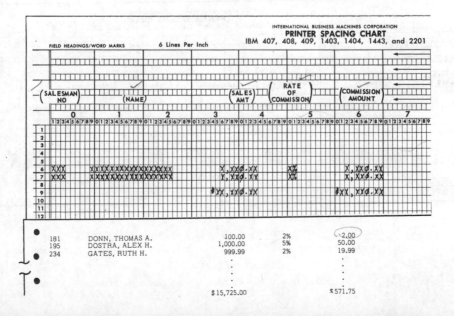

CHAPTER 4

FLOWCHARTING ASSIGNMENT 2

INSTRUCTIONS

On a Flowchart Worksheet draw a flowchart to illustrate the logic required to prepare a Weekly Payroll Report. Employees are to receive time and one-half for all work in excess of 40 hours. For example, an employee working 42 hours at $2.00 per hour would be paid for 40 hours work at $2.00 per hour, and 2 hours work at $3.00 per hour.

INPUT: Payroll Cards

Input is to consist of Payroll cards containing the Employee Number, Employee Name, Hours Worked, Rate of Pay, and Deductions. The format of the card is illustrated below.

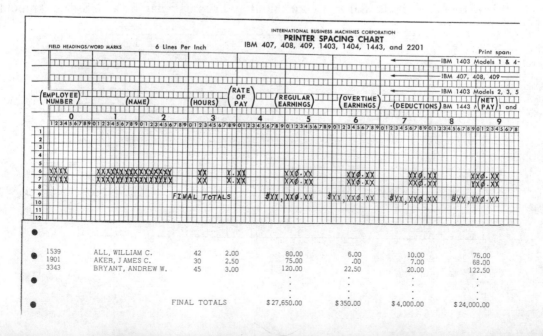

OUTPUT: Payroll Report

Output is to consist of a Payroll Report. The report is to contain the Employee Number, Employee Name, Total Hours Worked, Regular Rate of Pay, Regular Earnings, Overtime Earnings, Deductions, and Net Pay. Regular Earnings added to Overtime Earnings minus the Deductions will give the Net Pay. Final Totals are to be taken of Regular Earnings, Overtime Earnings, Deductions, and Net Pay.

1539	ALL, WILLIAM C.	42	2.00	80.00	6.00	10.00	76.00
1901	AKER, JAMES C.	30	2.50	75.00	.00	7.00	68.00
3343	BRYANT, ANDREW W.	45	3.00	120.00	22.50	20.00	122.50
	FINAL TOTALS			$ 27,650.00	$ 350.00	$ 4,000.00	$ 24,000.00

CHAPTER 5

CONTROL CODES

INTRODUCTION

In many applications, input records may be identified by special control punches or codes which are punched into the card. These codes may specify particular types of processing which are to take place dependent upon the code. For example, if a payroll report were to be prepared listing the employee name and the regular earnings, it may be also required to specify the bonus pay which an employee may receive if he works on a shift other than the day shift. The problem in this chapter illustrates an application of this type.

The input to the program is a file of data cards which contain the payroll information. The format of the card is illustrated below.

CARD INPUT

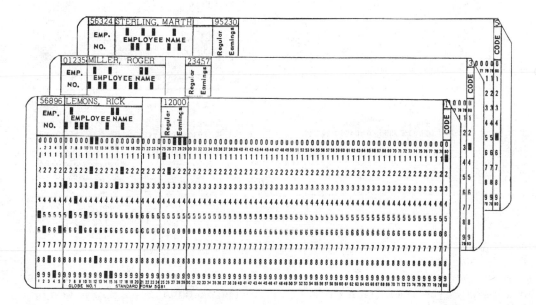

Figure 5-1 Card Input Format

In the example above it can be seen that the input cards contain the Employee Number in columns 1-5, the Employee Name in columns 6-20, the Regular Earnings in columns 25-29, and a "Code" in column 80. The Code is used to indicate the shift which the employee works. If the value in column 80 is "1," the employee works the day shift. A value of "3" indicates the second shift is worked by the employee and a value of "5" indicates the "graveyard" shift.

The output of the program is a report which contains the Employee Number, the Employee Name, the Shift Number, the Regular Earnings, the Bonus Earnings which an employee receives if he works on a shift other than the day shift, and the Total Pay for the employee. The format of the report is illustrated in Figure 5-2.

OUTPUT

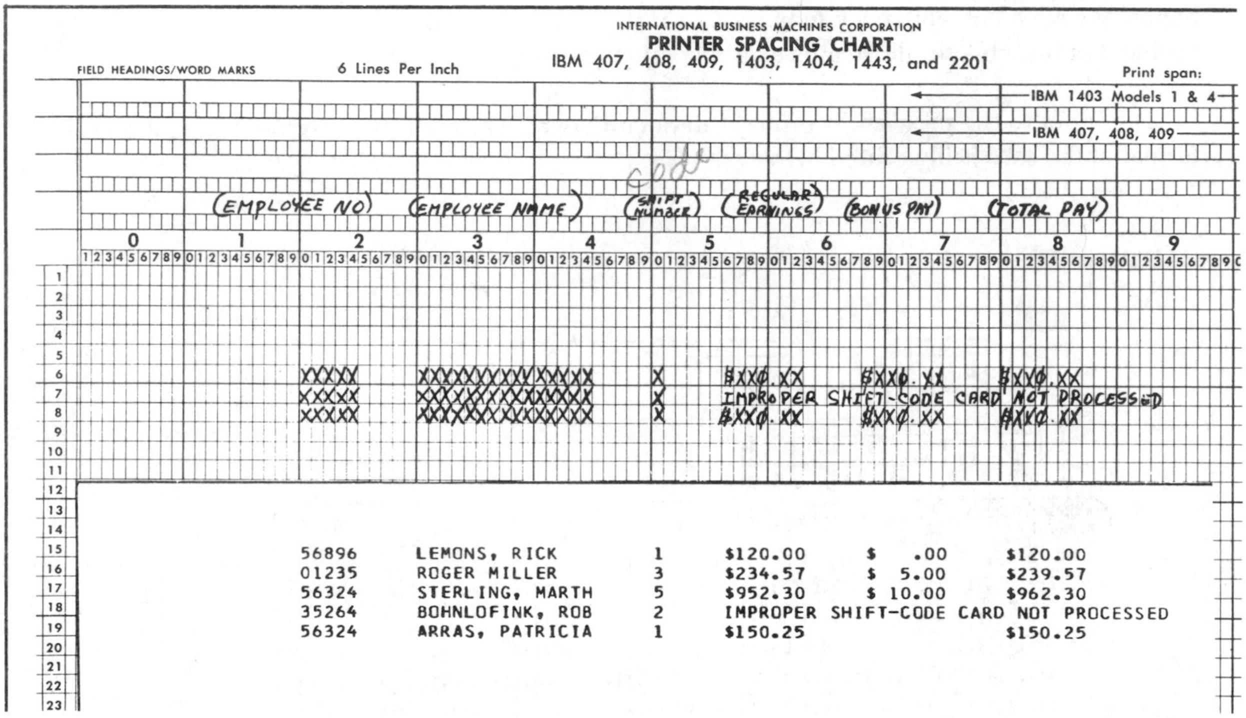

Figure 5-2 Printed Output

Note that if an employee works on the day shift (code = 1) he receives no bonus pay. If an employee works on the second shift (code = 3), he receives 5.00 in bonus pay and employees on the third shift (code = 5) receive 10.00 in bonus pay. Note the message "IMPROPER SHIFT-CODE CARD NOT PROCESSED." This message is printed on the report when the code in column 80 is not equal to 1,3, or 5.

The flowchart for the program is illustrated in Figure 5-3.

FLOWCHART

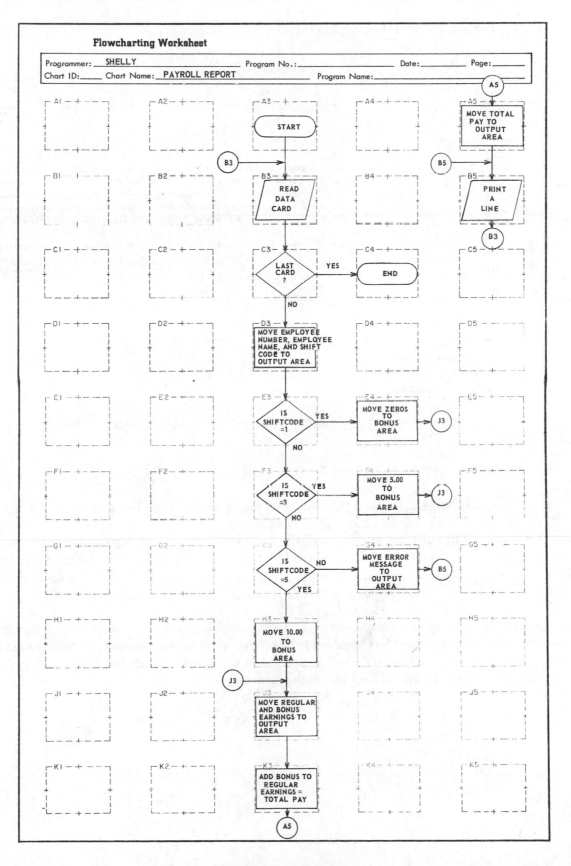

Figure 5-3 Flowchart

The processing within the program is explained in the following steps.

Step 1:   The beginning of the program is indicated and a card is read.

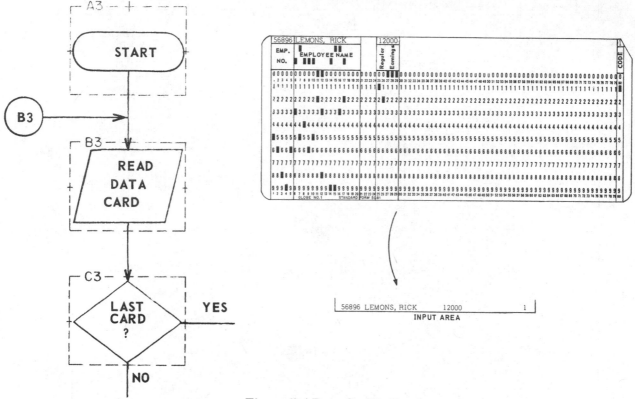

Figure 5-4 Data Card is Read

As with all programs illustrated thus far, the beginning of the program must be indicated with the terminal symbol. Since there is no initialization which must be performed, the next step is to read a data card. As noted previously, the data card contains the Employee Number, the Employee Name, the Regular Earnings, and a Shift Code in column 80 which indicates the shift worked by the employee. In the example in Figure 5-4, it can be seen that the value in the Shift Code field is "1" which indicates the employee worked the day shift.

Again, as in all programs which read input data files, a test must be performed to determine if the last data record or card has been read. The "yes" path of the decision symbol is taken if the last card has been read and the "no" path is taken if the last card has not been read. In the example, a data card is read, so the "no" path is taken.

Step 2: **The Employee Number, the Employee Name, and the Shift Code are moved to the output area.**

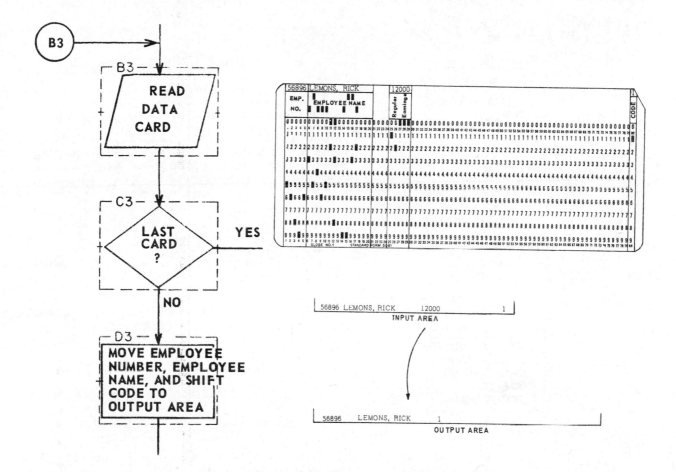

Figure 5-5 Data is Moved from the Input Area to the Output Area

Note from the example in Figure 5-5 that the fields are moved from the input data area to the output area. The fields moved are those which will always be contained on the report regardless of the value in the shift code field. As can be seen from Figure 5-2, the values in the other fields may vary dependent upon the Shift Code value.

Step 3:   A test is made to determine the value of the Shift Code.

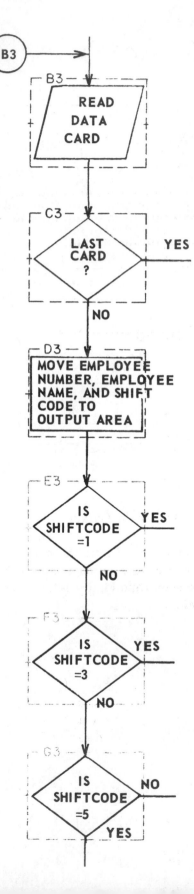

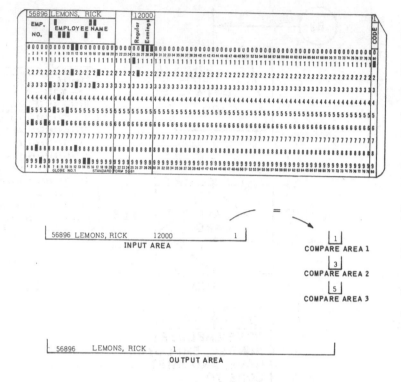

Figure 5-6 Shift Code is Compared

In the example it can be seen that the value in the Shift Code field may be compared to the values 1, 3, and 5, which are the valid values which may be contained in the Shift Code field. The "constants" 1, 3, and 5, which are used in the comparisons, are stored in main storage within the program. These are normally established when the program is compiled or assembled.

The portion of the flowchart illustrated indicates that if the shift-code in the input card is equal to 1, the comparisons to 3 and 5 will not take place, that is, if the shift-code is 1, the other two comparisons are bypassed. This is because it is not necessary to compare the shift-code to 3 and 5 because it is already known that the code is equal to 1. Thus, since an equal condition is found when the Shift-Code is compared to a "1," the comparisons to the constant values "3" and "5" do not take place and the "yes" path of the decision symbol in block E3 is taken.

Step 4: Zeros are moved to the Bonus Pay area.

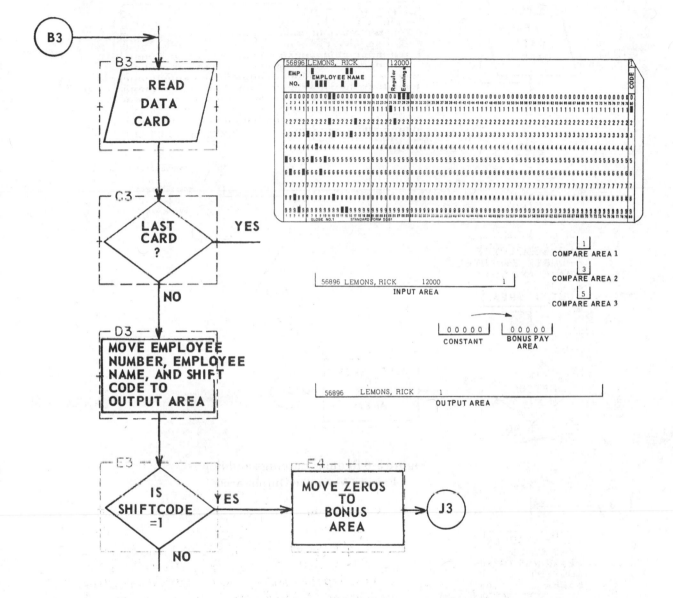

Figure 5-7 Zeros are Moved to Bonus Pay Area

As was noted previously, when the shift-code is equal to 1, it indicates that the employee worked the day shift and is not entitled to any bonus pay for working the second or third shifts. Therefore, as illustrated in Figure 5-7, zeros are moved to a bonus pay area, which will then be added to the regular earnings to determine the total pay for the employee. After the zeros are moved to the Bonus Pay Area, control is passed to block J3.

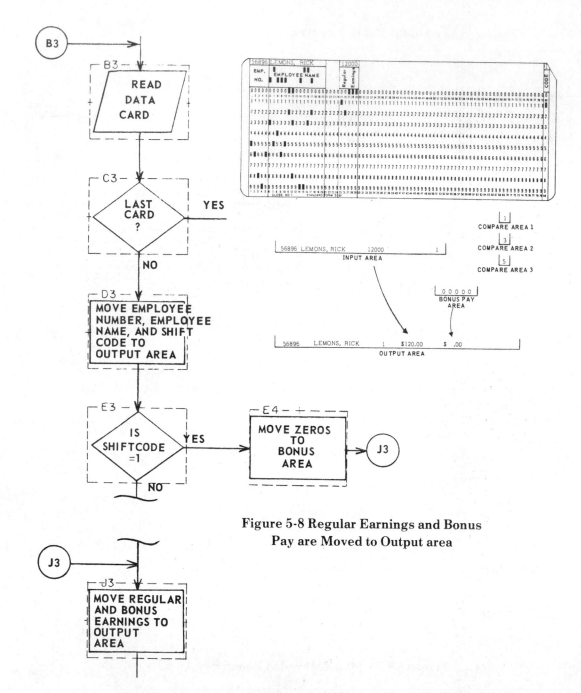

Figure 5-8 Regular Earnings and Bonus
Pay are Moved to Output area

Note from the example in Figure 5-8 that the Regular Earnings from the card input area and the zeros which were placed in the Bonus Pay area in Figure 5-7 are moved to the printer output area. Both of these numeric fields are edited. The regular pay in the output area contains the value 120.00 because the editing procedure inserts the decimal point at the desired location. When the zeros in the Bonus Pay Area are moved to the output area, the decimal point is again inserted in the correct location. Note also that the "leading zeros," that is, the zeros which precede the decimal point, are "suppressed," that is, they are not printed. Again, this type of editing of numeric fields is quite common on business reports and most programming languages have the capability of editing data in this manner.

Step 6: **The value in the Regular Earnings field is added to the value in the Bonus Pay area in order to determine a Total Pay.**

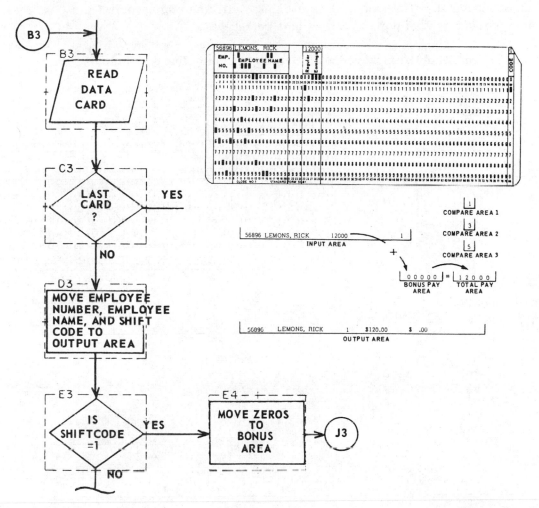

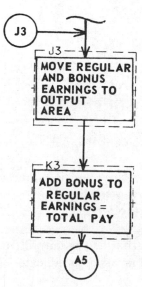

Figure 5-9 Regular Earnings is Added to Bonus Pay

In the example above it can be seen that the value in the Regular Earnings field, which is contained within the card input area, is added to the value contained within the Bonus Pay area. The sum of these two values is the Total Pay for the employee. Note in the example that the Regular Earnings of 120.00 is added to the Bonus Pay of 000.00 and the sum is the Total Pay, 120.00. The Bonus Pay is added to the Regular Pay even though the Bonus Pay is zero. This is because the same routine is used every time in the program regardless of the value which is stored within the Bonus Pay area. If, for example, the Shift-Code was 3, indicating that the employee worked the second shift, the value 5.00 would be stored in the Bonus Pay Area and this would be added to the Regular Pay. The use of a common routine to process data regardless of the values which may be stored in a particular area is normally a good programming technique.

Note also from the example in Figure 5-9 that after the addition operation is complete, control is passed to the block A5 on the programming flowchart worksheet. This is indicated by the connector symbol following block K3. The reason for this is that block K3 is the last block on the flowcharting sheet for column 3 (see Figure 5-3). Therefore, control must be passed to another block on another part of the flowchart worksheet.

Step 7: The Total Pay is moved to the output area, and a line is printed.

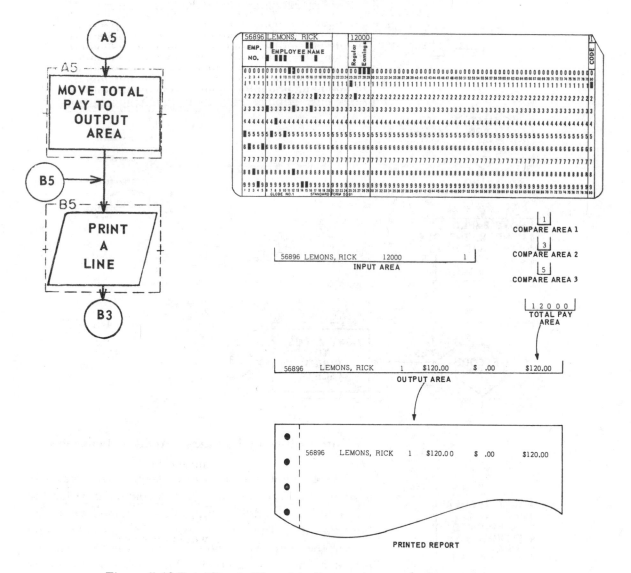

Figure 5-10 Total Pay is Moved to Output Area and a Line is Printed

Note from Figure 5-10 that the total pay is moved to the output area and is edited with a decimal point and a dollar sign. After the total pay has been moved to the output area, the entire print line has been completed and the line may be printed on the report.

As in previous examples, when a line is printed on the report, the data is moved from the output area to the report and the input/output trapezoid symbol is used to indicate that an input/output operation is to take place.

After the line has been printed on the report, the record has been completely processed. Therefore, the next step is to read another card. Note that the connector symbol is used to indicate that control is passed to block B3, which contains the Read instruction.

Step 8: The second card is read, and the Employee Number, Employee Name, and Shift Code are moved to the output area.

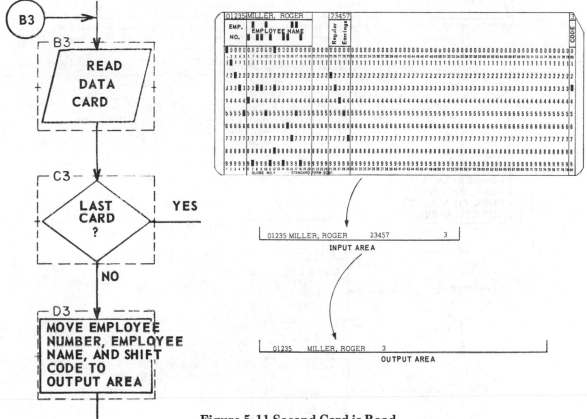

Figure 5-11 Second Card is Read

In Figure 5-11, the second data card is read from the card reader into the card input area, and selected fields are moved to the output area. Note that the Regular Earnings field contains the value 23457 and the Shift-Code field contains a 3.

Step 9: The second data card is processed. As this card contains a code 3, the employee is to receive $5.00 in bonus pay.

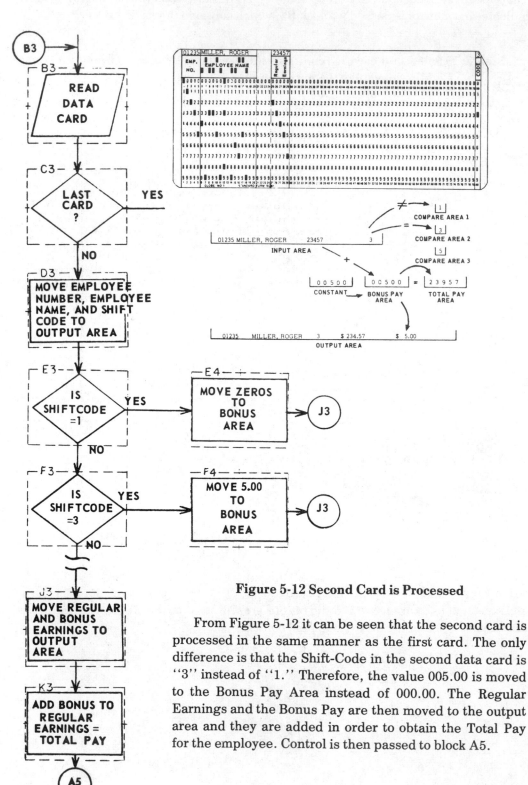

Figure 5-12 Second Card is Processed

From Figure 5-12 it can be seen that the second card is processed in the same manner as the first card. The only difference is that the Shift-Code in the second data card is "3" instead of "1." Therefore, the value 005.00 is moved to the Bonus Pay Area instead of 000.00. The Regular Earnings and the Bonus Pay are then moved to the output area and they are added in order to obtain the Total Pay for the employee. Control is then passed to block A5.

Step 10:   The Total Pay is moved to the output area and the line is printed.

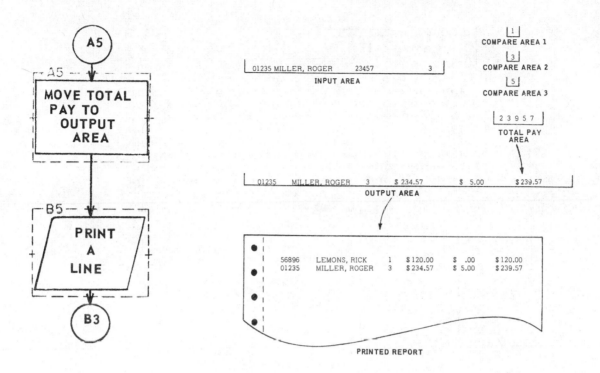

Figure 5-13 Line is Printed on the Printer

In Figure 5-13 it can be seen that after the Total Pay is calculated, it is moved to the printer output area and the print line is then printed. The third card will be processed in the same manner as the first two cards. The printed report after the third card is processed is illustrated in Figure 5-14.

Step 11:   The third card is read and processed and printed.

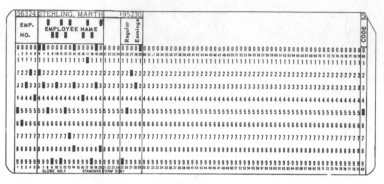

CARD INPUT

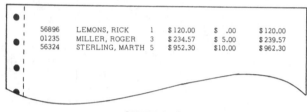

PRINTED OUTPUT

Figure 5-14 Third Card is Processed and Printed

As can be seen from Figure 5-14, the third card is processed in the same manner as the first two cards. Again the only difference is that the Shift-Code field in the third card contains a "5." Therefore, the employee worked the third shift and is entitled to 10.00 as Bonus Pay. This 10.00 bonus pay is added to the Regular Earnings of 952.30 and the Total Pay of 962.30 is printed on the report.

Whenever codes are punched within data cards to indicate a particular condition, such as the Shift-Code in the example, the possiblity exists that the value in the code field will not contain a valid value, that is, the Shift-Code may not contain a 1, 3, or 5. This may occur, for example, if the keypunch operator makes an error. Therefore, any program which is to use codes which are punched in a card must make provision for processing an invalid code. In the program in this chapter which creates the Payroll Report, the program checks for the values 1, 3, or 5 in the Shift-Code field. If none of these codes is found in the card, an error message "IMPROPER SHIFT-CODE CARD NOT PROCESSED" is printed on the report in place of the Regular Earnings, the Bonus Pay, and the Total Pay. The fourth card in the input stream contains an invalid code. The processing of this card is illustrated below.

Step 12: **The fourth data card is read.**

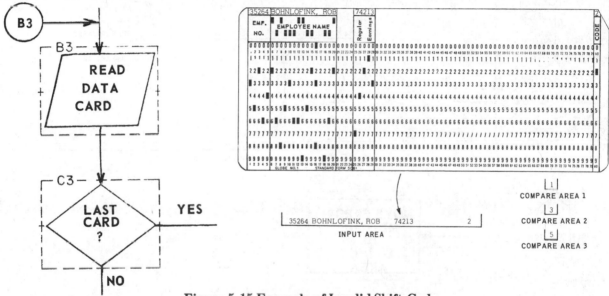

Figure 5-15 Example of Invalid Shift-Code

In the example above, it can be seen that the fourth data card is read into the Input Area in the same manner as the previous cards. Note also that the fourth card contains the value "2" in the Shift-Code field. This is an invalid value because only 1, 3, and 5 are valid. Therefore, the data card may not be processed in the normal manner since it is not known which shift the employee worked. When this occurs, an error message must be printed on the report. This processing is illustrated in Figure 5-16.

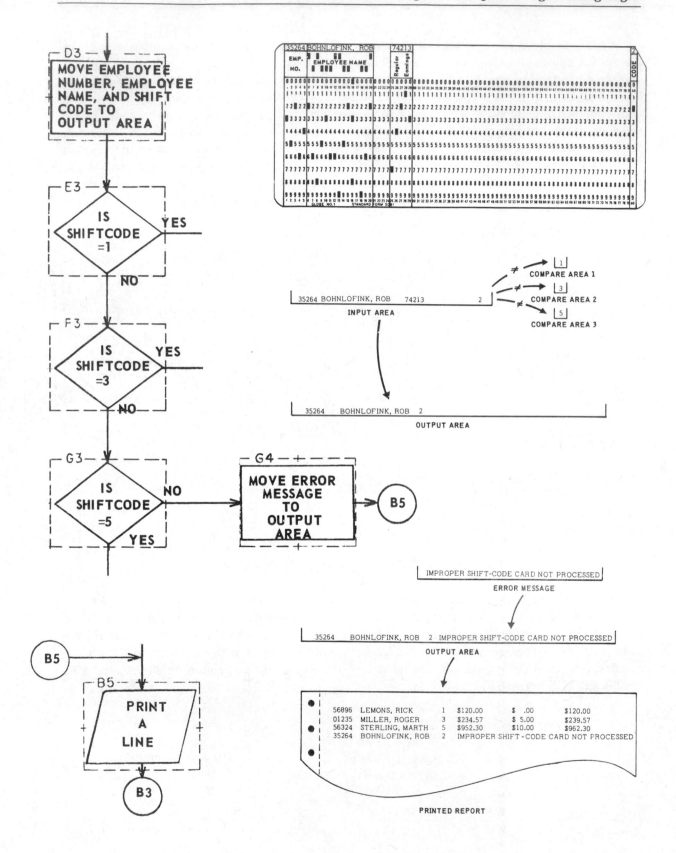

Figure 5-16 Invalid Shift-Code Is Processed

Note from the example in Figure 5-16 that the Employee Number, the Employee Name, and the Shift-Code are moved from the input area to the output area in the same manner as cards which contain a valid Shift-Code. This is done for two reasons: a) The data which is moved is correct regardless of whether the Shift-Code is correct or incorrect; b) The data moved to the output area may be used to identify the card in error so that it may be corrected and resubmitted in subsequent runs.

After the data is moved to the output area, the comparisons are performed on the value in the Shift-Code field. Note from Figure 5-16 that the value punched in the card, "2," is not equal to the valid values 1, 3, or 5. Therefore, the error message is moved to the printer output area. As noted previously, it is always necessary to check for all valid values within a field which contains codes because the possibility exists that an invalid value will be in the field. After the error message is moved to the output area, control is passed directly to block B5 which contains the instructions to write on the printer. Note that the Regular Earnings, the Bonus Pay, and the Total Pay are not moved to the output area. This is because there is no way of determining the correct Bonus Pay since the Shift-Code field does not contain a valid value. Thus, the Total Pay cannot be calculated properly.

After the line is printed on the printer, control is passed to block B3 which reads the next card. Processing will continue until the last data card is read.

Step 14: The last data card is read.

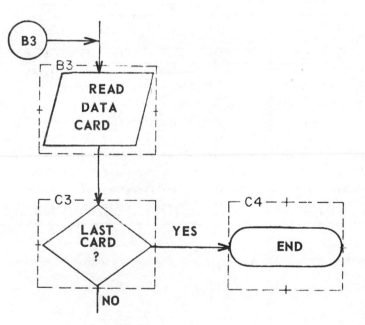

Figure 5-17 Last Card is Read

As with programs illustrated previously, when the last data card is read, the program is terminated. In the example, there is no special processing which must take place at the conclusion of the processing of the data cards so the program is ended.

CHAPTER 5

FLOWCHARTING ASSIGNMENT 1

INSTRUCTIONS

On a Flowchart Worksheet draw the flowchart to illustrate the logic required to produce a Customer Sales Report. Input cards will contain a control code indicating whether the customer balance punched on the card is current, whether the balance is over 30 days old, or whether the balance is over 60 days old. A "1" punch indicates a current account, a "2" punch indicates an account 30-60 days past due; and a "3" punch indicates an account over 60 days past due. If the account is current, a 3% cash discount is given. If the account is 30-60 days past due, no cash discount is given. For accounts over 60 days past due, a 1.5% service charge is added to the account.

INPUT: Customer Sales Cards

Input is to consist of Customer Sales Cards containing the Customer Number, the Customer Name, the Balance and a Code field containing a "1," a "2," or "3" punch. The format of the Sales Cards is illustrated below.

OUTPUT: Customer Sales Report

Output is to consist of a Customer Sales Report. The report is to contain the Customer Number, the Customer Name, the Balance, the Discount Percentage or Service Charge, and the Balance Due. The Balance Due is obtained by multiplying the Balance by the Discount Percentage and subtracting the answer obtained from the original balance, or by multiplying the balance by the Service Charge and adding the answer to the original balance. Each Customer is to be identified as being "Current," "30-60 Days" or "Over 60 Days."

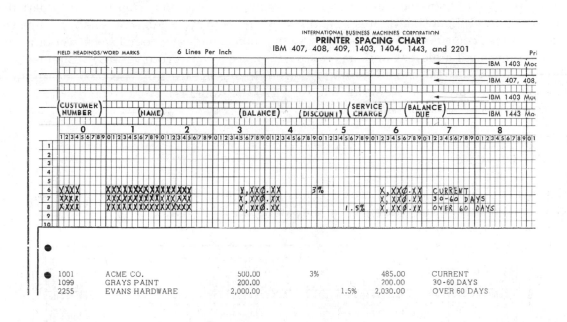

CHAPTER 5

FLOWCHARTING ASSIGNMENT 2

INSTRUCTIONS

On a Flowchart Worksheet draw the flowchart to illustrate the logic required to produce a Sales Commission Report. Input cards will contain a control code indicating the type of Employee. A "1" code indicates a part time employee. No commission is paid to part time employees. A "2" punch indicates a fulltime salaried employee. Fulltime salaried employees receive a 5% commission on all sales. A "3" punch indicates employees working on a commission only. Employees working on a commission only basis receives a 5% commission on all sales up to $1,000.00, and a 7% commission on all sales in excess of $1,000.00. For example, a "commission only" employee with sales of $1,200.00 would receive a commission of 5% on $1,000.00, and a 7% commission on $200.00.

INPUT: Sales Cards

Input is to consist of Sales Cards containing the Salesman Number, Salesman Name, and Sales Amount and a Code. The format of the Sales Cards is illustrated below.

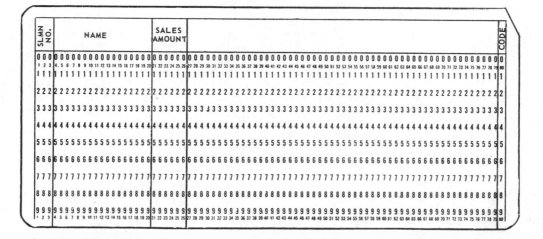

OUTPUT: Sales Commission Report

Output is to consist of a Sales Commission Report. The report is to contain the Salesman Number, Salesman Name, Sales Amount and Commission. Employee cards which contain a "1" punch are to be identified as PART-TIME on the report. Employee cards containing a "2" punch are to be identified as FULL-TIME on the report. Employee cards containing a "3" punch are to be identified as COMMISSION on the report. Final Totals are to be taken of the Sales Amount and Commission Amount.

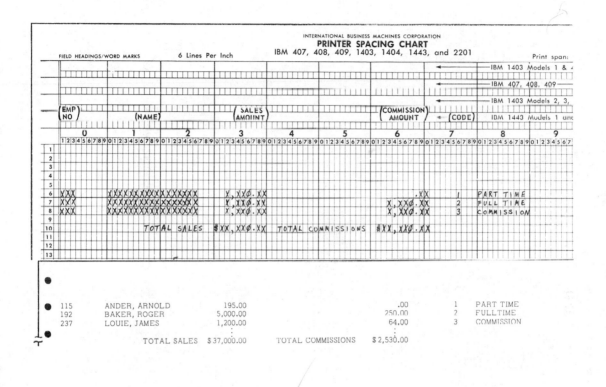

CHAPTER 6

REPORT HEADINGS AND SUBROUTINES

PROGRAM SWITCHES

INTRODUCTION

In the reports which have been created in previous examples, the information on the report was obtained from data read in input cards. Report headings and column headings or other identifying information were not printed. In many business applications it is desirable to utilize the computer to print headings on a report to identify the contents of the report. The use of headings is illustrated in Figure 6-1.

EXAMPLE

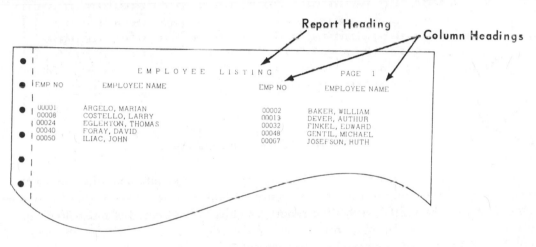

Figure 6-1 Example of Headings on Report

In the example above it can be seen that the title EMPLOYEE LISTING is printed as a part of the report on the first page and each subsequent page. In addition column headings and a page number are also included.

It will also be noted from examples illustrated previously that one line has been written on the report for each input record which is read. This does not necessarily have to occur, that is, more than one input record may be read for each line which is printed on a report. The example in this chapter will illustrate the programming technique which is required in order to place headings on a report and also the use of more than one input record to create an output line on a printed report.

The report to be created is an Employee Listing. The format of the input data cards which will be read is illustrated below.

CARD INPUT

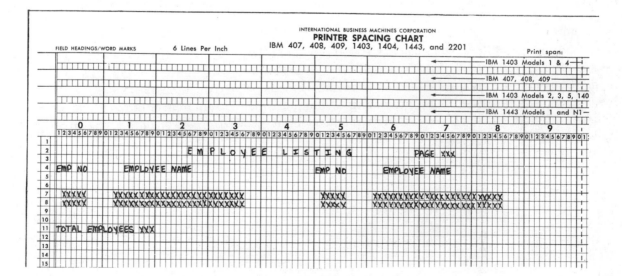

Figure 6-2 Format of Card Input

Note from the card format illustrated above that each card contains an Employee Number in columns 2-6 and the Employee Name in columns 12-36. As can be seen, there is one card for each employee. The Employee Listing report which is to be created is illustrated below. Note the use of page numbering, report and column headings and the message TOTAL EMPLOYEES after all cards have been processed.

REPORT

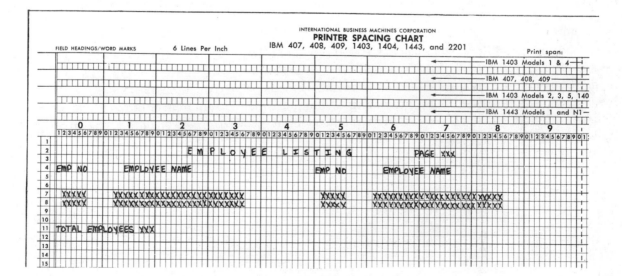

Figure 6-3 Format of Printed Report

As can be seen from the report illustrated in Figure 6-3, headings are used to identify the fields on the report. In addition, it should be noted that each line on the report contains the Employee Number and Employee Name for two employees. Thus, for each line printed on the report, two input cards will be read. The diagram below illustrates this concept.

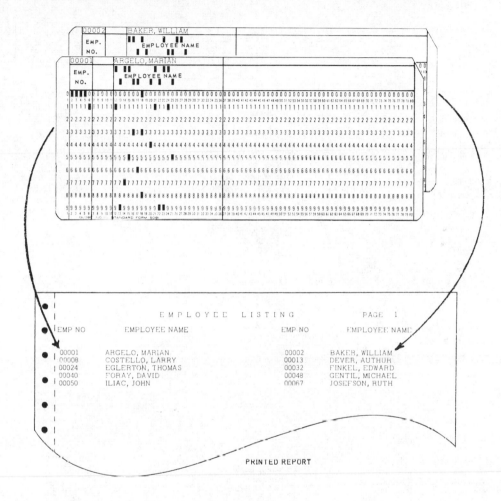

Figure 6-4 Two Input Cards Used in a Single Line of Print

As headings are to be printed on the report on the first page and each subsequent page, a programming technique utilizing what is commonly called a "closed subroutine" will be used. In addition, because two input cards are to be utilized to form a single line of printing the programmer must develop the logic to assure that all cards are properly processed at the end of the job. Thus, this flowchart also introduces an important programming concept called a "program switch." The flowchart is illustrated in Figure 6-5.

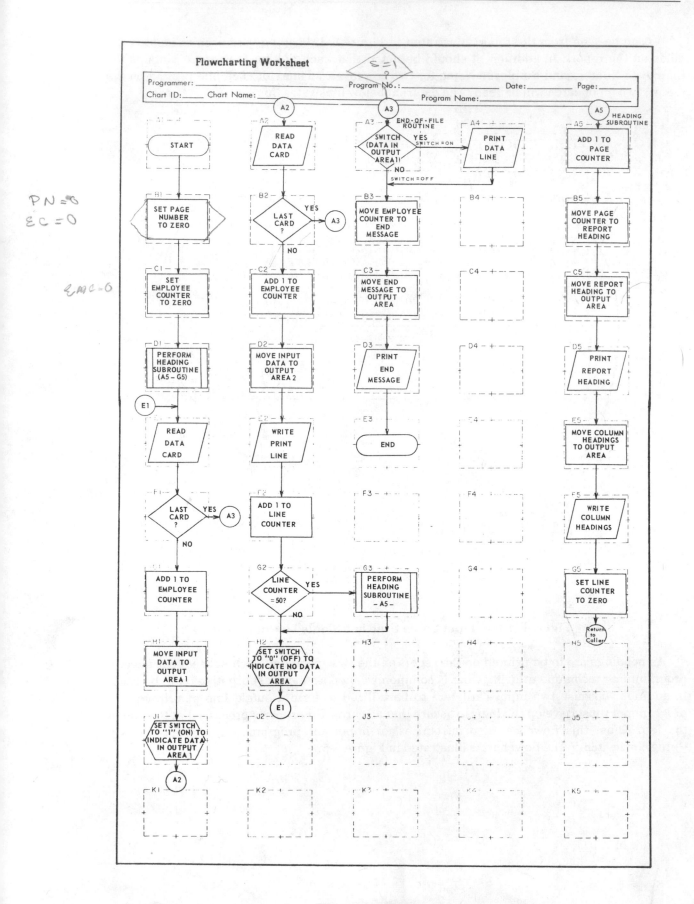

Figure 6-5 Flowchart

The step-by-step processing is described below and on the following pages.

Step 1: The beginning of the program is indicated and the initialization processing is performed.

Figure 6-6 Page Number and Employee Count Area are Zero

Note from the report format illustrated in Figure 6-3 that the report contains a page number in the upper right-hand corner and that, at the conclusion of processing, a total of the number of employees is to be printed. Whenever values are to be accumulated during the processing of data, the counters used to store the accumulated totals must be initialized to zeros prior to beginning processing. Thus, the counter for the page number and the counter for the employee count are set to zero prior to any processing within the program. It should be noted that these counters may be initialized to zero at the beginning of the processing of the program. The method of initialization is normally dependent upon the programming language used.

The page number counter will be incremented each time a new page is to be printed on the report. Thus, when the first page is printed, the page number counter will be incremented by 1 prior to moving it to the output line. As can be seen, this will result in the first page on the report being numbered 1, the second page being numbered 2, etc. As was noted previously, there is one input card per employee. Thus, the employee count is actually a count of the number of cards read. Therefore, each time a card is read in the program, the employee counter will be incremented by one and will reflect the number of employees.

Step 2: The Heading Subroutine is performed.

Note in Figure 6-7 that the rectangular symbol which normally indicates some type of processing is used to indicate that the Heading Subroutine is to be processed. The difference in this symbol is that two vertical lines are included within the rectangle. When this symbol is used, it indicates that the instructions within the program are to cause a Subroutine to be executed.

**Figure 6-7 PERFORM
Heading Subroutine**

A subroutine is defined as a "standardized set of instructions which may be used at more than one point in a program to direct the computer to execute a particular operation." Subroutines are used when the same set of instructions are required at several different points in a program. The Heading Subroutine which is used to print the headings on the report is a CLOSED SUBROUTINE. A Closed Subroutine is a set of instructions required by the program that is not stored in the main line of the program and may be utilized repeatedly when needed in the main program. This is illustrated in Figure 6-8.

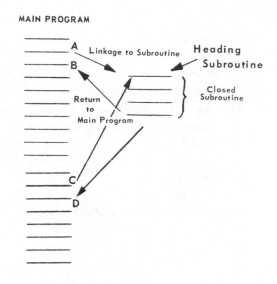

Figure 6-8 Example of Closed Subroutine

In the example above it can be seen that the Main Program must "link" to the closed subroutine. The term "link" is used because upon completion of processing within the subroutine, control is returned to the instruction following the instruction which caused control to be passed to the subroutine. Thus, the instructions within the subroutine may be executed from any point in the main program by merely linking to the subroutine. Control is always returned to the next instruction in the main program when the processing of the subroutine is completed.

In the example, the instructions which are to be used to write the headings on the report are set up as a subroutine. This is because the heading routine is to be called from more than one place within the main program, that is, a heading must be written for the first page prior to writing any data on the report and it must also be written on the subsequent pages after an entire page of data has been printed. Therefore, the heading subroutine must be called prior to processing any data, as illustrated in Figure 6-7, and also following the Write instruction to the printer if a full page of data has been written.

Step 3:   The heading routine is performed.

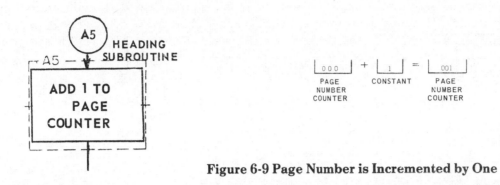

Figure 6-9 Page Number is Incremented by One

In Figure 6-6, the page number field was set to zero. In the example in Figure 6-9, one is added to the page number counter so that the first page on the report will be numbered 1. The constant value "1," which is always added to the page number counter, is stored in main storage within the program. This value is normally initialized when the program is assembled or compiled.

Step 4:   The page number is moved to the Report Heading area.

Figure 6-10 Page Number is Moved to First Heading

Note from the example above that the page number, which was calculated in Figure 6-9, is moved to the Report Heading line. This heading is a constant value which is stored in main storage within the program and is normally established when the program is assembled or compiled. Note also that the page number has been edited, that is, the leading zeros have been removed. Again, this editing capability is available with most programming languages.

Step 5:   Report Heading is moved to the output area and is printed.

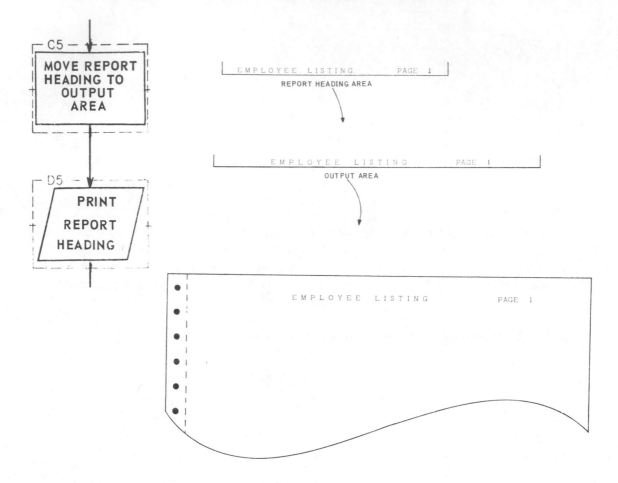

Figure 6-11 First Heading is Printed

Note in Figure 6-11 that the report heading is moved to the output area and is then printed as the first line on the report. The heading which is printed in the example above is the first line which is to be printed on the page. This requires that the page in the printer be positioned in such a way that the first heading line is always the first line on a new page. It order to accomplish this, the page must be ''skipped to head of forms,'' that is, it must be positioned at the first line of the new page. The process of causing the page to skip is performed by either a unique command to the printer to skip to a new page or by a portion of the instruction which is used to write the heading line. The method used is dependent upon the programming language in use.

Regardless of the method used in the program, there must be some type of mechanism on the printer itself which can recognize the beginning of a page. On most printers, the mechanism used is a carriage-control tape. This carriage control tape is placed on the printer on a special device which is able to sense holes in the tape in much the same manner as the holes in punched cards are sensed by the card reader. The holes in the carriage control tape indicate the relative position of the form which is being printed. The example in Figure 6-12 illustrates the carriage control tape which could be used by the program in this chapter.

CARRIAGE CONTROL TAPE

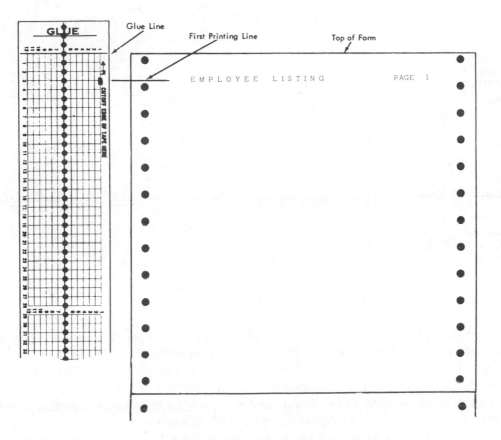

Figure 6-12 Example of Carriage Control Tape

In the example illustrated in Figure 6-12 it can be seen that the size of the carriage control tape corresponds to the size of the form being used. Each horizontal line on the carriage control tape corresponds to a single line of print on the form. Thus, for each line on the report there is a corresponding horizontal line on the carriage control tape. The vertical lines on the carriage control tape correspond to the read brushes which are on the printer and are called CHANNELS. In the carriage control tape illustrated in Figure 6-12, there are 12 channels. The number of channels in a carriage control tape may vary dependent upon the type of printer being used.

Holes are punched in the carriage control tape in much the same way as holes are punched in a card. These holes are then sensed by the brushes on the printer. A hole in a channel may be used to identify and line on a page. For example, note in Figure 6-12 that a hole is punched in channel 1 to correspond to the first line on the page. Therefore, when the printer is instructed to skip to channel 1, that is, skip the forms until the brushes sense the hole in channel 1 of the carriage control tape, the forms will be positioned at the first line of the new page. It is through the use of the carriage control tape that forms in the printer may be skipped to the proper line on the page.

Step 6:   The Column Headings are moved to the output area and printed.

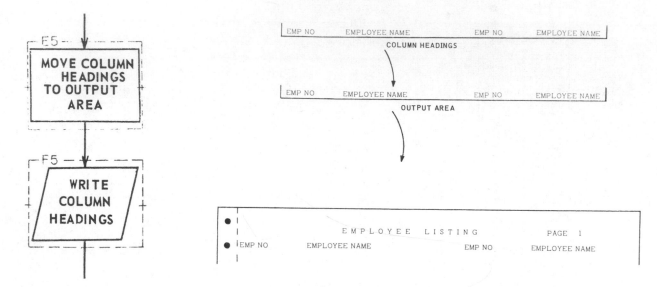

Figure 6-13 Column Headings are Printed

Note from the example in Figure 6-13 that the second line is printed on the report in the same manner as the first heading line, that is, the value which is stored in main storage is moved to the output area and the value which is moved to the output area is then printed. Note that the second heading line is double-spaced, that is, there is a single line of blanks between the first and second heading lines. Double spacing such as this is not normally controlled through the use of a carriage control tape. Instead, there are commands which can be issued to the printer to cause it to automatically space one, two, or three lines. These commands operate independently of the carriage control tape. The carriage control tape is normally used only when it is desired to space more than three lines or when it is necessary to skip to a new page.

Step 7:   The line counter is set to zero and control is returned to the main program.

Figure 6-14 Page Count is Set to Zero and Control is Returned

As was noted previously, the heading subroutine is to be entered whenever a heading is to be printed on the report. A heading must be printed each time the preceeding page has been fully printed. One method to determine if a page has been fully printed is to count the number of lines which have been printed on the page. When the required number of lines have been printed, the heading subroutine must be entered in order to skip to the next page and print the new headings. In the example, after the headings are printed, 50 detail lines will be printed and then the computer will be instructed to skip to a new page and again print the report headings on the next page.

When the number of lines printed is to be used to determine when the heading subroutine is to be entered, a counter is used. The counter is initialized to zero in the heading subroutine and when a line is printed on the report, the counter is incremented by 1. When the counter reaches a specified value, the heading subroutine is entered. In addition, the heading subroutine must reset the counter to zero so that the number of lines on the new page will be counted properly. Thus, in Figure 6-14, the line counter is set to zero so that when lines other than the headings are printed on the page, the counter will be incremented to indicate the number of lines printed. The line counter in Figure 6-14 should not be confused with the page number counter illustrated earlier. The page number counter is used to keep a count of the number of pages printed and to supply a page number to the first heading.

After the line counter has been set to zero, the heading subroutine returns control to the main program. As noted previously, the reason for using a subroutine is so that the instructions in it may be executed from more than one portion of the main program. Thus, the term "Return to Caller" is used to indicate that the subroutine returns control to the portion of the main program from which it was called. In this example, it will return control to block E1 because this is the block immediately following the instruction which called the heading subroutine.

Step 8:   A data card is read.

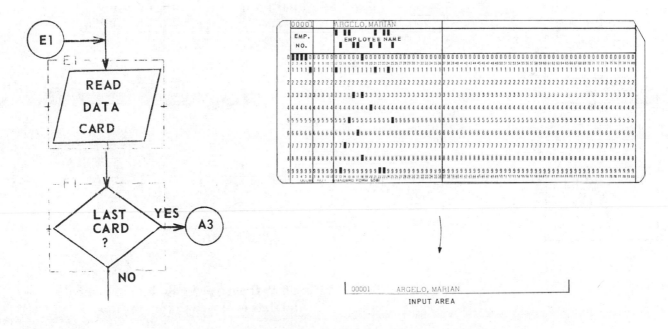

Figure 6-15 Data Card is Read

After the page number and employee count fields have been initialized to zero and the heading is printed on the first page, the program is ready to begin processing data. Therefore, the first data card is read. As with all programs which process input data, a test must be made to determine if the last data card has been read. In the example, the last data card is not read. Therefore, the "No" path of the decision symbol is taken.

Step 9: The Employee Count field is incremented by 1 and the input data is moved to the output area.

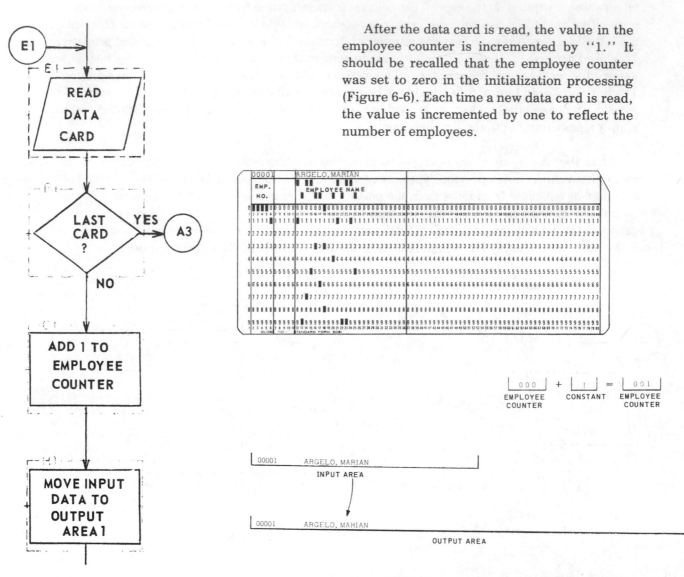

After the data card is read, the value in the employee counter is incremented by "1." It should be recalled that the employee counter was set to zero in the initialization processing (Figure 6-6). Each time a new data card is read, the value is incremented by one to reflect the number of employees.

Figure 6-16 Employee Count is Incremented And Data is Moved to Output Area

After the employee counter is updated, the input data is moved to the output area. The input data consists of the Employee Number and the Employee Name.

It should be noted that the term OUTPUT AREA1 in the flowchart is used merely to reference a portion of the Output Area which, in the example above, will contain the first portion of the line to be printed.

Step 10:   A switch is set to indicate that output data is in the output area.

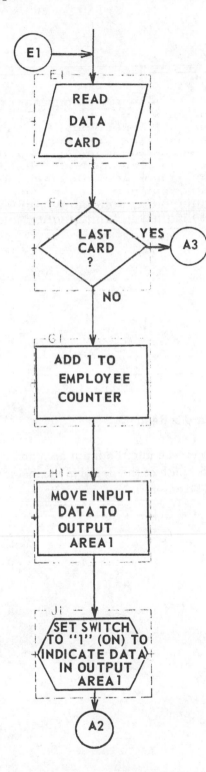

A program switch is a programming technique which is commonly used to allow alternative processing to be accomplished within a program dependent upon the value in the switch. In the example flowchart in this chapter, the use of a switch is necessary to allow for the printing of a record when the end of job routine is entered. At this point in the flowchart it is only necessary to understand that the purpose of the switch is to indicate that there is data in the output area to be printed.

In the example in Figure 6-17 it can be seen that the value "1" is moved to the Switch area to set the Switch "ON." The value "1" in this area indicates that a portion of the output line is stored in the output area. If the switch was not equal to "1," it would indicate that a portion of the output line was not in the output area. Thus, as can be seen, by placing a value in the "Switch" field, it can be specified that the output line must be printed by the end-of-file routine before the total employees line is printed. If the value is not in the Switch field, the output line will not be printed prior to printing the total employees line.

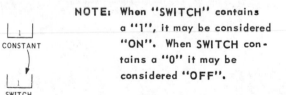

NOTE: When "SWITCH" contains a "1", it may be considered "ON". When SWITCH contains a "0" it may be considered "OFF".

Figure 6-17 Switch is Set

It should be noted that the value "1" in the switch area is not required, that is, any value may be used as long as it has meaning within the program. Thus, the switch could be set to any value in Step 10 as long as the end-of-file routine tests the proper value. The program switch is merely used to indicate a condition within the program which may be tested and which may control which processing is executed.

Step 11: The second data card is read.

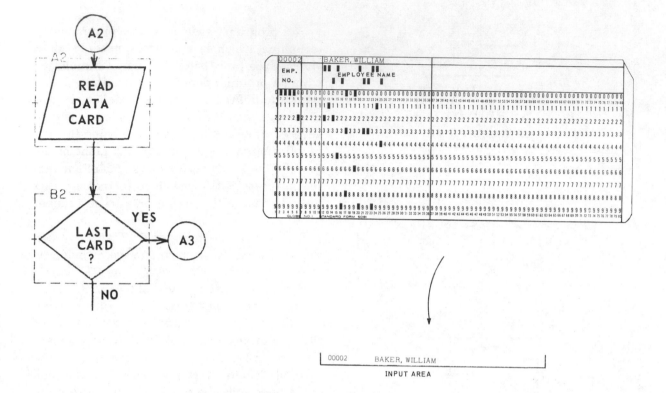

Figure 6-18 Second Data Card is Read

As can be seen from Figure 6-18, the second data card is read into the input area and a test is made for the last card. Since a data card is read, the ''no'' path of the decision symbol is taken. If it had been the last card, the end-of-file routine would be entered.

Step 12: **The Employee Counter is updated by one and the input data is moved to the output area.**

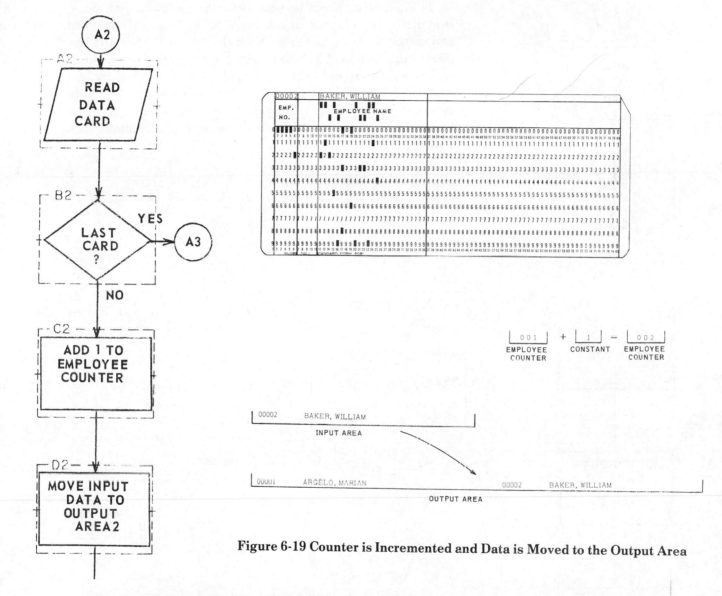

Figure 6-19 Counter is Incremented and Data is Moved to the Output Area

In the example above it can be seen that the employee counter is incremented by one because the second card has been read. As was noted previously, the value in this counter is incremented by one each time a card is read in order to reflect the number of employees. The input data is then moved to the output area. Note that the output area now contains the data from both the first and the second card.

Note in the flowchart in Box D2 that the term OUTPUT AREA 2 is used to refer to the right portion of the single OUTPUT AREA.

Step 13:   **The output line is printed and the line counter is updated by one.**

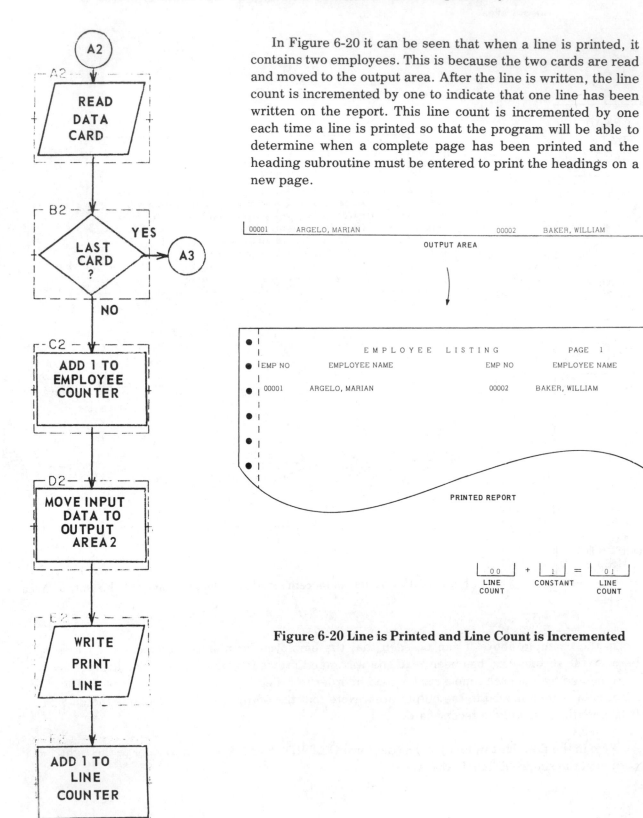

In Figure 6-20 it can be seen that when a line is printed, it contains two employees. This is because the two cards are read and moved to the output area. After the line is written, the line count is incremented by one to indicate that one line has been written on the report. This line count is incremented by one each time a line is printed so that the program will be able to determine when a complete page has been printed and the heading subroutine must be entered to print the headings on a new page.

Figure 6-20 Line is Printed and Line Count is Incremented

Step 14:   Determine if an entire page has been printed.

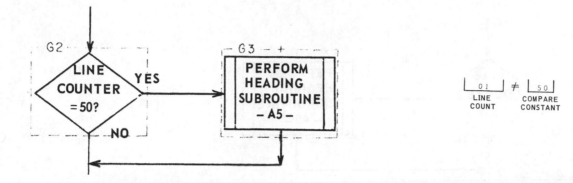

Figure 6-21 Line Count is Checked

In the example above, the value in the Line Count field is compared to a constant of 50 which is stored in main storage within the program. If the line count is equal to 50, it indicates than an entire page has been printed, that is, fifty lines of names have been printed on a single page. When this occurs, the heading subroutine is entered to skip to a new page and print the headings. As can be seen from the example above, the value in the Line Count field is "01" because only one line has been printed on the report.

Step 15:   Set Switch to "0" (off) to indicate no data in the output area and return to read the next card.

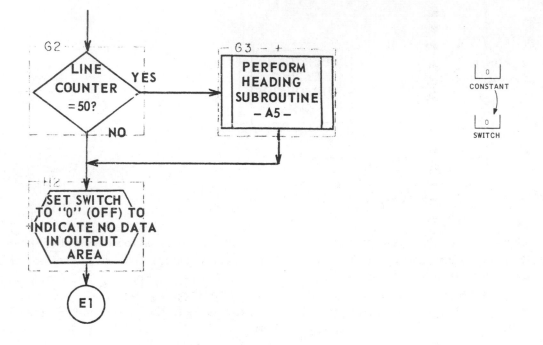

Figure 6-22 Indicate No Data in Output Area

It should be recalled that a program switch was set to indicate that data was in the output area after the first data card was moved to the output area (Figure 6-17). This switch was set so that if the second Read command resulted in an end-of-file condition, the first card would be printed. After the second card has been read and the entire line has been printed, however, there is no data in the output area **which remains to be printed.** Therefore, the switch must be set to indicate that no data is in the output area to be printed. In the example in Figure 6-22, this is accomplished by moving the value "0" to the switch area. It should be recalled that the value "I" was moved to the switch area to indicate that data was in the output area. As noted previously, the values used within a switch to indicate alternative processing within the program may be any value desired by the programmer. The only requirements is that the use of switches be consistent throughout the program. Thus, the choice of "0" to indicate that no data is in the output area and "1" to indicate that data is in the output area is merely an arbitrary choice.

Step 16: **The remaining forty-nine lines are printed on the first page of the report.**

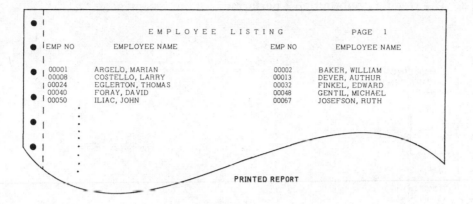

Figure 6-23 First Page of Report is printed

As noted, there will be 50 lines of detail printing on each page of the report. When the fiftieth line has been printed, the header routine will be entered. This is illustrated in Figure 6-24.

Step 17: **The Heading Subroutine is entered when 50 lines are printed.**

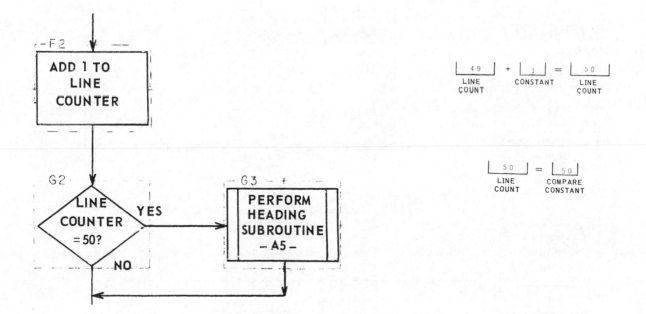

Figure 6-24 End of Page is reached

As can be seen from Figure 6-24, the line count will contain the value 50 when fifty detail lines have been printed on the report. Thus, the Heading Subroutine will be entered.

Step 18:   The Heading Subroutine is performed for the second page.

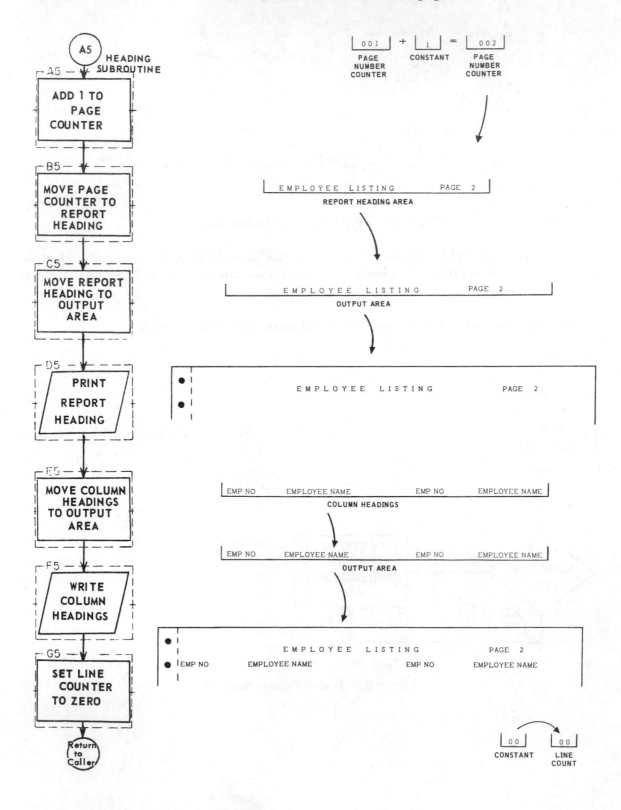

Figure 6-25 Heading Subroutine for Second Page

Note: If end-of-file routine is is entered here, the data card read by the instruction in Box E1 must be printed and then the program can be terminated.

In Figure 6-25 it can be seen that the page number is incremented from "1" to "2" to be printed in the heading. The first and second headings are then printed on the report. The last step in the Heading Subroutine is to reset the Line Count to a value of zero. This is done because fifty more lines are to be printed on page 2 before the heading routine is entered again. The counter must be reset so that it may be incremented to a value of fifty in the main program.

The program will continue to process data until the end-of-file is reached on the card input file. When this occurs, the end-of-file routine will be entered. As was noted, two situations may occur when the end-of-file routine is entered. If the end-of-file routine is entered after the first read instruction in the program, there will be no data in the output area which must be printed. If the routine is entered after the second read instruction, there will be data which is in the output area which must be printed (the data card which was read by the first read instruction). This status is indicated by the value in the Program Switch. If the value in the switch is equal to zero, there is no data in the output area and if the value in the switch is equal to one, there is data in the output area. Therefore, the first operation which must be performed in the end-of-file routine is to determine if there is data in the output area to be printed. For example, assume that one data card remains to be processed and that data card is read by the statement in Box E1.

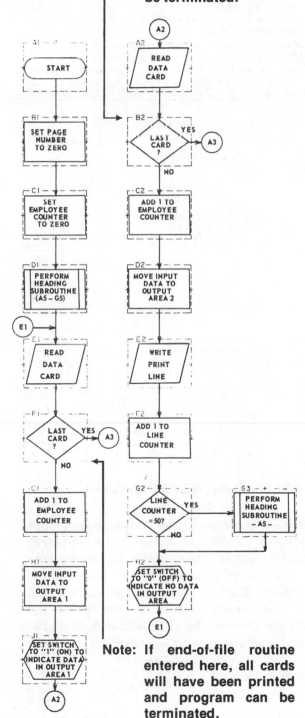

Note: If end-of-file routine entered here, all cards will have been printed and program can be terminated.

Figure 6-26 Flowchart

Step 19: Last data card is read.

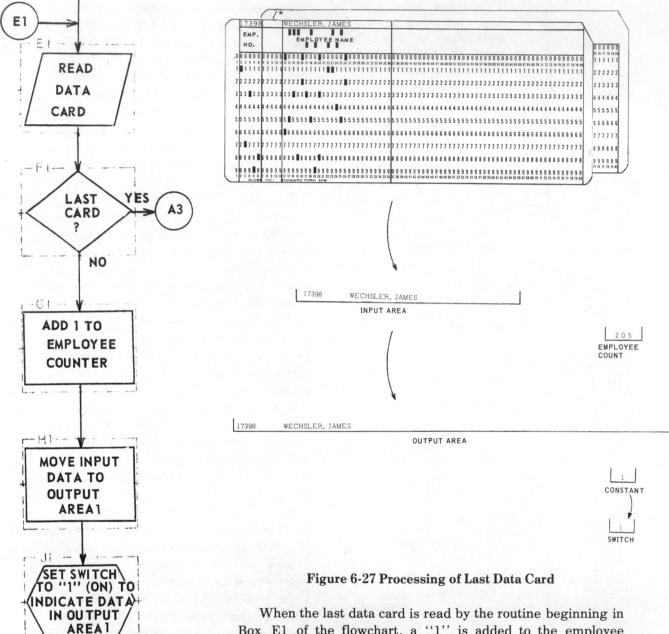

Figure 6-27 Processing of Last Data Card

When the last data card is read by the routine beginning in Box E1 of the flowchart, a "1" is added to the employee counter, the data in the input area is moved to the output area and the switch is set to "1" to indicate that there is data in the output area to be printed. The next step is to read another card through the read instruction specified in box A2 of the flowchart. As this is the /* card, the card used to indicate the end of the data cards to be processed, the end-of-file routine is entered.

Step 20: The end-of-file routine is entered and the status of the program switch is checked.

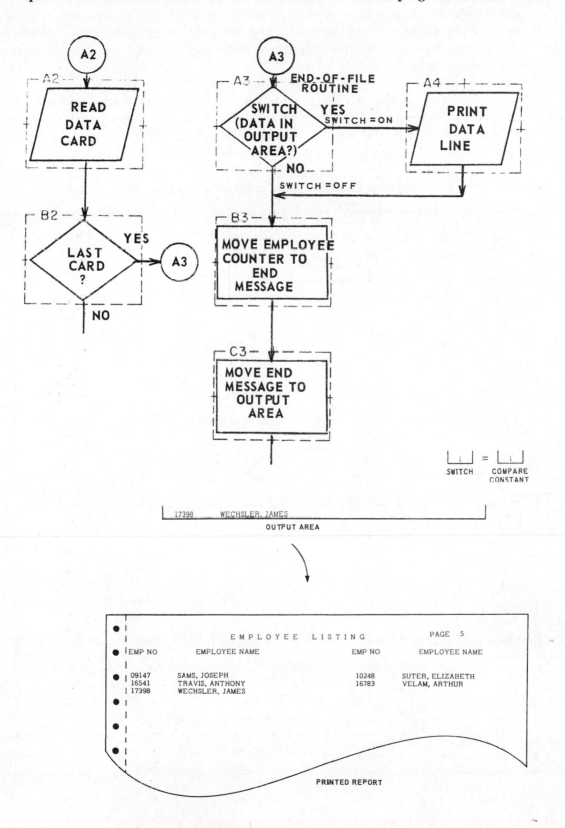

Figure 6-28 Last Data Line is Printed if Stored in Output Area

In the example in Figure 6-28 if the value in the Switch field is equal to 1, it indicates that there is data in the output area to be printed. Thus, the method used to determine if there is data in the output area is to compare the value in the Switch field to a constant "1." If they are equal, it means that there is data in the output area and if they are not equal, it means there is not data in the output area.

If there is data to be printed, the data is merely printed by a Write instruction in the same manner as all of the other detail lines have been printed. Note that if the switch contained a zero, the Print instruction would not be executed. This condition would occur if the read instruction in box E1 of the flowchart read the /* or end-of-file card.

Step 21:   The End Message is Printed and the program is terminated.

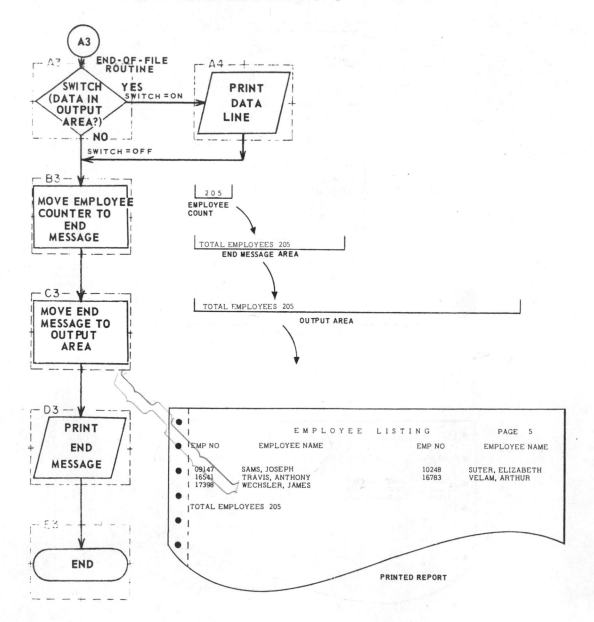

Figure 6-29 End Message is Printed

Note in Figure 6-29 that the Employee Count, which has been incremented by one each time a card is read, contains the value ''205,'' which indicates that there have been 205 cards read and processed. The value is moved to the End Message area and then the End Message is moved to the output area. It is then printed as the final line on the report.

After the End Message has been printed, there is no more processing to be done in the program, so it is terminated. The use of headings on printed reports is extremely common. It is very seldom that a report is prepared without some type of identifying headings. The use of a subroutine is also quite common since headings can many times be required at different points within the program.

The use of a programmed switch as an indicator within a program is the primary way in which program-created conditions may be tested. The use of a programmed switch should be thoroughly understood prior to beginning Chapter 7.

Example 2 - Programmed Switch

The previous example illustrated the use of a programmed switch to control the proper printing of the data at the end of file routine. Programmed switches are an effective programming technique and have many applications when programming business type problems. The effective use of switches in a program can often dramatically reduce the number of steps required in the solution of a problem by using routines or parts of routines that are common to several parts of the program.

In the previous example two READ steps were used in the solution of the problem. The first read was used to read the first data card, the second read operation was used to read the second data card (See Figure 6-5). Note in the flowchart that Steps E1, F1, and G1, and Steps A2, B2, and C2 are identical. By a slight modification to the Flowchart in Figure 6-5 through the use of a programmed switch, Steps A2, B2, and C2 can be eliminated. Figure 6-30 illustrates a modification of the flowchart in Figure 6-5. Note the use of the Switch in Step II1. The use of the switch at this point in the logic permits all processing to be performed using a single Read operation.

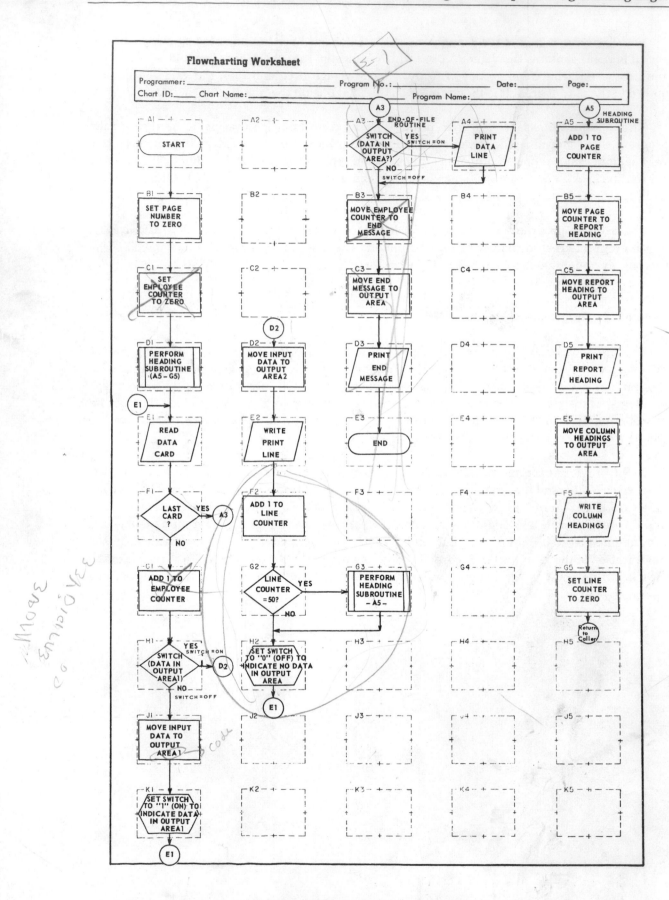

Figure 6-30 Flowchart - Example 2

CHAPTER 6

FLOWCHARTING ASSIGNMENT 1

INSTRUCTIONS

On a Flowchart Worksheet draw a flowchart to illustrate the logic required to produce a DAILY SALES REPORT.

(handwritten: Report HEADING)

INPUT: Salesman Name Cards and Sales Cards

Input is to consist of two types of Cards for each salesman: a Salesman Name Card and a Daily Sales Card reflecting the Amount sold to each customer contacted for the day. There is one Salesman Name Card for each salesman. This card is identified by a ''1'' control punch in card column 80. There will be one or more Daily Sales Cards for each Salesman. These cards will be identified by a ''2'' control punch in card column 80. The format of the cards is illustrated below.

NOTE: A ''2'' control punch in card column 80 identifies the Daily Sales Cards

A ''1'' control punch in card column 80 identifies the Salesman Name Cards

OUTPUT: Daily Sales Report

Output is to consist of a Daily Sales Report listing the Salesman Number and Salesman Name from the first card. The Date, Customer Number, and Sales Amount are to be printed for each of the Daily Sales Cards. Note that the Date which will be identical for each of the Daily Sales Cards is to be printed only on the first line for each Salesman. Include report and column headings and a page number.

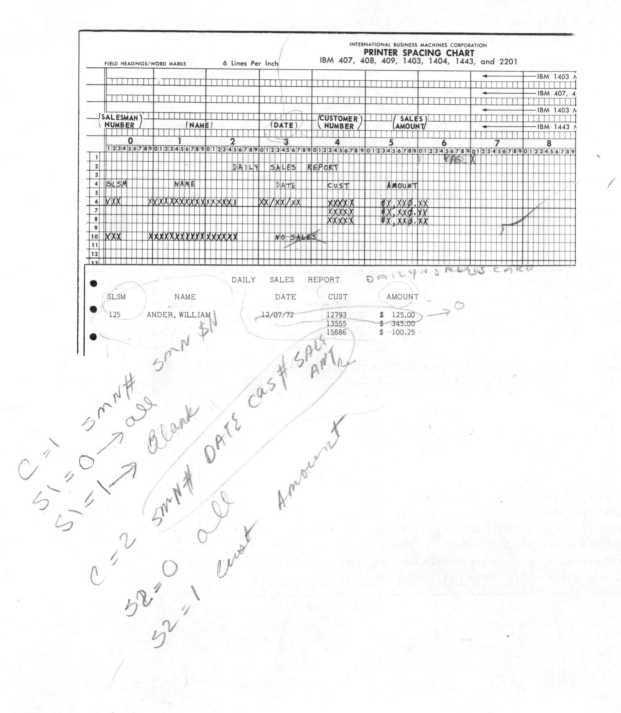

CHAPTER 6

FLOWCHARTING ASSIGNMENT 2

INSTRUCTIONS

Modify the problem presented in Flowcharting Assignment 1 to illustrate the logic to produce a Daily Sales Report in cases where there may be no sales for the day, that is, there may be a Salesman Name Card (code 1) but no Daily Sales Cards. If there are no Daily Sales Cards for the Salesman, the message "NO SALES" should be printed adjacent to the Salesman Number and Salesman Name.

OUTPUT: Daily Sales Report

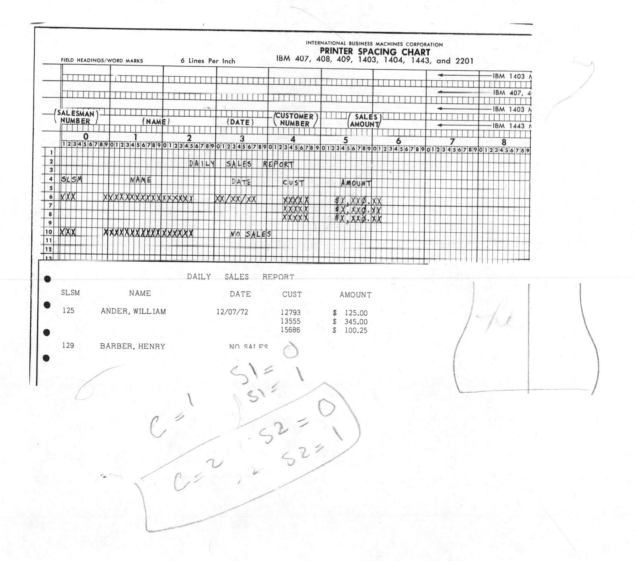

MINOR TOTAL

INTRODUCTION

As has been seen in previous examples, processing may take alternate paths dependent upon the relative values in two fields in main storage. One of the more common types of comparisons which are made to determine the path of processing concerns comparing the same field in each input record which is read and executing unique routines when the value in the field changes. The example in this chapter illustrates this concept of "control breaks" by creating an Accounts Receivable Register report and taking a minor total for each new customer. The input to the program is illustrated in Figure 7-1.

CARD INPUT

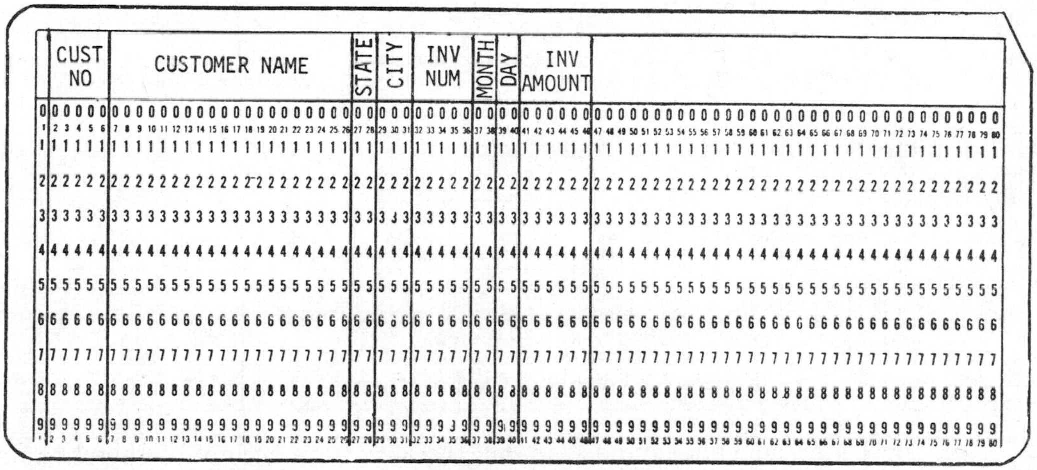

Figure 7-1 Card Input

From Figure 7-1 it can be seen that the input consists of the Customer Number, the State and City, an Invoice Number, the Month and Day, and an Invoice Amount. The output of the program is illustrated in Figure 7-2.

PRINTED REPORT

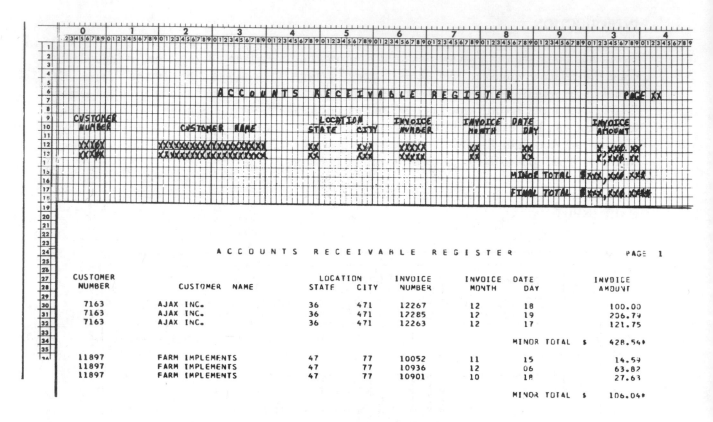

Figure 7-2 Format of Output Report

In the report illustrated above it can be seen that the data from each of the input cards is printed on the report. In addition, a total is accumulated for each customer invoice amount and when a new customer is read, that is, when the customer number changes, the total for the customer just processed is printed. This total is called a MINOR TOTAL. Note also that a Final Total of all of the invoice amounts will also be printed.

The basic logic involves reading the first card; storing the customer number from the first card in a "compare area"; processing the first card; reading the next card; comparing the customer number from the card just read to the customer number in the compare area; if the customer numbers are equal processing the card; if the customer numbers are unequal printing a minor total.

The flowchart for the program is illustrated on pages 119 and 120. Note that two pages are required for the flowchart and that an "off page" connector symbol is used when the sequence of operations continues from one page to another.

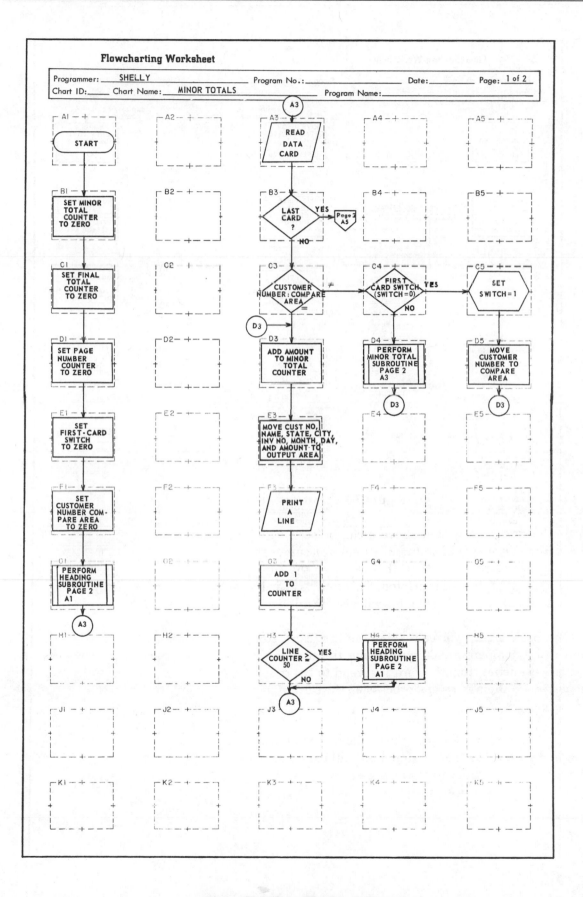

Figure 7-3 Flowchart (1 of 2)

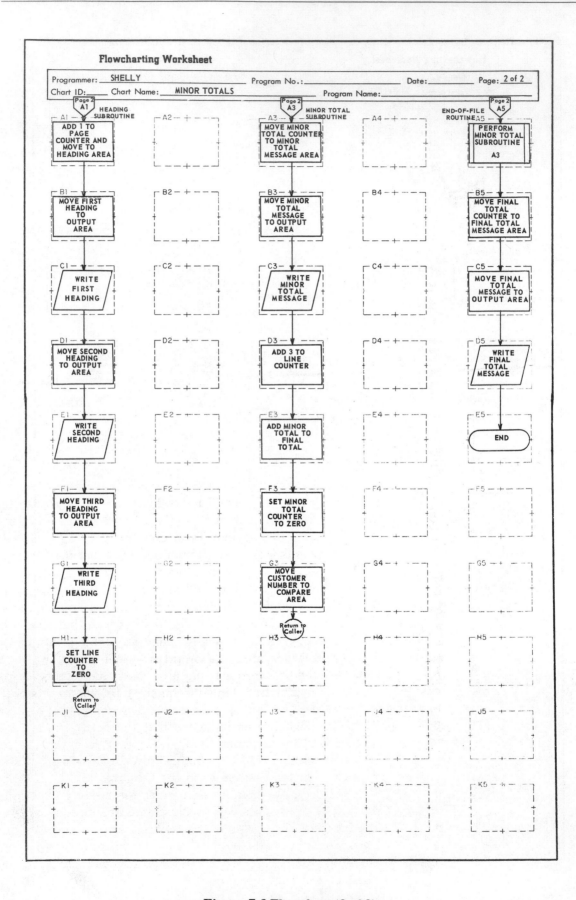

Figure 7-3 Flowchart (2 of 2)

The detailed processing within the program is illustrated in the following steps.

Step 1:   The Initialization of counters and a compare area is performed and the heading on the first page is printed.

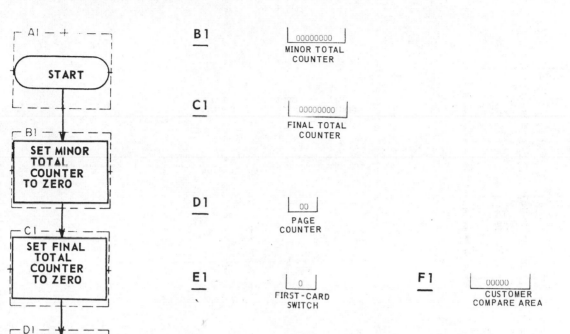

Figure 7-4 Initialization

In the example above it can be seen that initial values of zero are placed in a Minor Total counter, a Final Total counter, a Page Number counter, A First-Card Switch, and a Customer Compare Area. The Minor Total Counter is used to total the invoice amounts for each customer and the Final Total counter is used to total all of the minor totals. Both of these must be set to zero initially so that they will reflect the proper values when the invoice amounts are added to them. The page number is set to zero in the same manner as in Chapter 6 so that it may be incremented each time a new page is to be printed. The First-Time Switch area is a program switch which is used to indicate if the first card is being processed. Special processing, which will be illustrated in subsequent steps, is to take place if the first card is being processed. The value "0" in the First-Card Switch area indicates that the first card is being processed. The Customer Compare area is used to store the customer number which is being processed in the program. When the customer number in the Compare area is different than the customer number on a card, the minor total routine must be processed, as will be illustrated in subsequent steps. The value zero is moved to the compare area so that the first card, which cannot contain a customer number of zero, will cause an unequal comparison when compared with the customer compare area.

After the initialization has taken place, the Heading Subroutine is entered in order to print the heading on the first page.

Step 2:   The headings are printed on the first page of the report.

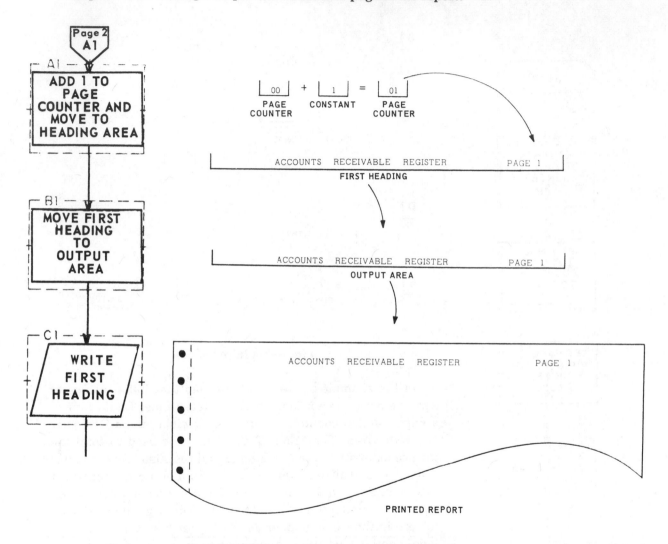

Figure 7-5a Report Heading is Printed on Report

After the report heading is printed, the column headings are moved to the output area and printed and the line counter is set to zero.

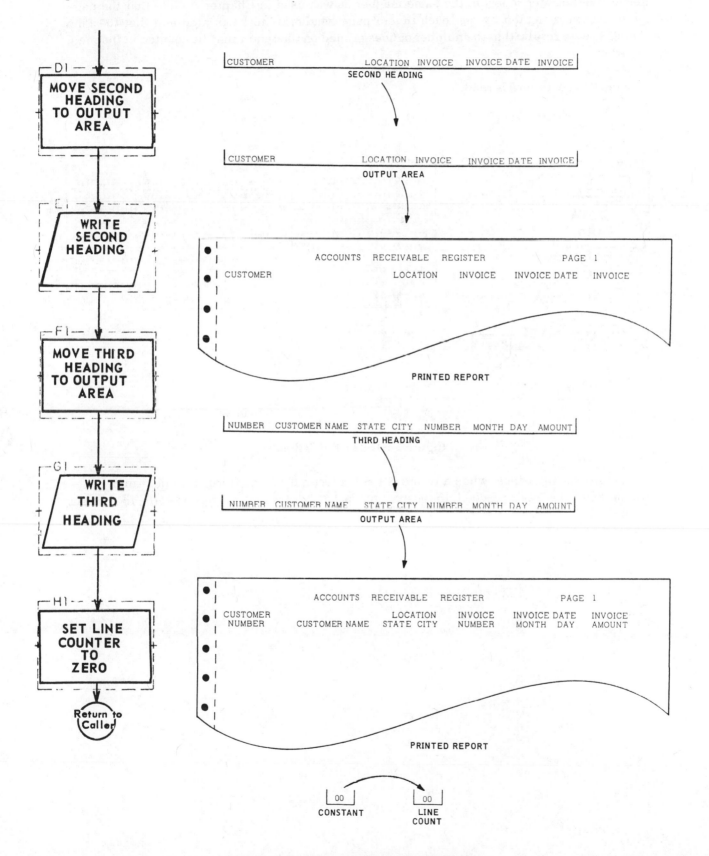

Figure 7-5b Column Headings are Printed

In the example in Figure 7-5, it can be seen that the headings are printed on the Accounts Receivable Register report in the same manner as was used in Chapter 6. Note that the page number is incremented by one each time a page heading is to be printed and that the Line Count is set to zero so that the number of lines printed on the report may be counted in the main program.

Step 3: A data card is read.

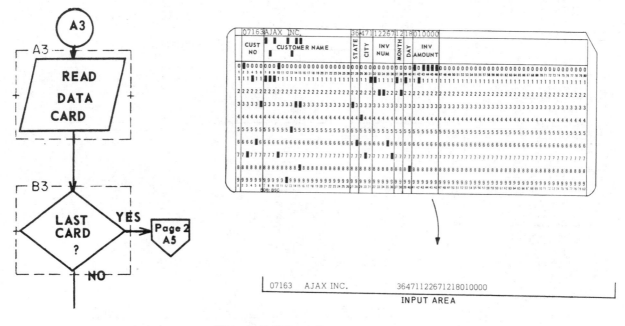

Figure 7-6 Data Card is Read

As with all input files, when a record is read, a test must be performed to determine if the end of the file has been reached. In the example, a data card is read so the end of the file has not been read.

Step 4: The Customer Number on the card is compared with the Customer Number in the Customer Number Compare area.

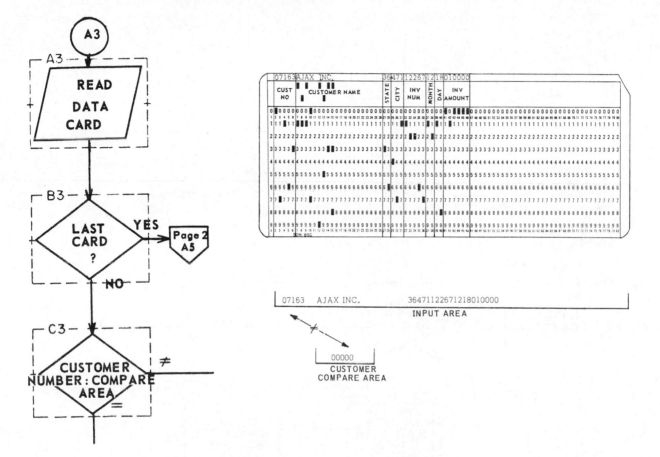

Figure 7-7 Customer Number in Card is Compared with Customer Compare Area

As noted previously, each card which is read contains a customer number. This customer number in the card is compared with the Customer Number contained in the compare area to determine when a new customer has been found and when the Minor Total for the previous customer should be printed. When the first card is read, however, there is no previous customer. Thus, the customer number in the data card is compared to the zeros which were placed in the Customer Number compare area in the Initialization routines (see Figure 7-40). Since the customer number in the card can never be zero, the comparison with the first data card will always produce an unequal comparison as illustrated in Figure 7-7.

Note in Figure 7-7 the use of a colon (:) to indicate that two values are to be compared to each other. This is an alternate method which may be used to indicate a comparison when an "equal-unequal" condition is to be tested. Note also the use of the equal sign (=) and the unequal sign (≠) to indicate the paths to be taken as a result of the comparison. When the colon is used to indicate that a comparison is to take place, the equal sign and the unequal sign must be used to identify the paths to be taken. In the example, it can be seen that the customer number in the compare area is not equal to the customer number in the input card. Therefore, the unequal path is taken.

Step 5: The unequal routine is entered to determine if the first card is being processed.

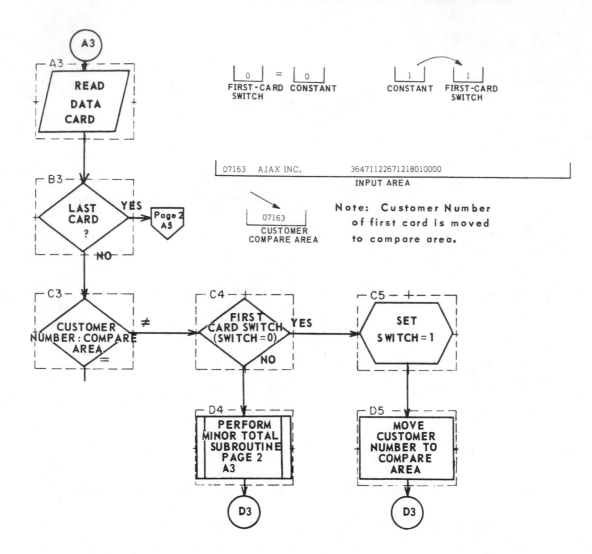

Figure 7-8 First Card is Processed

When the customer number in the input card is not equal to the customer number in the compare area, a routine is entered to determine if the first card is being processed. This is accomplished by testing a first-card switch for the value zero. If it is the first card, the switch is set to the value "1" and the customer number in the first card is moved to the compare area. If it is NOT the first card, a minor total routine is entered.

In the example in Figure 7-8 the first card is being processed; therefore, the first-card switch will contain a zero and the routine will be entered to set the first-card switch to a "1" and move the customer number of the first card to the compare area.

Step 6: The invoice amount is added to the minor total counter, the input data is moved to the output area, and the data line is printed on the report.

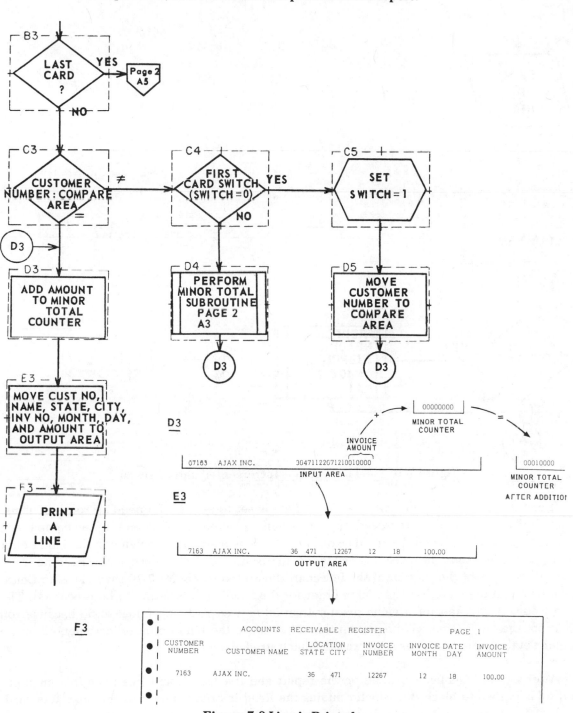

Figure 7-9 Line is Printed

Note in Figure 7-9 (Box D3) that the value contained in the Invoice Amount field in the input record is added to the Minor Total counter, which was set to zero in the initialization processing. The Minor Total counter is used to accumulate the total of the Invoice Amounts for each customer which is processed. The data in the input area is then moved to the output area and printed.

Step 7:   After a line is printed, the line count is incremented by one and a test is made to determine if a new page should be printed.

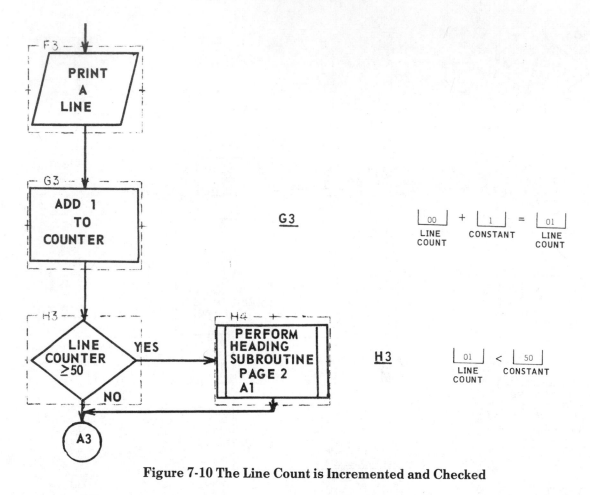

Figure 7-10 The Line Count is Incremented and Checked

It should be recalled that the Line Count field is set to zero in the heading routine. Thus, when the first data card is processed, the Line Count is incremented by one. In the comparison to determine if a new heading should be printed, it can be seen that the value in the Line Count field, "0," is less than the constant used for comparison, "50." Therefore, a new heading is not printed. Note from the portion of the flowchart illustrated in Figure 7-10 that the Line Count must be equal to or greater than 50 in order for the heading subroutine to be processed. The Line Count is checked for a value greater than 50 as well as being equal to 50 because, on occasion, the Line Count will be greater than 50 because the Line Count is incremented in the Minor Total routine as well as in the routine illustratred above.

After the line has been printed on the report and the Line Count has been incremented, control is passed to block A3, which contains the Read instruction to read the next data card.

Step 8:   The second and third data cards are read and processed in the same manner as the first data card. The results of the processing of the three data cards is illustrated below.

INPUT CARDS

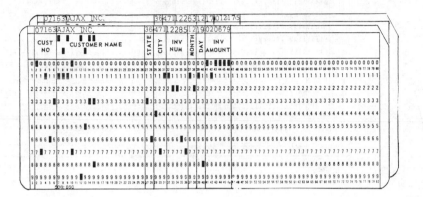

PRINTED REPORT

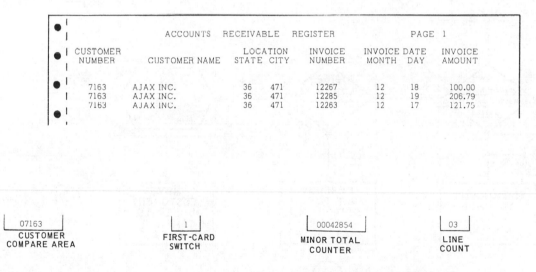

Figure 7-11 Processing after Three Cards are Processed

In the example above it can be seen that the second and third input cards are read and printed on the report. They are printed on the report with no Minor Total being printed because the customer number on the input card is the same as the Customer Number in the Customer Compare area. It should be recalled that a Minor Total is to be printed only when the customer number changes. Note also that the first-card switch is not changed and the Minor Total counter is incremented by the values in the Invoice Amount in each of the input cards. The line count is incremented by 1 each time a line is printed on the report.

When the fourth card is read, the Customer Number is different in the input card and a Minor Total will be printed on the report. This is illustrated in the next steps.

Step 9: The fourth data card is read and the Customer Number changes.

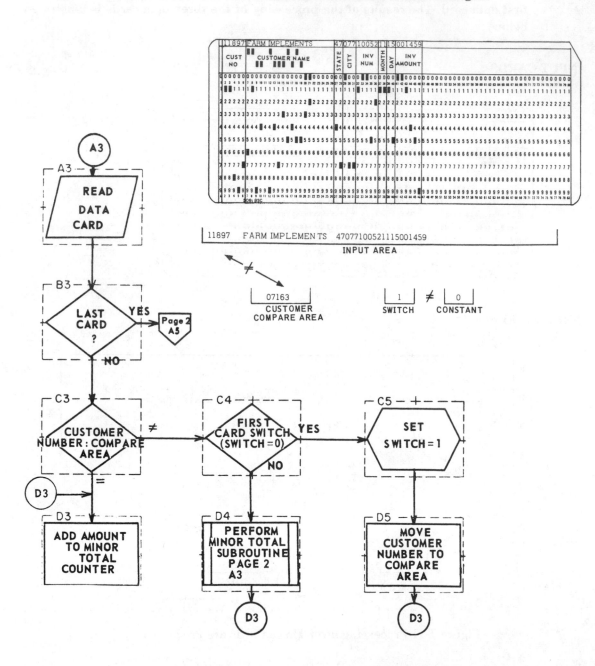

Figure 7-12 Data Card with New Customer is Read

Note from the example above that the fourth data card contains the customer number 11897. This customer number is different from the customer number for the first three cards which is contained in the Customer Number compare area. Therefore, a Minor Total must be printed for the Customer Number 07163. Note in block C3 that the comparison will indicate that the customer numbers are not equal. When the first-card switch is checked, it is found that it is not equal to 0. This is because the value "1" was moved to it when the first card was processed (Figure 7-8). Therefore, the answer to the question in block C4 is NO and the Minor total subroutine will be performed.

Step 10: **The Minor Total Subroutine is entered.**

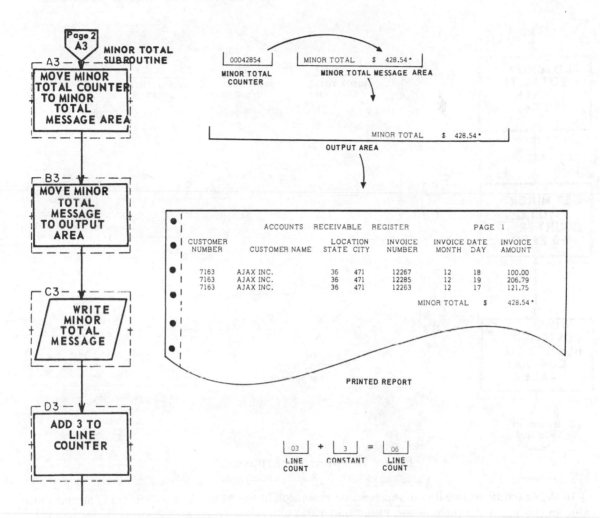

Figure 7-13 Minor Total Subroutine is Processed

Note from the example in Figure 7-13 that the value in the Minor Total Counter field is moved to the Minor Total message area and it in turn is moved to the output area. The Minor Total message is then printed on the report. After it is printed, the constant value "3" is added to the line count. The value "3" is added because a total of three lines are used for the Minor Total message—one for the blank line preceding the message, one for the message itself, and one for the blank line following the message. As noted previously, the check in the main program is made to determine if the line count is equal to or greater than 50. It can be seen how the line count may be greater than 50, that is, if it contained the value 40 when the Minor Total subroutine is entered, it would contain 52 after the subroutine has completed processing.

After the Minor Total has been printed for a Customer, it must be added to the Final Total counter which is an accumulation of all of the Minor Totals and will be printed at the conclusion of the program. In addition, the Minor Total counter must be reset to zero so that the total of invoice amounts for the next customer may be accumulated and the new customer number must be moved to the customer compare area. This is illustrated in Figure 7-14.

Step 11:   The Minor Total is added to the Final Total, the Minor Total Counter is reset to zero, and the new Customer Number is moved to the Customer Compare area.

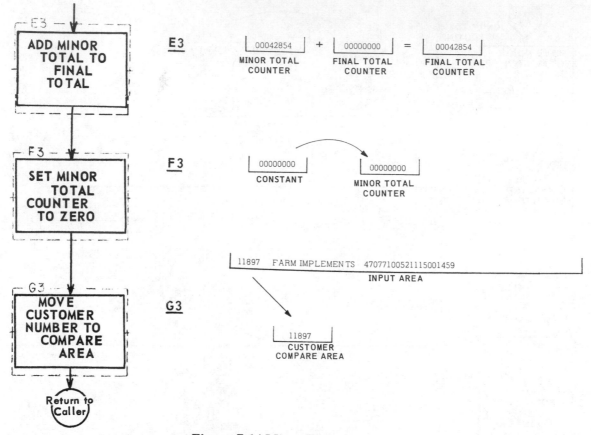

Figure 7-14 Minor Total Processing

In the example above it can be seen that the value in the Minor Total Counter is added to the value in the Final Total Counter. This Final Total will reflect the sum of all of the minor totals for all of the customers processed. The Minor Total Counter is then set to zero so that it may accumulate the total of the invoice amounts from the new customer. The new customer number is then moved to the Customer Compare area so that comparisons will take place properly for each subsequent card which is read. The Minor Total subroutine then returns control to the routine which called it. This routine then passes control to block D3 (see Figure 7-12).

Step 12: **The record (customer 11897) is processed and printed on the report and the Minor Total counter is incremented by the invoice amount from the card.**

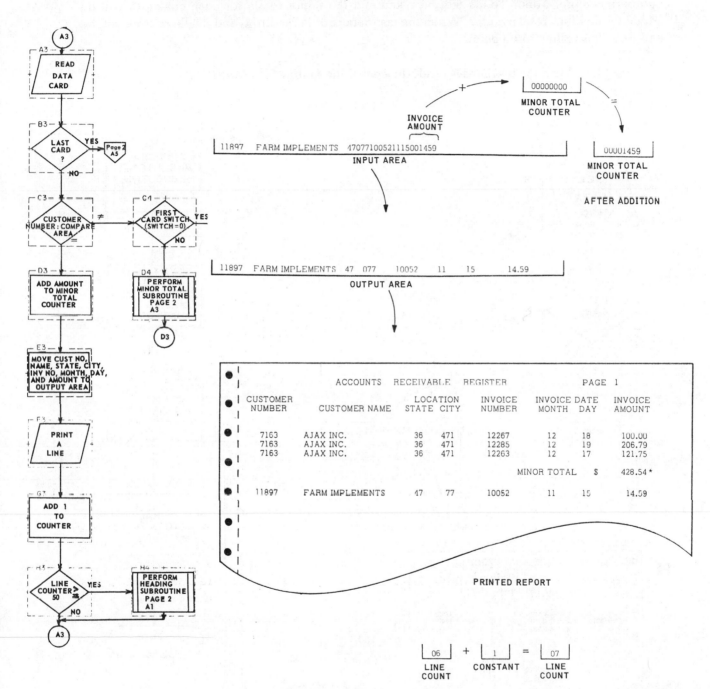

Figure 7-15 The First Record of the Second Customer is Processed

Note from the example in Figure 7-15 that the data from the fourth card is moved to the output area and printed. It is printed following the Minor Total message which was printed for the first customer. In addition, the line count is updated and the check is performed to determine if a new page must be started. In the example above it can be seen that the line count area will contain the value "7" because this is the number of lines which have been printed on the report.

Processing will continue with the remainder of the card file as has been illustrated. When the line count is equal to or greater than 50, a new page will be printed. As the customer numbers change, Minor Totals will be taken and the minor totals for each customer will be added to the Final Total counter. When the last data card is read, the end-of-file routine will be entered. This is illustrated below.

Step 13:   When the last card is read, the end-of-file routine is entered.

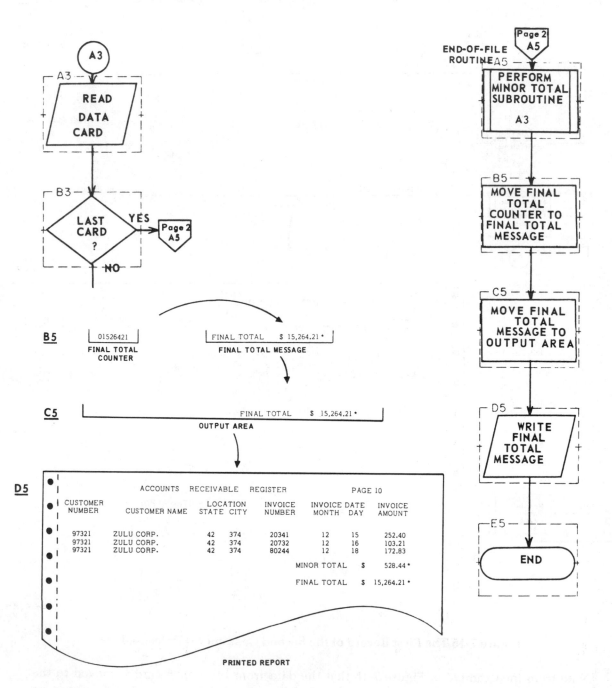

Figure 7-16 End-of-File Routine is Processed

From Figure 7-16, it can be seen that the first operation performed by the end-of-file routine is to call the Minor Total Subroutine. This must be done because a Minor Total must be printed for the last customer which is processed, that is, when end-of-file is reached for the card input file, the last customer to be processed must also have a Minor Total printed. In addition, this last minor total must be added to the final total so that a final total reflects all of the minor totals on the report.

After the last customer is processed in the Minor Total Subroutine, the final total, which has been accumulated for each customer, is moved to the Final Total message area and this message is printed on the report. The Final Total is the last line which is to be printed on the report, so the program is terminated.

CHAPTER 7

FLOWCHARTING ASSIGNMENT 1

INSTRUCTIONS

On a Flowchart Worksheet draw the logic to produce a Group Indicated Report of the sample problem illustrated in the text on pages 117, 118, and 119. Group indication refers to the process of printing identifying, repetitive information from the first card only of each control group. Note in the output illustrated below that the Customer Number, the Customer Name, and the State and the City are group indicated.

INPUT: Sales Cards

OUTPUT: Group Indicated Accounts Receivable Register

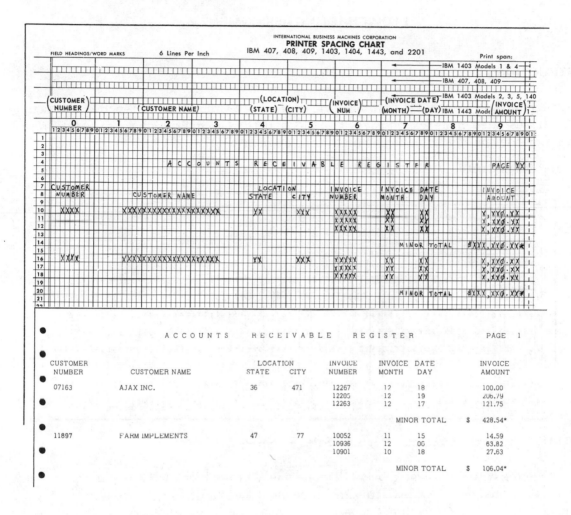

CHAPTER 7

FLOWCHARTING ASSIGNMENT 2

INSTRUCTIONS

On a Flowchart Worksheet draw the logic to produce a Group Printed report of the sample problem illustrated in the text on pages 117, 118, and 119. Group Printing refers to the process of printing one line of information for each group of cards.

INPUT: Sales Cards

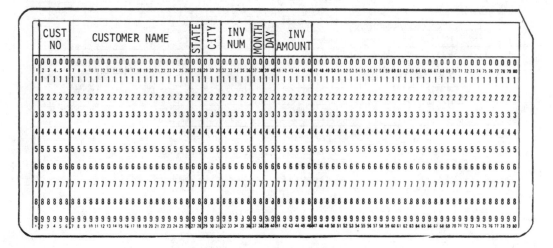

OUTPUT: Accounts Receivable Register, Sales Summary Card

Note in the output illustrated below that one line is printed for each group of cards. Thus, one line is printed for AJAX INC. from the three input data cards. See Figure 7-2. The Invoice Number, Month, and Day will not appear on the report. A Sales Summary Card is also to be punched when there is a change in Customer Numbers. The Sales Summary Card is to contain the Customer Number, Customer Name, State, City and Total Amount.

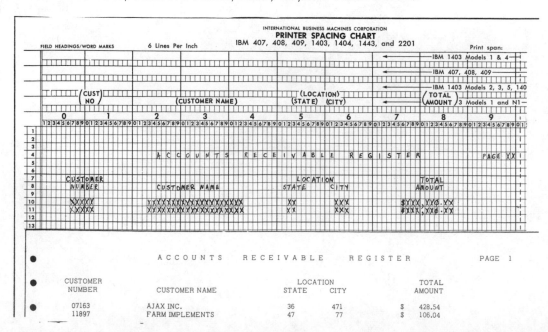

CHAPTER 8

MAJOR, INTERMEDIATE, MINOR TOTAL

INTRODUCTION

An extension of the Minor Total logic illustrated in Chapter 7 involves the taking of higher levels of totals, that is, the taking of totals for more than one control break. The flowchart example in this chapter illustrates the logic of taking major, intermediate, and minor totals. The input is illustrated in Figure 8-1.

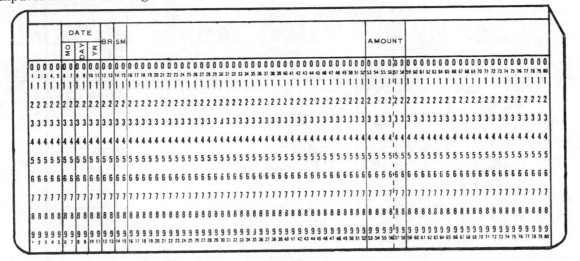

Figure 8-1 Input

The printed output to be obtained is illustrated below.

```
 ● |              WEEKLY SALES ANALYSIS REPORT          PAGE  1
 ● |
 ● |       DATE      BRANCH     SALESMAN      AMOUNT
 ● |     12/10/71      15          21          40.00
         15          21         150.00
 ●                                      $ 190.00 *
 ● |                 15          41          50.00
                               $  50.00 *
 ● |                                            $   240.00 * *
 ● |                 16          37         205.00
                               $ 205.00 *
 ● |                                            $   205.00 * *
 ● |
                  TOTAL SALES FOR THE DAY       $  445.00 * * *
 ● |     12/12/71      15          21         382.00
                               $ 382.00 *
 ● |                                            $   382.00 * *
 ● |
                  TOTAL SALES FOR THE DAY       $  382.00 * * *
 ● |
                               FINAL TOTAL      $   827.00 * * * *
 ● |
 ● |
```

Figure 8-2 Major, Intermediate, Minor Total Report

139

Note from the report illustrated in Figure 8-2 that a total is taken each time the Salesman Number changes (Minor Total), each time the Branch Number changes (Intermediate Total) and each time the Date changes (Major Total). In addition, a Final Total is to be printed. The flowchart for this program is illustrated in Figure 8-3.

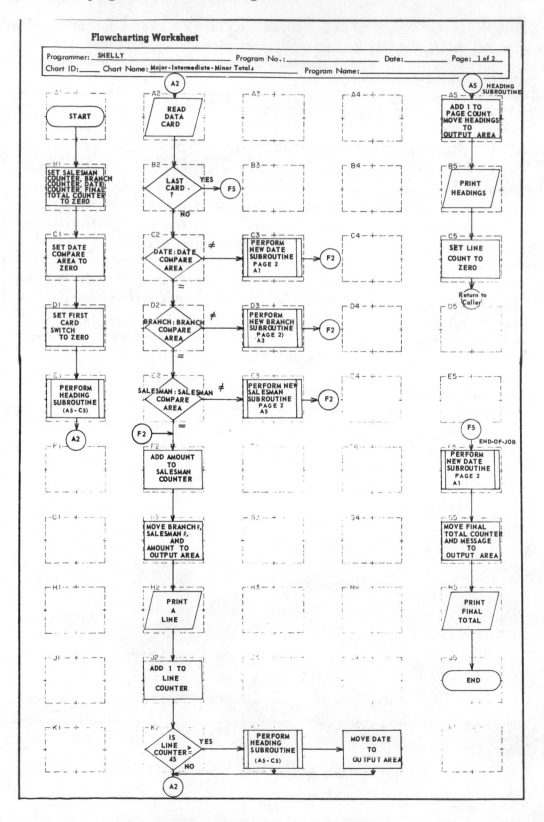

Figure 8-3 Flowchart (Page 1 of 2)

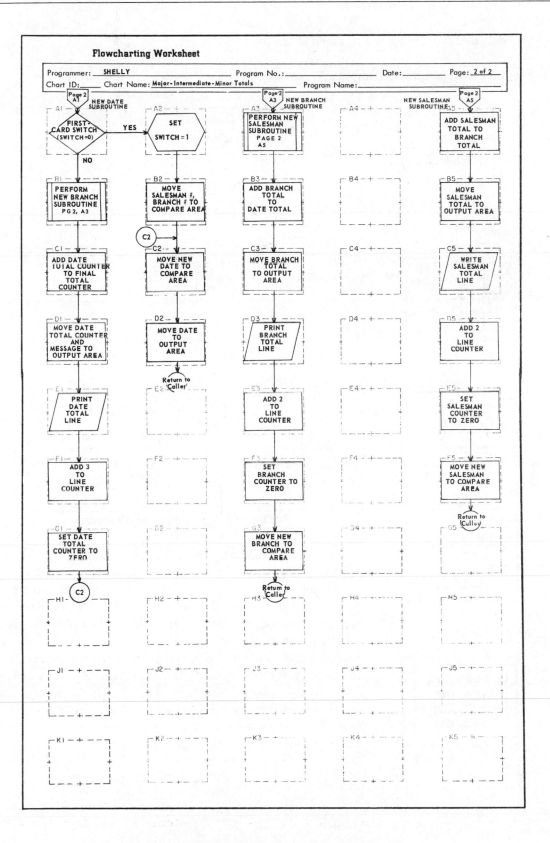

Figure 8-3a Flowchart (Page 2 of 2)

The detailed processing is explained in the following steps.

Step 1:   **The Counters, Compare Areas, and First-Card Switch are initialized.**

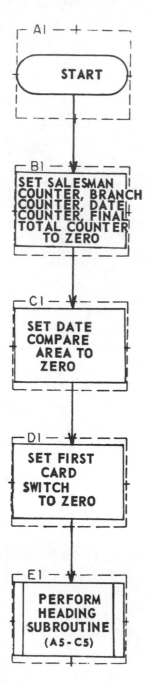

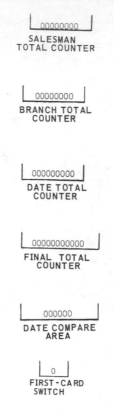

Figure 8-4 Initialization Procedures

In the Initialization processing illustrated above, it can be seen that the areas which are to be used to accumulate totals are all set to zero, that is, totals are to be accumulated for the Salesman, the Branch, the Date, and a Final Total. Each of the areas to be used to accumulate these totals are set to zero. In addition, the Date Compare Area is set to zero for the same reason as the Customer Number Compare Area was set to zero in the program in Chapter 7, that is, so that the first card read will cause an unequal situation to occur. The first-card switch, which will indicate that the first card is being processed, is also set to zero. After the initialization has taken place, the headings will be printed on the first page of the report.

Step 2: **The headings are printed on the first page.**

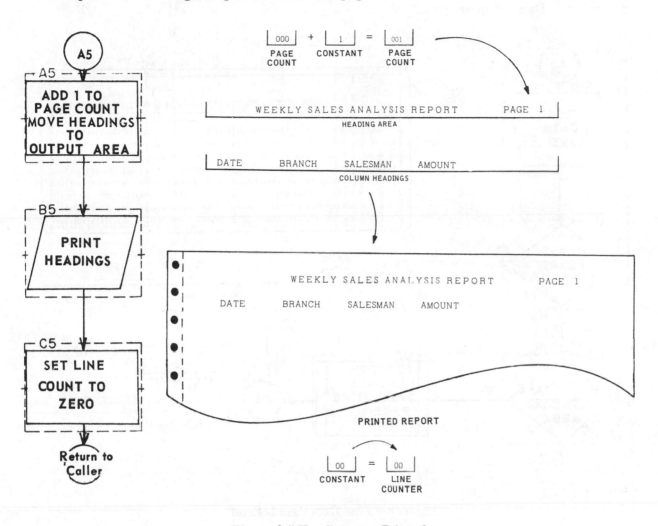

Figure 8-5 Headings are Printed

In the example above it can be seen that the page number is incremented by one as in previous programs and then the headings are printed on the report. It should be noted that, although not shown explicitly in the illustration, the headings would have to be moved to the output area in the same manner as in previous programs. The line count is then set to zero so that it may be used to indicate when a new page must be printed.

Step 3:   The first data card is read and the date in the card is compared with the date in the Date Compare Area.

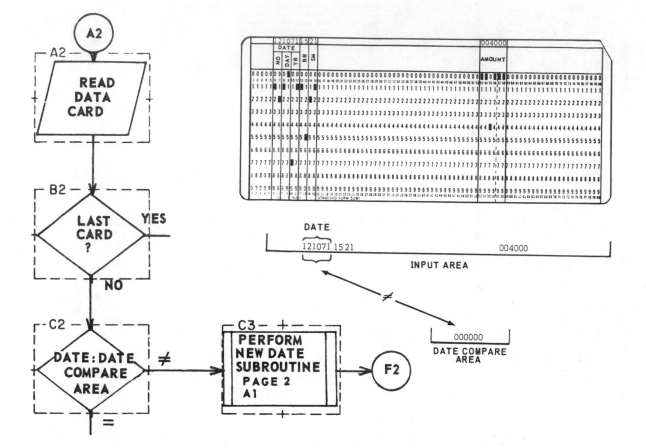

Figure 8-6 First Data Card is Read

Note from Figure 8-6 that the first data card is read into the Input Area. As with all input files, a test must be made to determine if the end of the file has been reached. In the example above, it has not because a data card was read. A comparison is then performed between the date which is contained in the input card and the date which is stored in the Date Compare Area. It can be seen that they are not equal because the Date Compare Area contains the zeros which were placed in it during the initialization (Figure 8-4). Thus, as is desired, the first card read causes an unequal condition and the New Date Subroutine is processed.

Step 4:   The New Date Subroutine is entered to process the first data card.

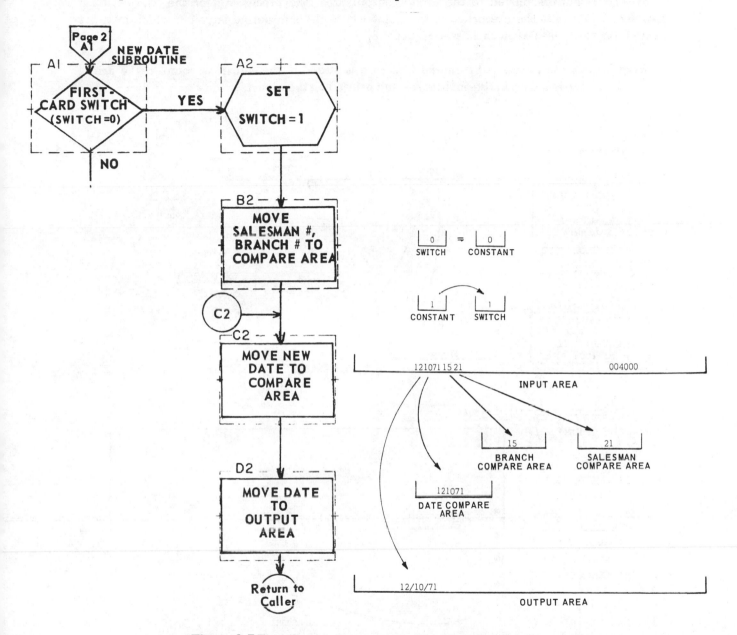

Figure 8-7 First Card is Processed in New Date Subroutine

The New Date Subroutine illustrated above is entered whenever a card with a new date is read. As noted previously, it is entered when the first card is read because the value in the Date Compare Area is zero. If the first card is being processed, the value in the First-Card Switch is zero. This is because the switch was initialized to a value of zero in the initialization processing and has not been changed. Therefore, the "yes" path of the decision symbol is taken in block A1. When the first card is processed, the value in the First-Card Switch is changed from zero to one. The Salesman Number and the Branch Number from the first input card are then moved to their respective compare areas to be used for comparisons when subsequent cards are read. The date from the first card is then moved to the Date Compare Area so that it too may be used for comparisons. The date on the card is then moved to the output area. As noted previously, the date in the output area is to be printed only once for each new date that is processed. Therefore, the date is moved in this routine so that it will be printed on the first line for each new date which is processed.

After the date is moved to the printer output area, the processing for the first card is complete. Control is then returned to the point where the subroutine is called which in turn causes control to pass to block F2 (see Figure 8-6).

Step 5:   The sales amount from the first card is added to the salesman counter, the print line is set up in the output area and printed on the report.

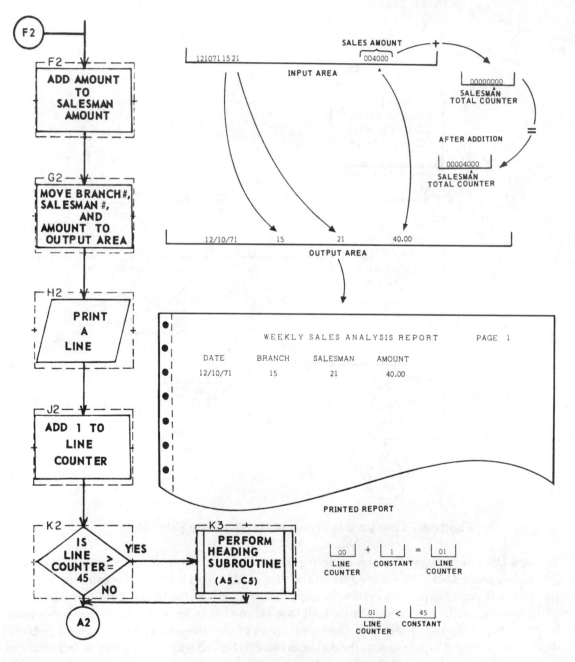

Figure 8-8 Line is Printed on Report

From the example in Figure 8-8 it can be seen that the sales amount in the card is added to the Salesman Total Counter to accumulate the total sales for each salesman. The Branch Number, the Salesman Number, and the Sales Amount are then moved to the output area. Thus, the only time a date will appear on the report is for the first line of the printed report for each new date. The subsequent lines will have only the branch and the salesman numbers. This is called "group-indication."

After the line is printed, the value in the Line Counter is incremented by one to indicate the number of lines printed and it is then checked to determine if a new page should be printed. In the example, the value in the Line Counter is 01, which is not equal to or greater than 45. Therefore, a new page is not printed. Instead, control is passed to block A2 where a second card is read and processed.

Step 6:   A second card is read and processed

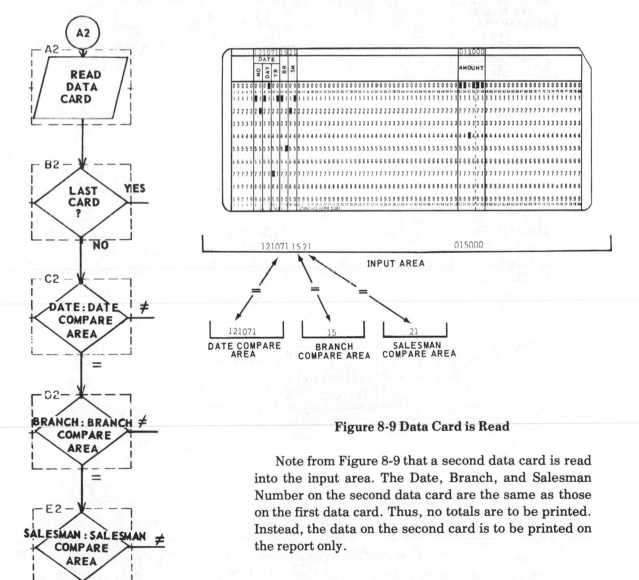

Figure 8-9 Data Card is Read

Note from Figure 8-9 that a second data card is read into the input area. The Date, Branch, and Salesman Number on the second data card are the same as those on the first data card. Thus, no totals are to be printed. Instead, the data on the second card is to be printed on the report only.

Step 7:   The amount is added to the Salesman Counter and the data from the second card is
          moved to the output area and printed. The result of this processing is illustrated
          below.

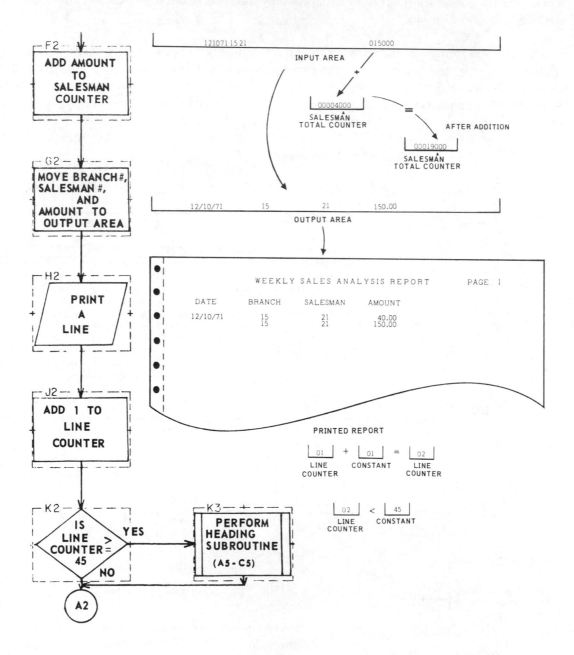

Figure 8-10 Second Data Card is Processed and Printed

Note in the example above that the sales amount on the second data card is added to the
Salesman Counter and then the line is printed. The Line Counter is again updated by 1 to
indicate that two lines have been printed. Note also that the date is not printed on the second
line. It is printed on the first line only because it was not moved to the output area for the
second card.

Step 8:   The third data card is read and a change in salesman number is processed.

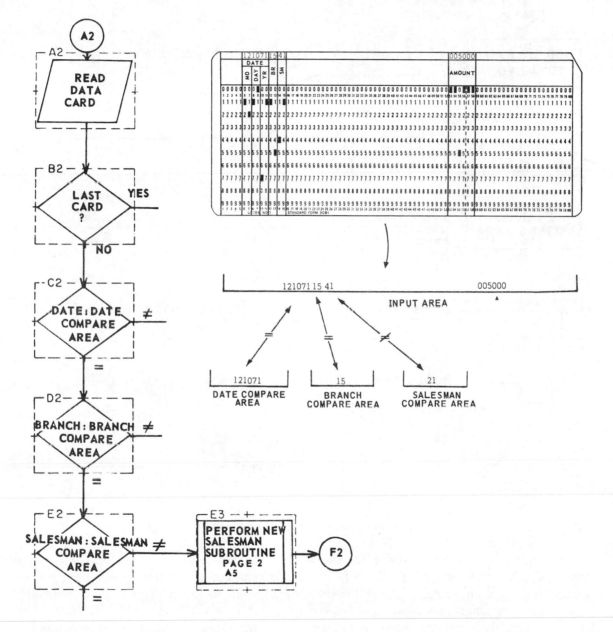

Figure 8-11 Change in Salesman Number

Note in the example above that the third data card is read and that the Salesman Number is different from that stored in the Salesman Compare Area, that is, the 41 in the input record is not equal to the 21 in the Salesman Compare Area. Thus, the New Salesman Subroutine must be processed. Note that the Date and the Branch are equal.

Step 9:   The New Salesman Subroutine is processed.

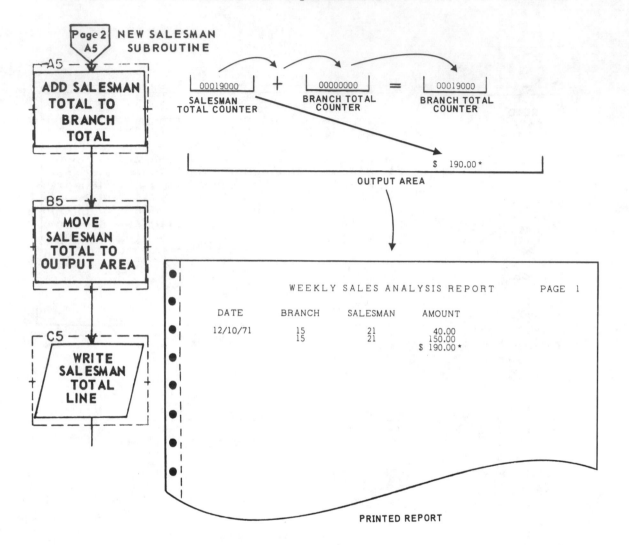

Figure 8-12 New Salesman Subroutine is Processed

As can be seen from Figure 8-12, the total which has been accumulated for the first salesman in the main-line program is added to the Branch Total Counter. This counter was set to zero in the initialization portion of the program and has not been processed so it contains zeros. After the salesman total is added to the counter, it contains the total for the first salesman within the branch. The salesman total is then moved to the output area and printed on the report. Note that the amount accumulated in the Branch Total Counter will be the total of all of the salesmen in that branch.

Step 10:   The New Salesman Subroutine is completed.

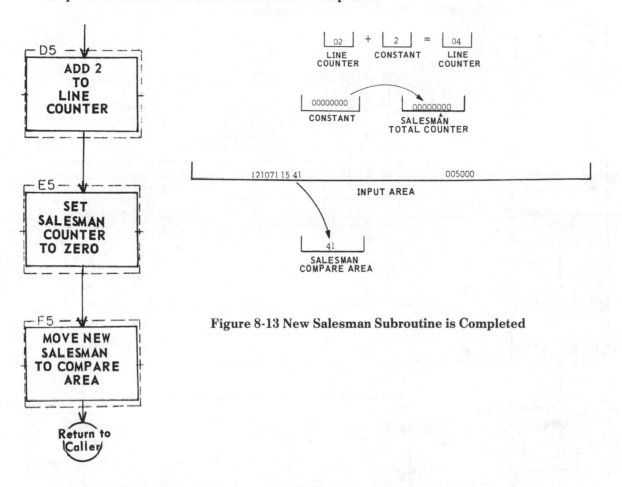

Figure 8-13 New Salesman Subroutine is Completed

In the example above it can be seen that after the salesman total is printed on the report, the line Counter is incremented by 2. This is because two lines are printed as a result of the total being printed—the total itself and one blank line after the total. The Salesman Total Counter is then set to zeros so that the total for the next salesman will be accumulated properly and the new salesman number is moved to the Salesman Compare Area to be compared with the next card which is read. Control is then passed back to the caller, which in turn gives control to block F2 (see Figure 8-11).

Step 11:   The third card is then processed and printed on the report. The results are illustrated below. (See Figure 8-3 for the flowchart.)

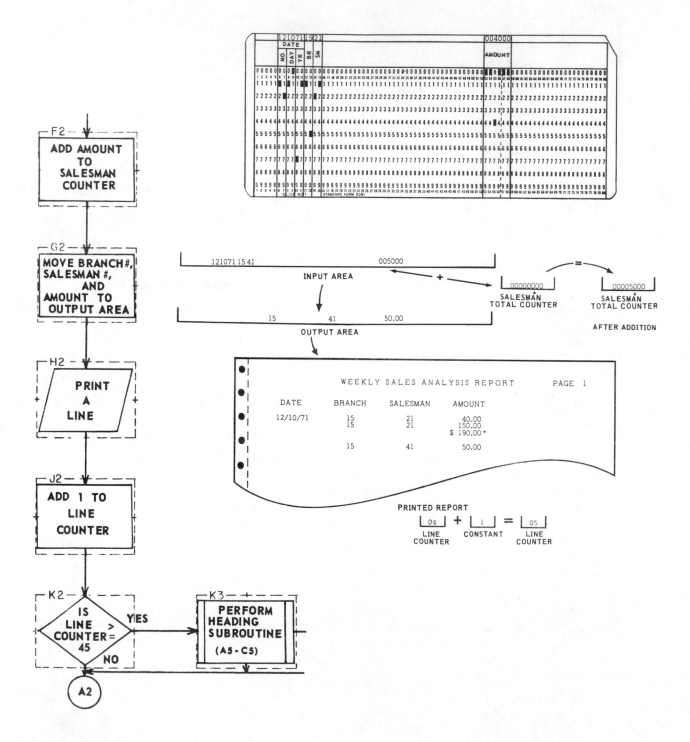

Figure 8-14 Card Data is Printed

Step 12:   The next card is read and a change in Branch is found.

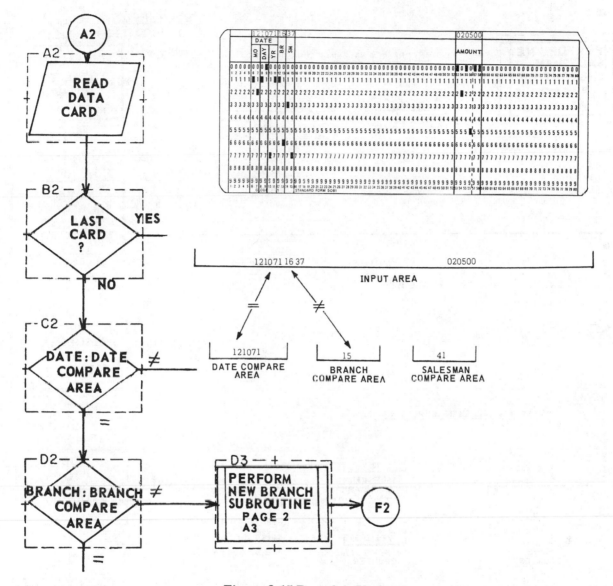

Figure 8-15 Branch is Unequal

Note in the example above that the fourth card read results in an unequal condition when the Branch in the input card is compared with the Branch in the Branch Compare Area. When this occurs, it means that there is both a change in Branch and a change in Salesman, since salesman cannot be in two different branches of the company. Therefore, totals must be taken for both the salesman and the branch. This is accomplished by performing the New Branch Subroutine.

Step 13:   The New Branch Subroutine is processed.

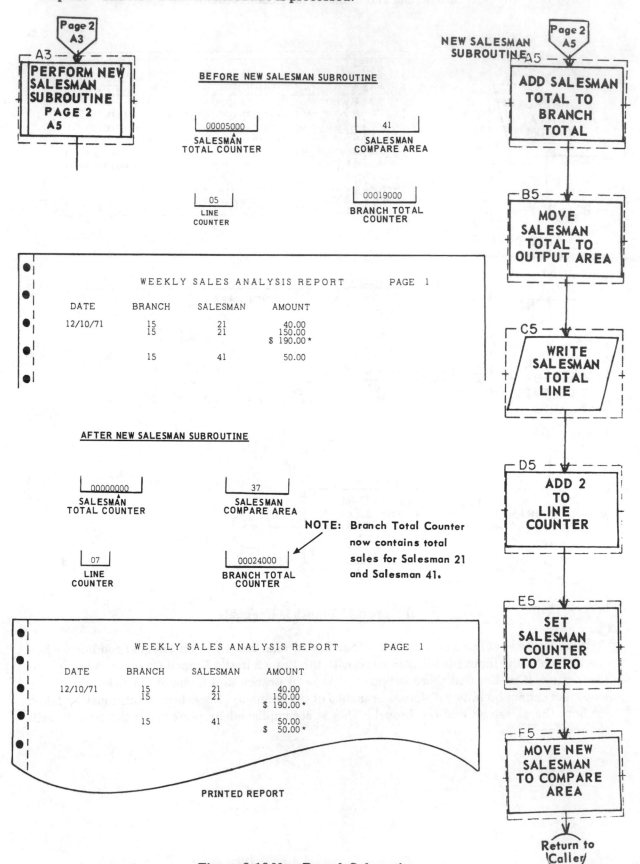

Figure 8-16 New Branch Subroutine

Note from Figure 8-16 that the first processing which is accomplished in the New Branch Subroutine is that the New Salesman Subroutine is performed. As noted previously, whenever a change in branch number occurs, a change in salesman number will also occur, therefore, a total for the Salesman must be taken. In the New Salesman Subroutine the Salesman Total is added to the Branch Total Counter, the Salesman Total is moved to the output area and a line is printed. In addition, the line counter is incremented, the Salesman counter is set to zero, and the Salesman Number from the card that caused the control break is moved to the Salesman Compare Area.

After the New Salesman Subroutine has been processed, control returns to Step B3 in the flowchart where the contents of the Branch Total Counter are added to the Date Total Counter. It should be recalled that the Date Total Counter was set to zero in the initialization processing at the beginning of the program. Thus, when the branch total is added to the Date Total Counter, the Date Total Counter reflects the total for the first branch on the report. It should be noted that the date total Counter will eventually contain the total of all of the branches within a given date.

The branch total is then moved to the output area and printed on the report as illustrated. After it is printed, the Line Counter is incremented, the Branch Total Counter is set to zero and the new branch number is moved to the Branch Compare Area.

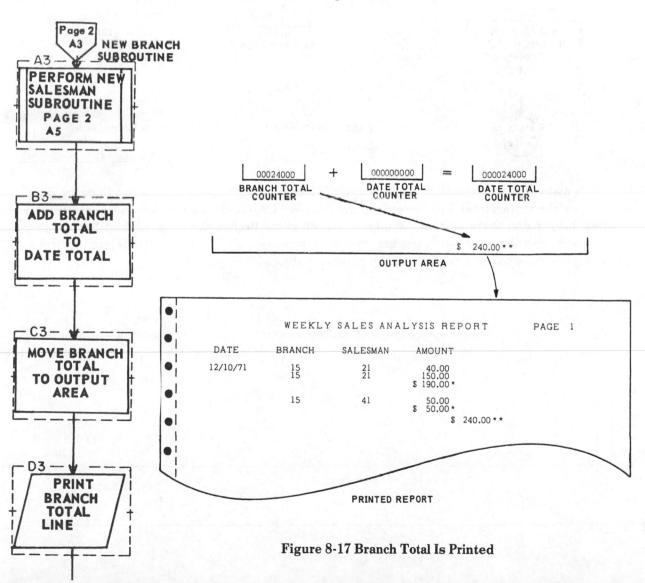

Figure 8-17 Branch Total Is Printed

Step 14:   The remainder of the New Branch Subroutine is processed.

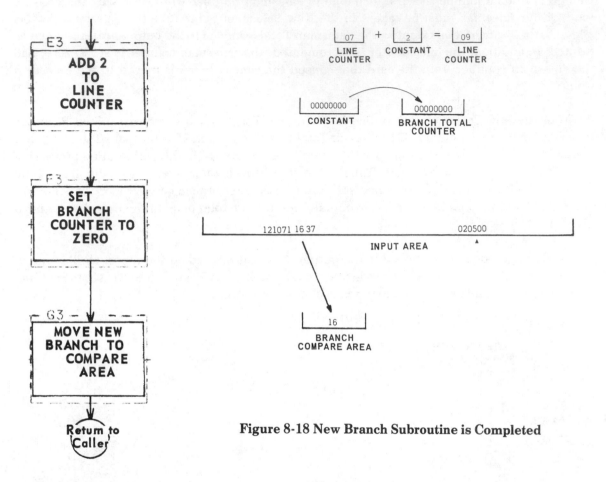

Figure 8-18 New Branch Subroutine is Completed

Note in Figure 8-18 that the Line Counter is incremented by two because two lines are used to print the branch total. In addition, the Branch Total Counter is reset to zero to be used for the next branch and the new branch number is placed in the Branch Compare Area. All processing has been completed and the program is ready to process the next branch. Therefore, control is returned to the caller which in turn gives control to block F2 on page 1.

Step 15: **The first card of the new branch is printed on the report. The results are illustrated below.**

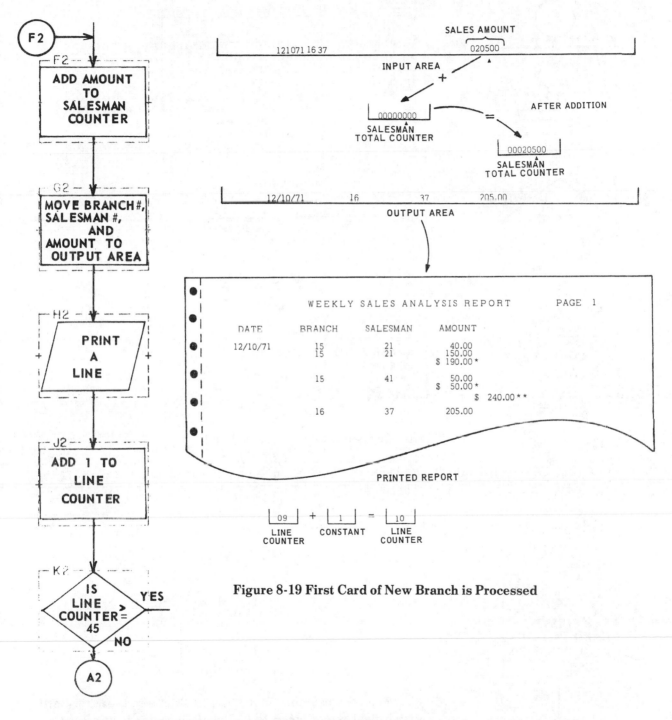

Figure 8-19 First Card of New Branch is Processed

As can be seen from Figure 8-19, the first card of the new branch is processed in the same manner as previous input cards, that is, the Salesman Total Counter is incremented by the Sales Amount from the input card and the Branch, Salesman Number, and Sales Amount are printed on the report. The Line Counter is incremented by 1 to indicate that 10 lines have been printed on the first page of the report. It should again be noted that printing will continue on the first page until the value in the Line Counter is equal to or greater than 45. At that point, a new page will be begun by processing the Heading Subroutine.

Step 16:   The next card is read and it contains a new date.

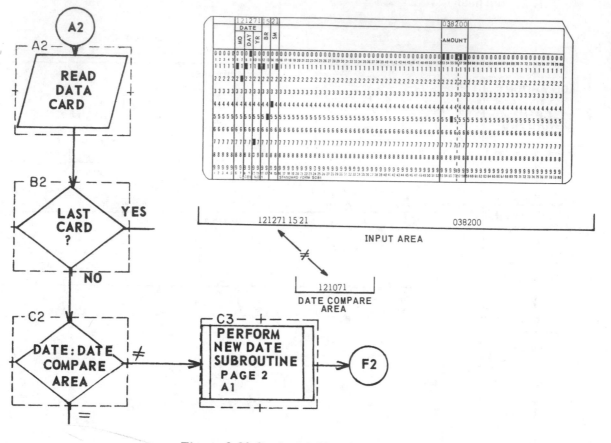

Figure 8-20 Card with New Date is Read

As can be seen from the example above, the date on the next card read is not equal to the date in the Date Compare Area. Therefore, the New Date Subroutine must be performed.

Step 17:   The New Date Subroutine is entered.

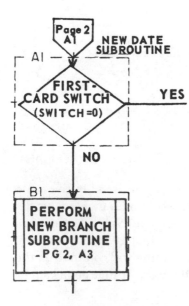

Figure 8-21 New Date Subroutine is Entered

Note in the example above that the value in the First-Card Switch field is not equal to 0. This is because it was set to 1 when the New Date Subroutine was entered at the beginning of the program (see Figure 8-7). Therefore, the "no" path of the decision symbol is taken and the New Branch Subroutine is performed. This is done because whenever a new date is read, a branch total and a salesman total for that date must be printed.

Step 18:   When the New Branch Subroutine is entered, its first step is to perform the New
            Salesman Subroutine (see Figure 8-3). The results from the processing of the New
            Branch and New Salesman subroutines are illustrated below.

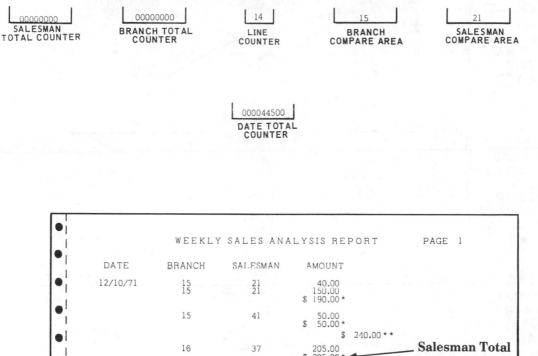

Figure 8-22 Results of Processing New Branch and New Salesman Subroutines

Note from the example above that the Salesman total and the Branch total have been printed
on the report and they are then set to zero so that they may accumulate the totals for the next
salesman and branch to be processed. The Branch Compare Area contains the new branch
number and the Salesman Compare Area contains the new salesman number. As always, the
Line Counter is incremented to reflect the number of lines printed on the report. Note also that
the Date total is a sum of all of the records which have been processed for the date, that is, it is
the sum of the branch totals which in turn are the sum of the salesman totals. Thus, it can be
seen that the minor total (the salesman total) is added to the intermediate total (the branch
total) which in turn is added to the major total (the date total).

Step 19:   After the New Branch and New Salesman Subroutines have been processed, the New Date Subroutine is processed.

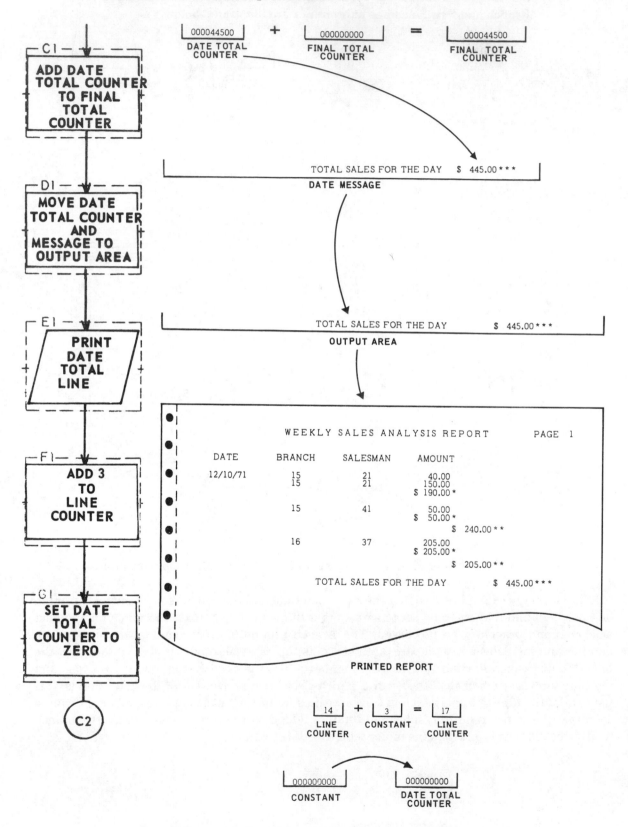

Figure 8-23 New Date Subroutine is Processed

From Figure 8-23 it can be seen that the Date total is added to the Final total which will be printed at the conclusion of the program. The Date total message is then printed on the report and the Line Counter is incremented. The Date Total Counter is then set to zero so that it may be used to accumulate to total for the next day.

Step 20:   **The new date is moved to the Date Compare Area and the date is moved to the printer output area.**

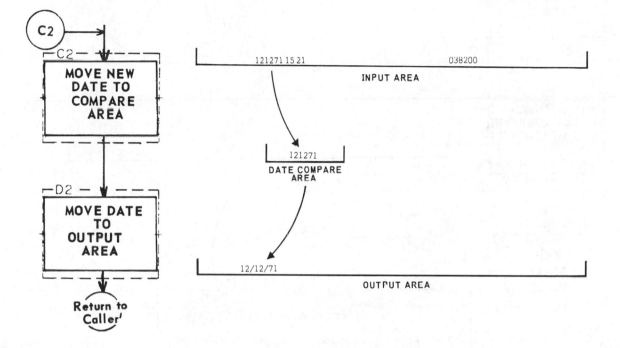

Figure 8-24 New Date Subroutine is Completed

Note from Figure 8-24 that the date in the input area which caused the New Date Subroutine to be processed is moved to the Date Compare Area to be used for comparisons to subsequent input records. The date is also moved to the output area so that it will appear on the first detail line for the new date. As was noted previously, the date is moved to the output area only in the New Date routine so that it will appear only on the first detail line.

The remainder of the input file will be processed in the same manner as described for the first date in the input file. A minor total will be printed for each change in salesman, an intermediate total will be printed for each change in branch, and a major total will be printed for each change in date. In addition, the final total of all of the amounts will be accumulated in the Final Total Counter. When the last card is read, the end-of-file routine will be entered as illustratred in Figure 8-25.

Step 21:   The end-of-file routine is entered when the last card is read.

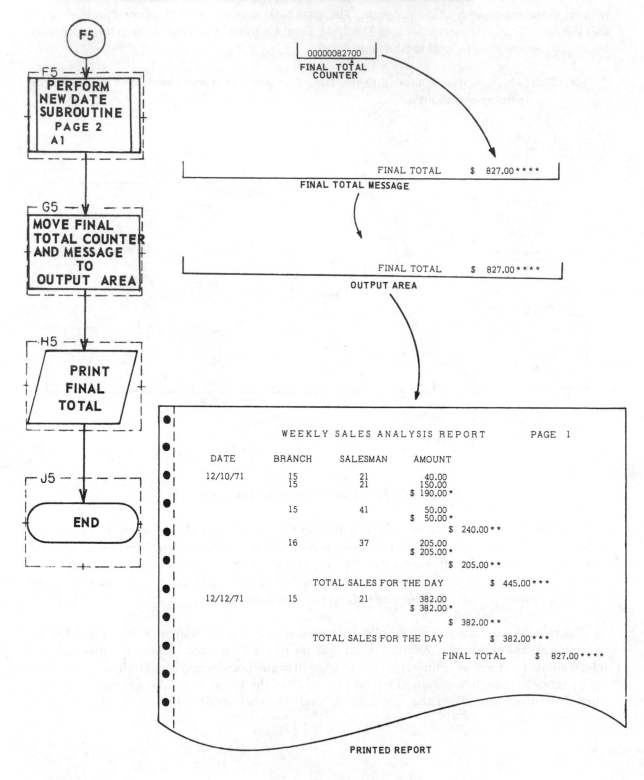

Figure 8-25 Final Total is Printed

Note from Figure 8-25 that the first thing done in the end-of-file routine is to perform the New Date Subroutine. This is done because when end-of-file is found, it signals the end of the date which was being processed. Therefore, the totals for the Salesman, the Branch, and the Date must be printed. After these totals are printed, control is returned to the end-of-file routine. The final total and the accompanying message are then moved to the output area and are printed on the report. Since there is no more data to be processed, the program is terminated.

As noted at the beginning of the chapter, the process of taking alternative action based upon values in a record being compared to values from previous records is a very common occurrence in business programming. The use of these comparisons and the concept of a "control break" should be thoroughly understood prior to studying the sequential update logic in Chapter 9.

CHAPTER 8

FLOWCHARTING ASSIGNMENT 1

INSTRUCTIONS

On a Flowchart Worksheet draw a flowchart to illustrate the logic required to produce a Sales Analysis Report listing the Salesman Number and Items Sold.

INPUT: Sales Analysis Cards

Input is to consist of Sales Analysis Cards containing the Salesman Number, the Item Number, the Item Description and the Sales Amount.

OUTPUT: Sales Analysis Report

Output is to consist of a Sales Analysis Report listing the Salesman Number, the Item Number, the Item Description and the Sales Amount. A minor total is to be taken when there is a change in Item Number and an intermediate total is to be taken when there is a change in Salesman Number. A final total is to be printed after all cards have been processed.

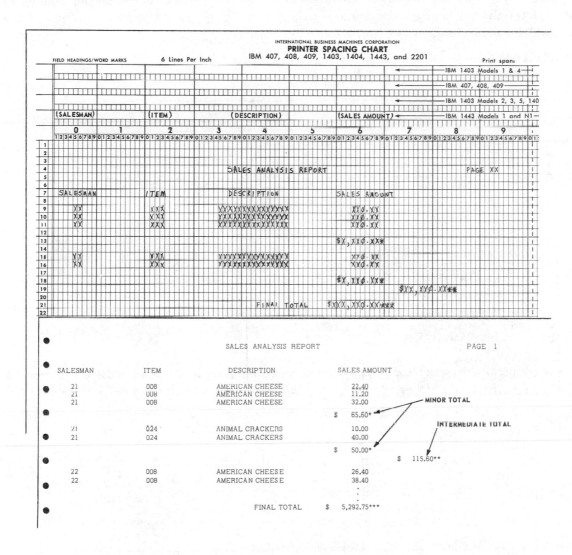

CHAPTER 8

FLOWCHARTING ASSIGNMENT 2

INSTRUCTIONS

Modify flowcharting assignment 1 to group print the Item Number and Item Description. In addition, the Current Date is to be printed on the report. The date is to be obtained from a Date Card which will be placed before the Sales Analysis Cards.

INPUT: Date Card and Sales Analysis Cards

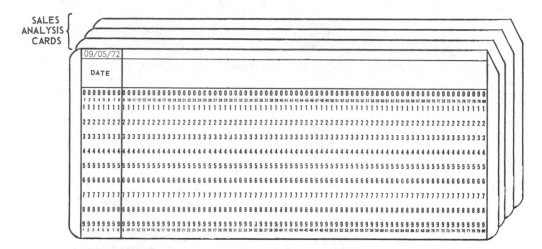

OUTPUT: Sales Analysis Report

The format of the report is illustrated below. Note that after all cards have been processed a message and the total number of cards processed is to be printed on the same line as the final total.

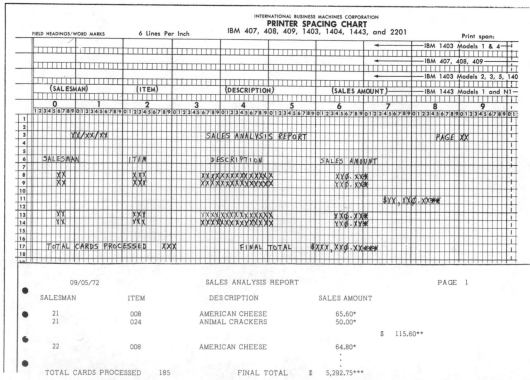

CHAPTER 9

SEQUENTIAL FILE UPDATING LOGIC

INTRODUCTION

In the examples in the previous chapters, the input data has been stored on punched cards and the output has been written on the printer. Two other types of devices which are commonly used with computer systems are magnetic tape and magnetic disk storage devices. On both types of devices, files may be stored in a sequential manner, that is, records on the tape or direct-access device are stored one after another and are processed one after another. Thus, the records are processed in the same manner as a card file. In addition, the records are normally arranged in some sequence based upon some control field or "key" such as a customer number. The sequential arrangement of records on a tape file are illustrated in Figure 9-1.

EXAMPLE

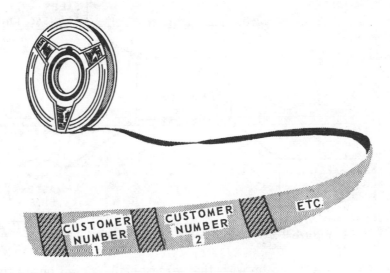

Figure 9-1 Data Stored on Tape

Magnetic tape is commonly used to store sequential master files. A Master File is a file consisting of records which contain up-to-date information relating the status of a system of which a master record is a part. For example, in a customer sales system, the master file could contain a record for each customer reflecting year-to-date sales.

Once a master file has been created, it is periodically necessary to update this file with current information so that the file always contains the most recent data. Typically, file updating procedures take three forms: additions, deletions, and changes.

An addition takes place when a new record is added to an already established master file. For example, in a customer sales system, if a new customer is acquired, it would be necessary to add a record to the master file reflecting the acquisition of the new customer.

167

A deletion becomes necessary when data currently stored on the master file is to be removed. For example, if a customer no longer purchases from the company, it would be necessary to delete the corresponding master record from the file.

A change must be made to the master file whenever the data on the master file no longer contains accurate, up-to-date information. For example, in a customer sales system, when a new sale is made, the sales amount must be added to the year-to-date sales amount in the master record to reflect a sale to the customer.

Sequential updating involves the reading of a sequential master file, the reading of a sorted sequential transaction file, and the creating of a new, updated master file. Normally, an exception report which lists transaction errors, such as invalid transaction codes, is also created. An example of a sequential file update is illustrated in Figure 9-2.

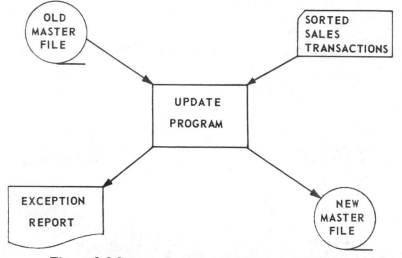

Figure 9-2 System Flowchart of Sequential Update

In the example above it can be seen that a master file stored on magnetic tape is to be updated by a sorted sales transaction file stored on punched cards. Output is to consist of the new updated magnetic tape master file and an exception report. The exception report lists transaction records in error such as cards containing invalid codes, cards with no related master records, etc.

The program presented in this chapter illustrates a technique to sequentially update a master file stored on magnetic tape with sorted transaction records stored on punched cards. The master file contains the year-to-date sales amounts for customers. This master file is to be updated with the new sales figures for the month. In addition, the update program will add customers or delete customers from the master file as needed. An error listing will also be produced which contains a list of any transaction records with errors such as invalid transaction codes. The format of the master file is illustrated in Figure 9-3.

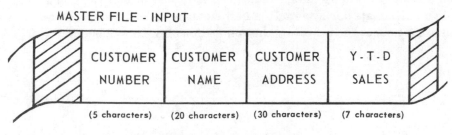

Figure 9-3 Master File

As can be seen from Figure 9-3, the master file consists of a Customer Number field which is five characters in length, a Customer Name field which is 20 characters in length, a Customer Address field which is 30 characters in length and the Year-To-Date Sales field which is 7 characters in length. The card format of the transaction file, which is used to update the master file, is illustrated in Figure 9-4.

TRANSACTION FILE - INPUT

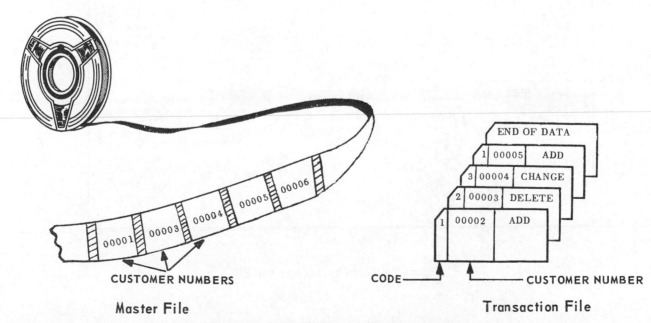

CODE 1 = ADDITION
CODE 2 = DELETION
CODE 3 = CHANGE

Figure 9-4 Format of Transaction Record

The transaction record contains the same field as the master record. In addition, it contains a transaction code which is used to indicate the type of processing which is to occur. A "1" in the Transaction Code field indicates that the transaction record is an addition; "2" indicates a deletion, and a "3" indicates a change to the Sales Amount field.

The flowchart logic for a file updating procedure is illustrated on the following pages. The logic requires the following steps: 1) a transaction record is read; 2) a master record is read; 3) the Customer Number of the master record and the transaction record are compared to determine if the master record is equal to, less than, or greater than the transaction record; 4) the required processing is performed based upon the comparison.

The steps in processing a sequential update are explained on subsequent pages. The data which will be used in the examples is illustrated below.

CUSTOMER NUMBERS

Master File

END OF DATA
1 | 00005 | ADD
3 | 00004 | CHANGE
2 | 00003 | DELETE
1 | 00002 | ADD

CODE —⟶   ⟵— CUSTOMER NUMBER

Transaction File

Figure 9-5 Test Data for Sequential Update

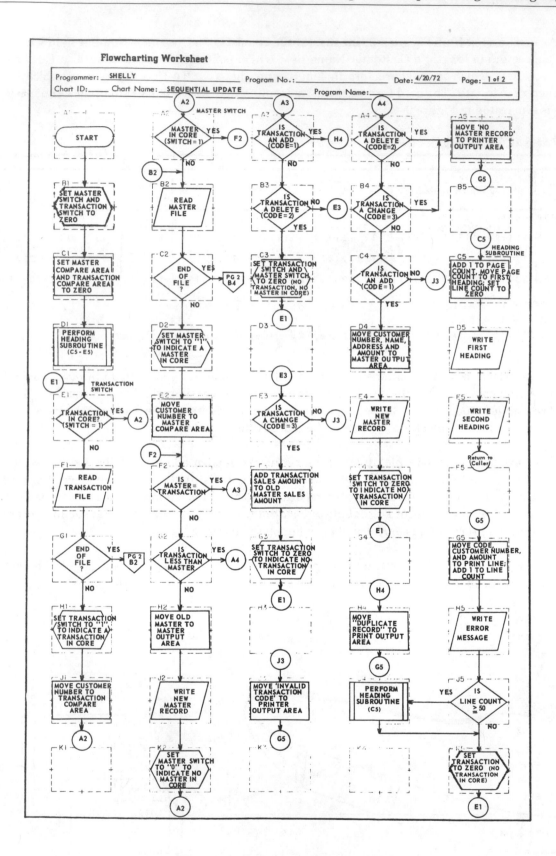

Figure 9-6 Flowchart (Page 1 of 2)

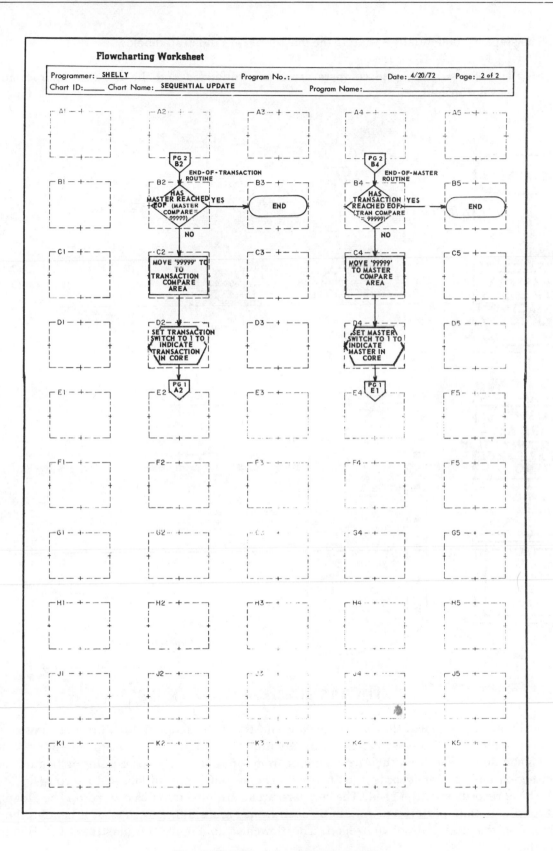

Figure 9-7 Flowchart (Page 2 of 2)

The steps in sequentially updating the master file are illustrated below.

Step 1:   **The switches and compare areas are initialized and the heading subroutine is performed.**

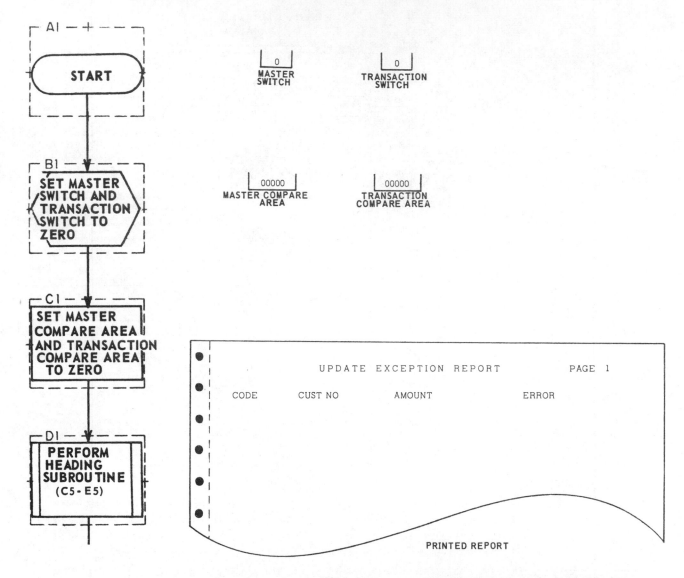

Figure 9-8 Initialization Processing

In the example above, the Master Switch and the Transaction Switch are both initialized with the value "0." These switches are used within the program to indicate whether or not a record should be read from the card reader or from the tape. When processing is begun, both transaction and master records must be read. The switches are initialized to zero to indicate that these records must be read. The compare areas are also initialized to zero. The Heading Subroutine is then performed. As can be seen from Figure 9-8, it results in a heading being printed on the first page of the report. The flowchart in Figure 9-6 illustrates the Heading Routine.

Step 2:   A transaction record is read from the card reader.

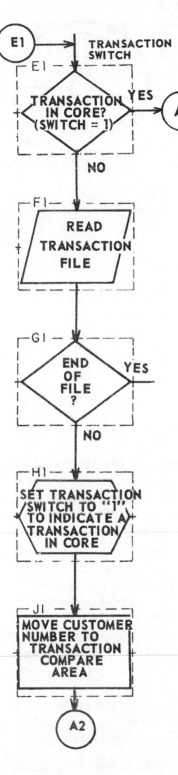

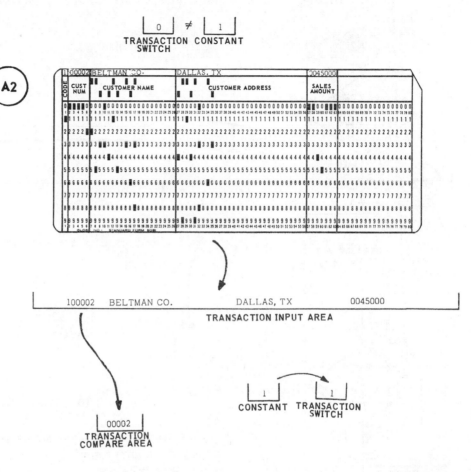

Figure 9-9 Transaction Record is Read

In the example above it can be seen that the first operation is to check the value in the Transaction Switch. The purpose of the transaction switch is to allow a transaction record to be read when the switch is set to "0" and to bypass the reading of the transaction record when the switch is set to 1. If the switch contains a zero, a record will be read and if the switch contains a "1," a transaction record will **not** be read. In the initialization processing, the value in the Transaction Switch was set to zero, so a record will be read.

After checking for End-of-File, the value in the switch is set to "1" because a transaction record is not in core storage to be processed. The Customer Number in the input record is then moved to the Transaction Compare Area in core storage so that it may be compared to the Customer Number which will be read from the master file. Control is then passed to block A2.

Step 3:   A record is read from the master file which is stored on tape.

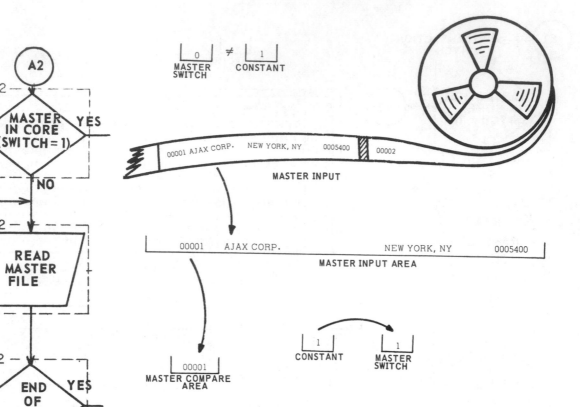

Figure 9-10 A Master Record is Read

Note from the example above that the Master Switch is tested in a manner similar to that used for the Transaction switch. When the switch contains a zero, as it will as a result of the initialization processing, a master record will be read. If the switch contained a "1," a master record would not be read. After the record is read into the master input area, the switch is set to "1" to indicate that a master record is in core storage. The Customer Number in the master record is then moved to the Master Compare Area so that it may be compared to the Customer Number in the Transaction Compare Area.

It should be noted from the examples is Figure 9-9 and Figure 9-10 that two input areas are used in the program—one for the transaction record and one for the master record. This is because the two records must be in core storage at the same time in order for them to be processed. This, of course, differs from previous examples when only one input area was required for the card input.

Step 4:   The Customer Numbers in the Transaction Compare Area and the Master Compare Area are compared and the appropriate action is taken.

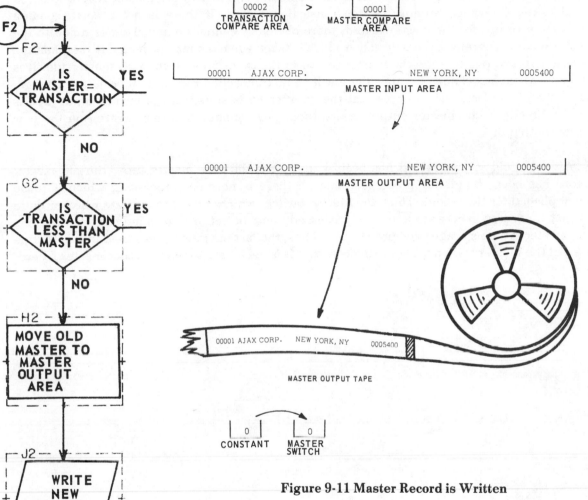

Figure 9-11 Master Record is Written

In the example in Figure 9-11, the Customer Number in the Transaction Compare Area is compared to the Customer Number in the Master Compare Area. As can be seen, the Customer Number in the Transaction Compare Area which contains 00002, is greater than the Customer Number in the Master Compare Area, which contains 00001. Thus, both "no" paths of the decision symbols are taken because the number in the Master Compare Area is not equal to the number in the Transaction Compare Area (Box F2 in the flowchart) and the number in the Transaction Compare Area is not less than the number in the Master Compare Area (Box G2).

As was noted previously, the three operations which may be performed when updating a sequential master file are adding a record, deleting a record, and changing a record. In order to delete or change a master record which is stored on the master file, there must be a corresponding transaction record, that is the Customer Number in the master record must be equal to the Customer Number in the transaction record. If there is not a corresponding transaction record for the master record, there obviously cannot be any changes made to the master record. Therefore, the only action which is taken when the master record is less than the transaction record is to write the master record in the input area on the new master file. It is written without any change because there will be no transaction record to indicate any change. Note, therefore, from the example that the data which is stored in the master input area is moved directly to the master output area without any change. It is then written on the new master output tape.

After the old master record has been written onto the new master tape, the old master record has been completely processed, that is, there is no more processing which is to be accomplished for the record. Thus, the Master Switch, which is used to indicate whether there is a master record in core storage to be processed, must be set to zero to indicate that there is ''no master in core storage to be processed.'' Thus, the last operation performed in this routine is to set the Master Switch to zero to indicate that it is necessary to read another master record.

Step 5:   Another master record is read.

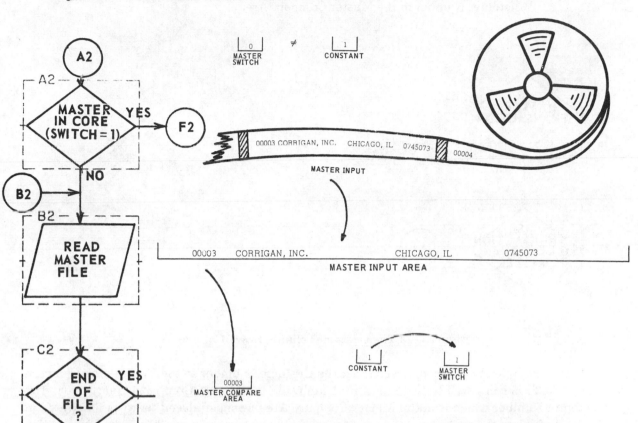

Figure 9-12 Second Master Record is Read

Note in the example above that a second master record is read because the Master Switch contains a zero, which indicates that there is not a master record ready to be processed in core storage. The switch was set to zero when the first master record was written on the new master file. After the second master record is read, the Master Switch is then set to one to indicate that a master record is in core storage. The Customer Number in the master record is then moved to the Master Compare Area to be used in comparisons with the transaction record.

Step 6:   The Customer Number in the Transaction Compare Area is compared with the Customer Number in the Master Compare Area.

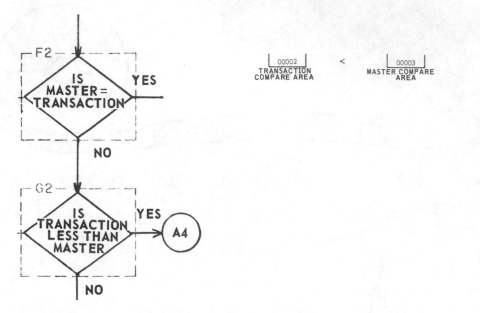

Figure 9-13 The Customer Numbers are Compared

In the example above it can be seen that the Customer Number in the Transaction Compare Area, 00002, is compared to the Customer Number in the Master Compare Area, 00003. The Customer Number which is in the Master Compare Area was just placed there as illustrated in Figure 9-12 when the second master record was read. The customer number in the Transaction Compare Area was placed there as illustrated in Figure 9-9 when the first transaction record was read. Note that even though a record has been written on the new master file, a second transaction record has not been read. This is because the first transaction record has not yet been processed.

In the comparison in Figure 9-13, the Customer Number of the transaction record is less than the customer number of the master record. When this condition occurs, it indicates that there will never be a master record which will be equal to the transaction record. This is because the master file is sorted in an ascending sequence, that is, each subsequent record in the master file has a higher customer number than the previous record, and when the transaction is less than the master, any record which follows on the master record will be higher than the transaction. When the transaction record is less than the master record, the only valid operation which may be performed is the addition of the transaction record to the master file. Since there will never be a corresponding master record, the transaction record cannot be used to delete or change an existing master record. When the transaction is less than the master record, the routine beginning in block A4 of the flowchart is entered.

Step 7:   The Transaction Code in the transaction record is checked to verify that the trans-action record contains a "1" to indicate that the record is to be added to the master file.

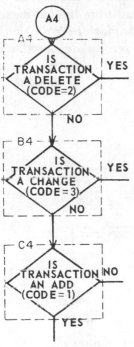

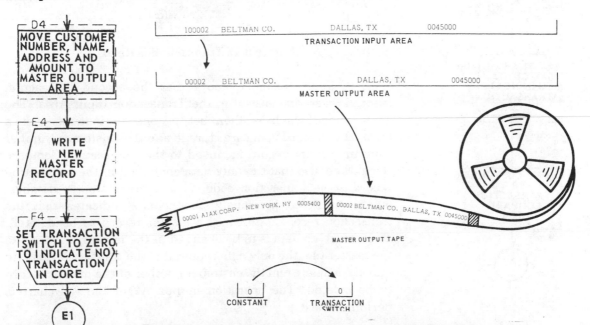

Figure 9-14 Transaction Code is Checked for an Add

As was noted previously, the Transaction Code in the transaction record is used to indicate the function of the transaction record. The three types of operations which may be performed by transaction records are to add a record (code = 1), delete a master record (code = 2), or change a master record (code = 3). Again, in order for a transaction record to delete or change a master record, the Customer Number in the transaction record must be equal to the Customer Number in the master record. Since the transaction Customer Number is less than the master record, the only function which may be performed is to add the transaction record to the master file. Thus, the comparisons illustrated in Figure 9-14 ensure that the Transaction Code is equal to "1," which indicates that the transaction is to be added to the master file. Any other Transaction Code will be treated as an error and a message will be printed on the error report. As can be seen from the example, the Transaction Code is valid because it is equal to "1."

Step 8:   The transaction record is added to the new master file.

Figure 9-15 Transaction Record is Added to Master Output File

Note from Figure 9-15 that the Customer Number, the Customer Name, the Customer Address and the Amount are moved from the Transaction Input Area to the Master Output Area. The record is then written on the master output tape. Note also that the transaction record which has been added to the master file is written immediately following the first record which was written on the file. The second master record which was read from the old master file, with the Customer Number 00003, has not yet been placed in the new master file. After the record is written on the new master file, the Transaction Switch is set to zero to indicate that an unprocessed transaction record is no longer in core storage, that is, the transaction record which was in the Transaction Input Area has been completely processed by being added to the new master file. Therefore, another transaction record must be read.

Step 9:   A second transaction record is read

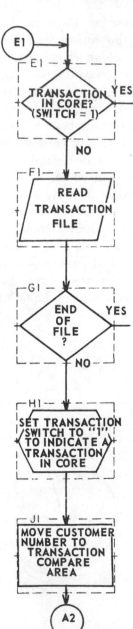

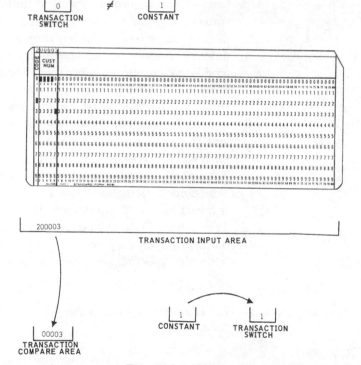

Figure 9-16 Transaction is Read

Note in the example above that the second transaction record is read and placed in the Transaction Input Area. The Transaction Switch is then set to one to indicate that a transaction record is in core storage and the Customer Number from transaction record is moved to the Transaction Compare Area. Note also that the only data contained in the transaction record is the transaction code, 2, and the customer number, 00003. As noted previously, the code 2 indicates that the transaction record is to cause a master record to be deleted. Thus, since no data is to be changed in the master or added to the master file, the only data required is the transaction code to indicate a delete and the customer number of the master record to be deleted. The operation in Box A2 of the flowchart is performed next.

Step 10: **The reading of a master record is bypassed.**

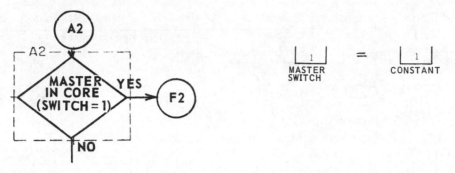

Figure 9-17 Master Read is Bypassed

Note in the example above that after the transaction record is read, the master switch is tested to determine if a master record is in core storage. In Figure 9-12, a master record was read and it has not yet been processed. Therefore, the master switch which was set to "1" in that example has not been reset to zero to indicate that a master need be read. Therefore, the reading of a master record is bypassed since the one in core storage has not yet been processed.

Step 11: **The Customer Number in the Transaction Compare Area is compared with the Customer Number in the Master Compare Area.**

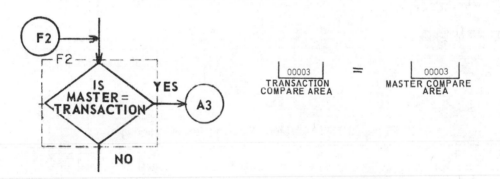

Figure 9-18 Customer Numbers are Compared

Note in the example in Figure 9-18 that when the Customer Numbers in the Transaction Compare Area and the Master Compare Area are compared, they are found to be equal. When the Customer Number in the transaction record is equal to the Customer Number in the master record, the two valid operations are to change the master record by adding the amount in the transaction record to the amount in the old master record or to delete the master record from the new master file. Thus, the next step in block A3 is to determine the type of operation to be performed on the master record.

Step 12:   The Transaction Code is checked.

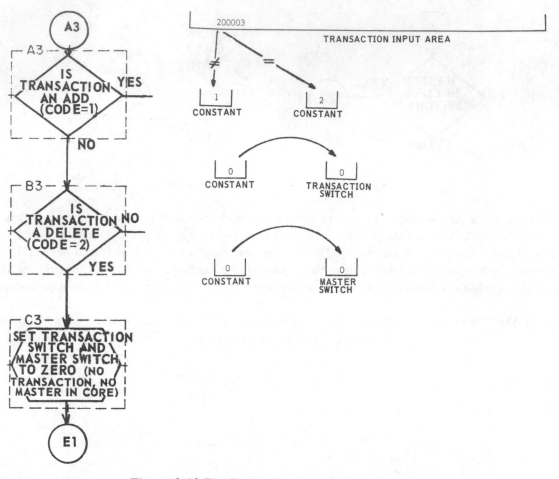

Figure 9-19 The Delete Transaction is Processed

In the example above, the Transaction Code in the transaction record is compared to a constant value of "1" to determine if the record is an "add" record. If it is, it is in error because it is not possible to add a record which already exists on the master file. Note from the example, however, that the transaction code is a "2," which indicates that the transaction record is to cause the master record to be deleted from the master file. Thus, when the code is checked for the value "2," which indicates a deletion, an equal condition is found.

It should be recalled that when a master record is deleted from the master file, it is not to be written on the new master file. Thus, the result desired from the deletion processing is to have the old master record not written on the new master file. In order to accomplish this, the next record on the old master file must be read while the master record currently in the Master Input Area is not moved to the Master Output Area and written. In order to do this, the Master Switch is set to zero, which indicates that the master record in core storage has been "processed." The Transaction Switch is also set to Zero to indicate that the transaction record has been processed. Note again that the master record which was read in Figure 9-12 is not written on the new master. Thus, the record is effectively deleted from the new master file.

After the switches have been set to zero, control is returned to block E1 where the next transaction record is read.

Step 13: The next transaction record is read.

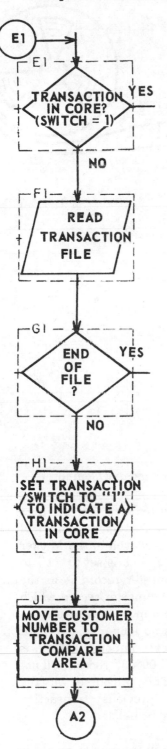

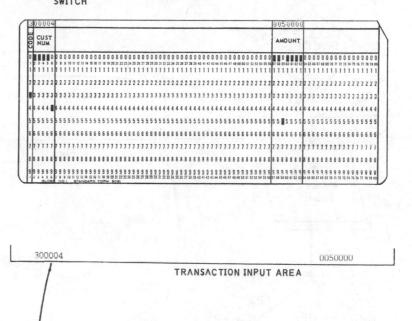

Figure 9-20 Transaction Record is Read

Note in the example above that the Transaction Switch contains a zero which indicates that there is not a transaction record in core which has not been processed. Thus, a transaction record must be read. The switch is then set to "1" and the Customer Number is moved to the compare area as in the previous steps. Note also that the Transaction Code is equal to "3," which indicates a change record. As mentioned previously, a change means that the amount field in the corresponding master record is to be incremented by the Amount field in the transaction record. Since the Amount field is the only field which is to be acted upon in this transaction, the Name field and the Address field do not contain any values.

After the transaction record is read, a check is made to determine if a master record must be read.

Step 14:   **Another master record is read and compared.**

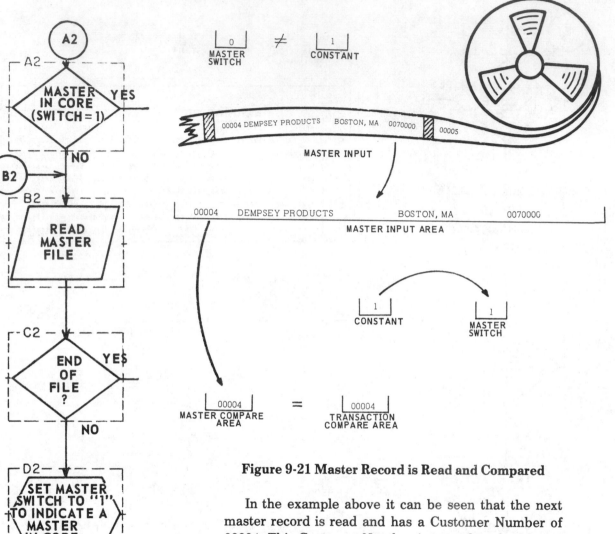

Figure 9-21 Master Record is Read and Compared

In the example above it can be seen that the next master record is read and has a Customer Number of 00004. This Customer Number is moved to the Master Compare Area and the Master Switch is set to "1" to indicate that an unprocessed master record is in the Master Input Area. Note that the master record which was previously in the Master Input Area, with the Customer Number "00003," is no longer in the input area when the record customer number "00004" is read. Thus, as can be seen, the "00003" record will not be written on the new master. This, of course, was the desired result because the previous transaction requested that the master record be deleted.

When the Customer Number in the master record is compared to the Customer Number in the transaction record, they are found to be equal, that is, they are both 00004. Thus, the routine in block A3 is entered.

Step 15:   **After the Customer Numbers are compared and found to be equal, a check is made of the code field in the transaction record.**

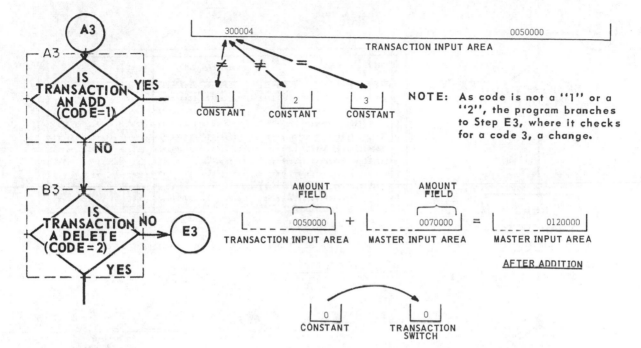

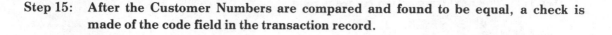

Figure 9-22 Master Record is Changed

In the example above it can be seen that the Transaction Code in the transaction record indicates that a master record is to be changed, that is, the Amount field in the master record is to be incremented by the Amount field in the transaction record. Therefore, the Amount in the Transaction Input Area is added to the Amount in the Master Input Area. The Transaction Switch is then set to zero to indicate that there is no unprocessed transaction record in core storage. This is because the Amount in the transaction record has been added to the master record and there is no more to be done with the transaction record. Note that the Master Switch is not set to zero. This is because the master record is not moved to the new master output area and written on the new master file. Since the old master record has not been written on the new master, it is still considered an unprocessed record even though the Amount field has been updated. The reason that the old master record is not written after the Amount is updated is that the possibility exists that there may be more than one transaction record to update a master record, that is, the Amount in the master record may be incremented by more than one transaction record. Thus, the master record should not be written on the new master file until all of the transaction records which reference that record are processed. This happens only when the Customer Number in the master record is less than the Customer Number in the transaction record. When this occurs, all of the transaction records will have been processed for the master record.

Step 16:   **The next transaction record is read.**

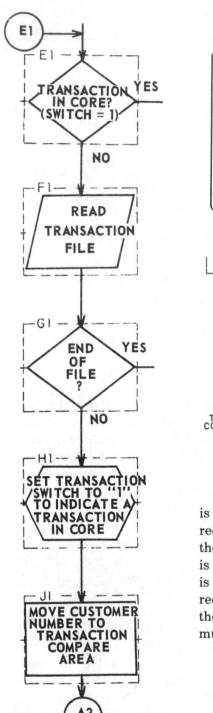

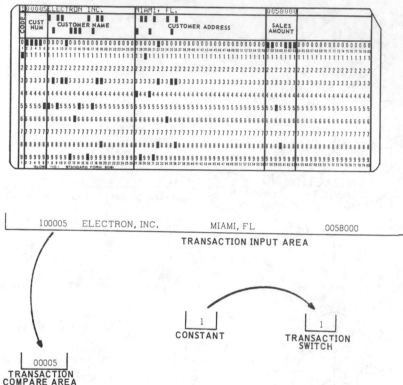

Figure 9-23 Transaction Record is Read

As in the previous examples, when the Transaction Switch is equal to zero, it indicates that there is not a transaction record in core storage. Thus, a transaction record is read into the Transaction Input Area. In addition, the Transaction Switch is set to "1" to indicate that an unprocessed transaction record is in core storage and the Customer Number in the transaction record is moved to the Transaction Compare Area. Control is then passed to block A2, which determines if a master record must be read.

Step 17: The master file is not read because a master record is in core storage. The Customer Numbers are compared to determine the action to be taken.

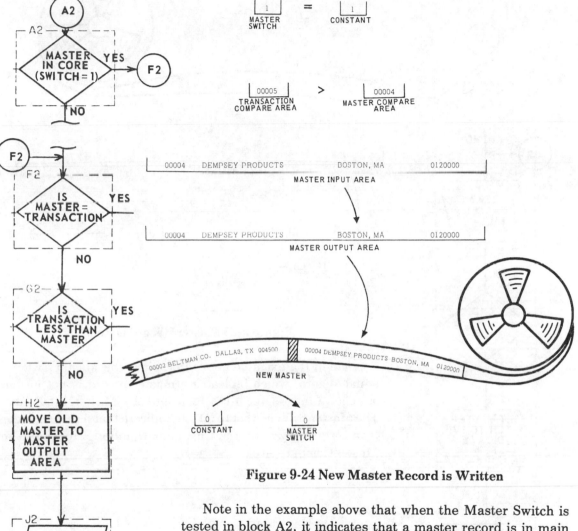

Figure 9-24 New Master Record is Written

Note in the example above that when the Master Switch is tested in block A2, it indicates that a master record is in main storage. Therefore, it is not necessary to read another record and control is passed to block F2. When the Customer Numbers are compared, it is found that the Customer number in the Master Compare Area is less than the Customer Number in the Transaction Compare Area. Thus, since there are no more transaction records to update the master record, the new master record with the updated Amount may be written on the new master file. The Master Switch is then set to zero to indicate that a master record must be read and control is passed to block A2.

Step 18: The next master record is read.

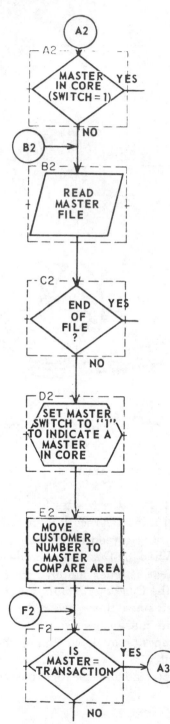

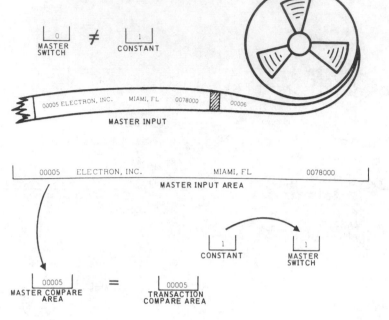

Figure 9-25 Master Record is Read

Note in the example above that since the Master Switch is equal to zero, which indicates a master record is not in main storage, a master record is read into the Master Input Area. The Master Switch is set to "1" to indicate that a master record is in core storage and the Customer Number is moved to the Master Compare Area.

Step 19: **The Customer Numbers in the Transaction Compare Area and the Master Compare Area are found to be equal. The "equal" routine is then entered and the appropriate action taken.**

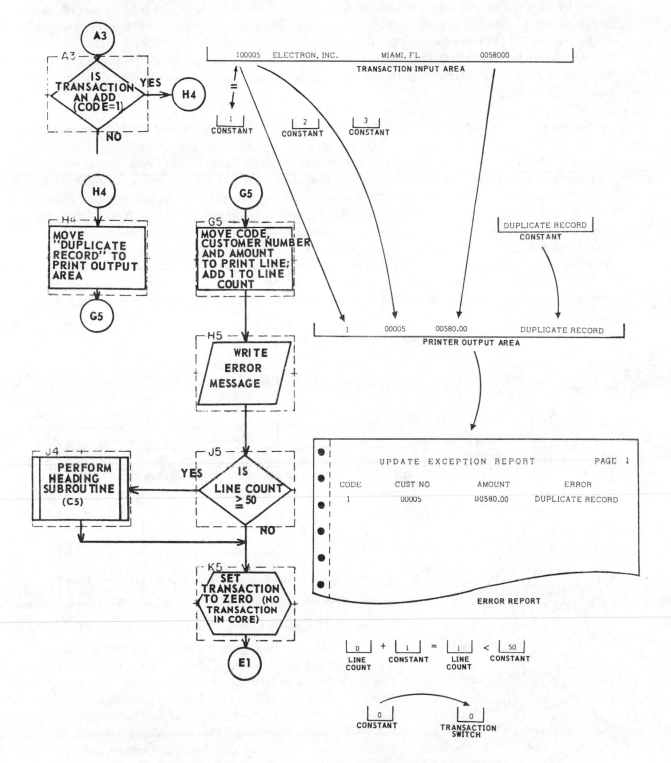

Figure 9-26 Invalid Transaction Record is Processed

In the example in Figure 9-26, it can be seen that the routine in block A3 is entered when the customer numbers are equal. As was noted previously, the valid operations when the customer numbers are equal are to delete the master record from the master file and to update the master record by adding the amount in the transaction record to the amount in the master record. An add transaction is invalid because a record cannot be added to the master file if it already exists on the master file. In the example, the transaction code is equal to a "1," which indicates that the record is to be added to the master file. Therefore, the transaction record contains an invalid transaction code. When this occurs, an entry is made on the Update Exception Report to indicate the error.

The statement in block H4 indicates that the message "Duplicate Record" is to be moved to the printer output area. This message is used to specify that the transaction record is attempting to add a duplicate record to the master file. The Transaction Code, the Customer Number and the Amount are then moved to the printer output area in order to identify the transaction record in error and the line is printed on the exception report. The line count is incremented by one and checked to determine if a new page is to be printed. In the example, this is the first line to be printed on the report, so the value in the Line Count field is only 1 and a heading will not be printed on a new page. After the line is printed on the report, the Transaction Switch is set to zero to indicate that the transaction record has been processed. It has been processed because it has been found to be in error. Thus, it cannot be used to perform any valid operation in the update processing. It is necessary, therefore, to read the next transaction record.

Step 20:   **The next transaction record is read**

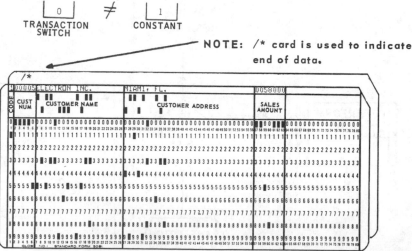

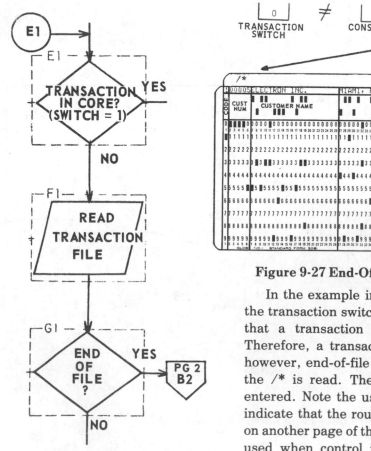

NOTE: /* card is used to indicate end of data.

Figure 9-27 End-Of-File is Found in Transaction File

In the example in Figure 9-27, it can be seen that the transaction switch is equal to zero, which indicates that a transaction record is not in main storage. Therefore, a transaction record is read. In this step, however, end-of-file is reached, that is, the card with the /* is read. Therefore, the end-of-file routine is entered. Note the use of the "off-page connector" to indicate that the routine is to be entered is illustrated on another page of the flowchart. This symbol is always used when control is to be transferred to a routine which is illustrated on a page of the flowchart other than the one where the transfer of control takes place.

Step 21: **The end-of-file routine for the transaction file is entered.**

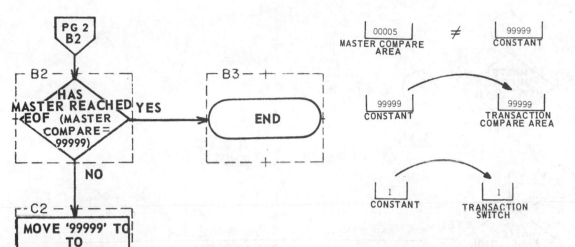

Figure 9-28 Transaction End-of-File is Processed

When two files are being processed within the same program, such as the transaction file and the master file in this example, the program cannot be ended when only one file has reached the end. Both files must reach end-of-file before the program can be ended. Thus, when end-of-file is reached for the transaction file, the first operation to be performed is to test if the master file has reached end-of-file. It it has, then the program can be terminated. If it has not reached end-of-file, then the remainder of the master file must be processed before the program can be terminated. In this example, in order to test if the master file has reached end-of-file, the value in the Master Compare Area is compared to the value "99999." This is a value which is moved to the Master Compare Area when the master file has reached end-of-file. Thus, if the value is not equal to "99999," as in the example above, it indicates that the master file has not yet been completely processed. If the master has not reached end-of-file, the value 99999 is moved to the Transaction Compare Area. This value accomplishes two objectives: first, it indicates that the transaction file has reached end-of-file, so that when the master file reaches end-of-file, the master end-of-file routine will be able to determine that the transaction file has been completely processed and the program will be terminated; second, it ensures that when the customer Number in the Master Compare Area is compared to the value in the Transaction Compare Area, the master will always be low. This is required because there are no more transaction records to be processed against master records. Therefore, the remaining master records will always be treated as if they are less than the transaction records and cause the writing of the remaining master records on the new master tape.

The Transaction Switch is then set to "1" to indicate that there is a transaction record in core storage. Even though there is not actually a record in core storage, the transaction file must not be read again because there are no more records to be processed. Therefore, the switch is set so that a transaction record will not be read. Control is then passed to block A2 on Page 1 so that the remaining master records may be processed.

Step 22:   The remaining master records are read and processed.

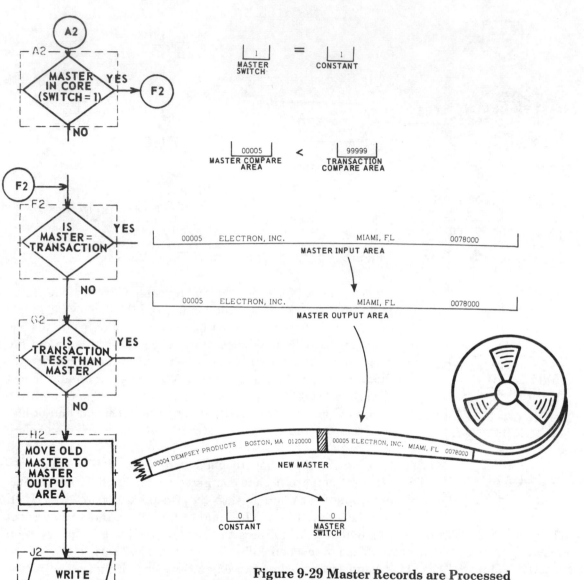

Figure 9-29 Master Records are Processed

As can be seen from the example above, the first test when the routine in block A2 is entered is to determine if there is a master record in main storage. In the example, there is a master in core storage, so a master record is not read. When the Customer Number in the Master Compare Area is compared with the value in the Transaction Compare Area, it is found that the master is less than the transaction. This will always be true when the transaction file has reached end-of-file because the value "99999" is moved to the Transaction Compare Area. Thus, the records which remain on the old master will merely be rewritten on the new master because there are no transaction records to update the records on the old master file.

Step 23: The master file is processed until the end of the master input file is found. The master end-of-file routine is then entered.

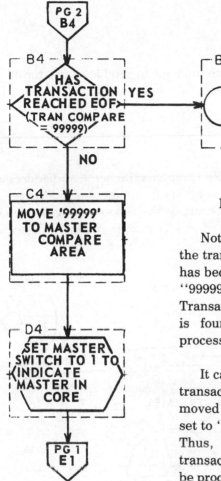

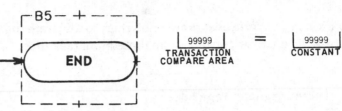

Figure 9-30 Master End-of-File Routine is Entered

Note in Figure 9-30 that the first test performed is to check if the transaction file has reached end-of-file. In this example, it has because the Transaction Compare Area contains the value "99999." As was noted previously, this value is moved to the Transaction Compare Area when the end of the transaction file is found. Thus, since both files have been completely processed, the program is terminated.

It can be seen from the flowchart in Figure 9-30 that if the transaction file had not reached end-of-file, the value 99999 is moved to the Master Compare Area and the Master Switch is set to "1" in the same manner as used for the transaction file. Thus, if the master file reached end-of-file before the transaction file, the remainder of the transaction records must be processed.

It should be noted that since the Customer Number of the transaction records will always be less than the Customer Numbers in the Master Compare Area after the master has reached end-of-file, the only valid transaction code for a transaction record after the master has been completely read is an "add" (Transaction code = 1). Any other code will cause an error message to be written on the Update Exception Report (see Figure 9-6). This is because there are no master records to be changed or deleted since there are no more master records.

The process of sequentially updating master files is quite common in business applications and should be thoroughly understood for the basic file update logic presented in this chapter can be applied to many types of business programming problems such as payroll, inventory control, etc.

CHAPTER 9

FLOWCHARTING ASSIGNMENT 1

INSTRUCTIONS

On a Flowchart Worksheet draw a flowchart to illustrate the logic to produce a master name and address file on magnetic tape from three input tape files.

INPUT: Three Magnetic Tape Files

Input is to consist of three magnetic tape files. Tape File 1 contains the name and addresses of customers in the Western United States. Tape File 2 contains the name and addresses of customers in the Central United States, and Tape File 3 contains the name and addresses of customers in the Eastern United States. Each File contains a customer number, customer name, and customer address.

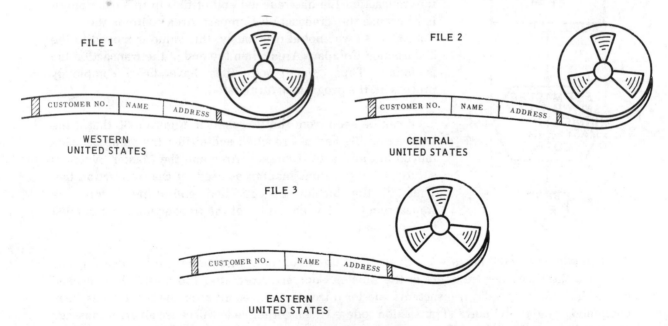

FILE 1

| CUSTOMER NO. | NAME | ADDRESS |

WESTERN
UNITED STATES

FILE 2

| CUSTOMER NO. | NAME | ADDRESS |

CENTRAL
UNITED STATES

FILE 3

| CUSTOMER NO. | NAME | ADDRESS |

EASTERN
UNITED STATES

OUTPUT: Master Name and Address File on Magnetic Tape

Output is to consist of a single magnetic tape containing the Customer Numbers, Customer Names, and Customer Addresses that were previously contained on the three input tapes. Each of the files is arranged in ascending order in Customer Number sequence.

| CUSTOMER NO. | NAME | ADDRESS |

UPDATED MASTER
NAME AND ADDRESS FILE

CHAPTER 9

FLOWCHARTING ASSIGNMENT 2

INSTRUCTIONS

On a Flowcharting Worksheet draw a flowchart to illustrate the logic to update a Master Employee file with transaction records containing additions, deletions, and changes to the master file.

INPUT: Master Employee File on Magnetic Tape, Transaction File containing additions, deletions, and changes on punched cards. The Master and Transaction File are in Employee Number sequence.

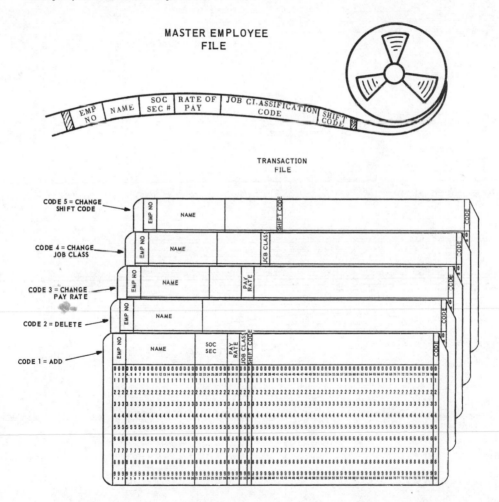

OUTPUT: Updated Master Employee File, Exception Report listing invalid transaction records.

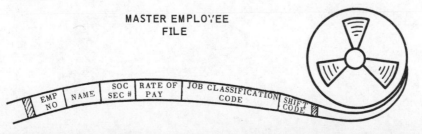

CHAPTER 10

SEQUENTIAL TABLE SEARCH

INTRODUCTION

In the previous examples of programs, the data to be processed and referenced within the program was read from card or tape files. In many business applications, it is desirable to organize reference data in the form of a "table," store the table in main storage, and retrieve those portions of the table that are needed in the solution of a problem. A table is a series of similar types of information which are stored in consecutive locations within main storage. The elements within a table may be any desired in order to solve a given problem. For example, in this chapter, a report is to be prepared listing item numbers of grocery merchandise and the respective description of the merchandise. The item numbers will be punched on input data cards. The description of the items is to be retrieved from a table. The chart below illustrates the item numbers and the corresponding descriptions.

ITEM #	DESCRIPTION
008	American Cheese
017	Sweet Butter
024	Asparagus
064	Coffee
069	Dried Peaches
073	Horse Radish
086	Carrots
095	Peas
101	Sweet Potatoes
110	Pineapples
116	Hot Peppers
125	Soda Crackers
137	Rice
138	Tomato Soup
139	Sugar
145	Pears
146	Cocoa
149	Tapioca
152	Nutmeg

Figure 10-1 Items and Descriptions

Note from the table illustrated above that for each item number there is a corresponding description which describes the product involved, that is, item #008 corresponds to American Cheese, item #145 corresponds to Pears, etc.

In order to incorporate this information into the program to be referenced, it can be stored in the form of a table, that is, each item and description will be followed by another item and description within the table. This is illustrated below.

EXAMPLE

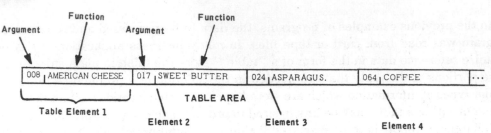

Figure 10-2 Example of Table Stored in Main Storage

In the example above it can be seen that a table area is reserved in main storage within the program and the item numbers and the descriptions are included in the area. Each item number within the table is called an ARGUMENT because the item number is to be used to identify the entry within the table. The descriptions are called FUNCTIONS because they are the values to be extracted from the table and used in the program. Each group of item number and description in the table is called a TABLE ELEMENT. Note from Figure 10-1 that there are 19 table elements because there are 19 item number and description combinations.

In some programming languages, reference to the table elements is often made by use of a subscript, that is, a number contained within parentheses. For example, the subscript entry (1) would be used to reference the first table element, the subscript entry (2) the second table element, etc.

In the program presented in this chapter, a file of cards containing the item number and a sales amount are read. The item number in the card is to be used to extract the appropriate description from the table and a report is to be created. The input and the report are illustrated in Figure 10-3.

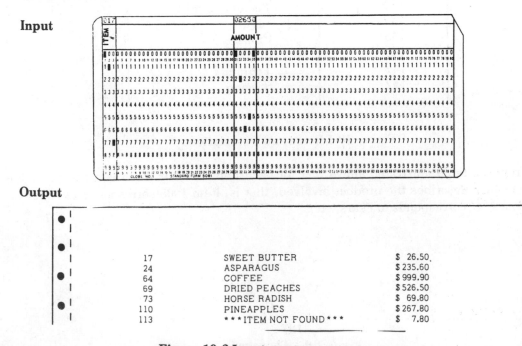

Figure 10-3 Input and Output of Program

Note from Figure 10-3 that the input cards contain an Item Number field and an Amount field. The item number in the input data is to be used to find the corresponding description in the table as illustrated in Figure 10-2. The flowchart of the program is illustrated in Figure 10-4.

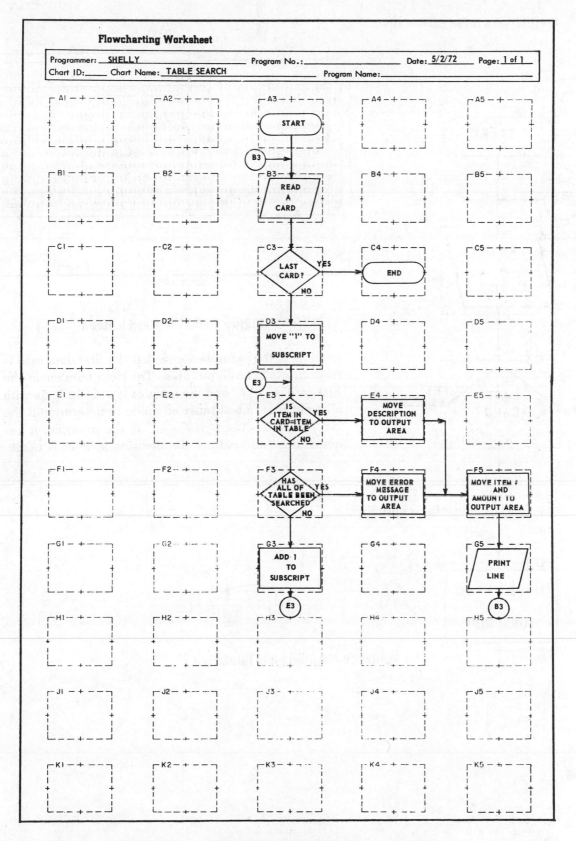

Flowcharting Worksheet

Programmer: __SHELLY__   Program No.: _____   Date: __5/2/72__   Page: __1 of 1__
Chart ID: _____ Chart Name: __TABLE SEARCH__   Program Name: _____

Figure 10-4 Flowchart

The steps involved in searching the table and extracting the desired description to be placed on the report are illustrated below.

Step 1:   An input card is read.

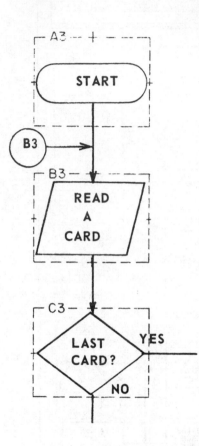

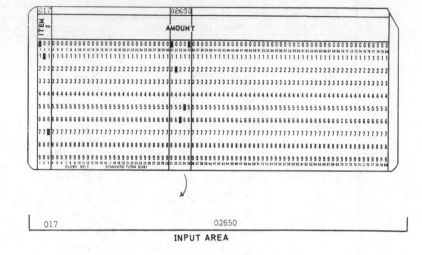

Figure 10-5 First Card is Read

Note in the example above that the first data card is read into the card input area. The item number in the first card is "017" and the amount is "02650." As with all input files, a test must be made to determine if the last record has been processed. In the example, it has not so the "no" path of the decision symbol is taken.

Step 2:   The subscript is initialized.

Figure 10-6 Subscript is Initialized

In the example in Figure 10-6, the SUBSCRIPT is initialized to the value "01." A Subscript is a value which can be used to reference each element within a table. This is illustrated below.

EXAMPLE

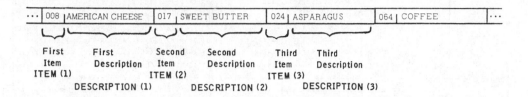

Figure 10-7 Example of the Use of SUBSCRIPTS

Note from the example in Figure 10-7 that each element within the table is broken down into the argument, which is called ITEM, and the function, which is called DESCRIPTION. When processing tables, it is normally not desirable to give a unique name or identification to each element within the table. Instead, the function is given one name and the argument is given another name and the required element within the table is referenced through the use of the name and a subscript which indicates which element within the table is to be referenced. Thus, the identifier ITEM(1) indicates that the first item within the table is to be referenced, the identifier ITEM(2) indicates the second item within the table is to be referenced, etc. The use of a subscript allows the table to be processed and searched within one single routine instead of referencing each element in the table with a different name, which would not allow this.

In most programming languages, the subscript need not be an absolute value such as ITEM(1). Instead, a variable subscript may be used, that is, an area in main storage within the program may be designated as the subscript and the value in this area serves as the value of the subscript. This is the use of the Subscript field illustrated in Figure 10-6. The value in this field will be used to determine which item and description, that is, which element, within the table is to be processed.

After the subscript is initialized, the "table search" may begin. The table search consists of basically comparing the value in the Item Number field in the input card with the Item Number values in the table. When an equal value is found, the corresponding description from the table is moved to the printer output area to be printed on the report. Thus, the next step, as illustrated in Figure 10-8, compares the Item Number in the input card to the first Item Number in the table.

Step 3: The first item number in the table is compared to the item number in the input record.

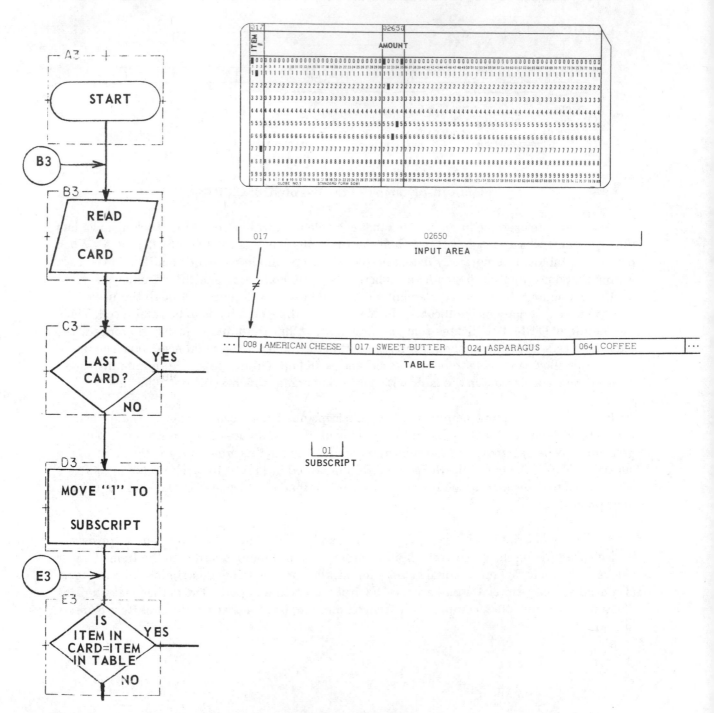

Figure 10-8 First Item Number in Table is Checked

In the example above it can be seen that the value in the Subscript field is "01." Thus, when the comparison takes place, the first item number in the table is compared to the item number in the input area. As can be seen, the item number in the input area, 017, is not equal to the first item number in the table, 008. Thus, the "No" path of the decision symbol is taken.

Step 4:   A test is made to determine if the entire table has been searched.

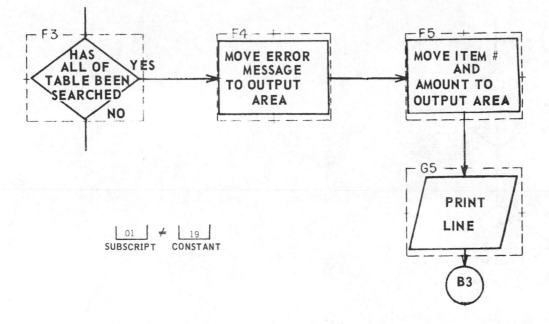

Figure 10-9 End of Table Test is Made

Whenever a table is to be searched, the possibility exists that the item number in the input data card will not be equal to any of the item numbers which are stored in the table. Therefore, whenever table searching is to take place, provision must be made to process records which do not contain a valid item number. One method of testing to determine if the entire table has been searched and the desired item number not found is to test if the value in the subscript field contains the maximum value which it can contain, that is, if it is equal to the number of elements in the table. Thus, in this example, the value in the subscript is compared to the value "19," which is the number of elements within the table. If the subscript is equal to nineteen, it means that all of the item numbers in the table have been compared to the item number in the input data and none have been found to be equal. Thus, an error message will be printed on the report (see Item #113 in Figure 10-3). Since the subscript is not equal to 19 in this example, the "No" path of the decision symbol is taken.

Step 5:   The subscript is incremented by 1 and control is returned to test the next item
          number in the table.

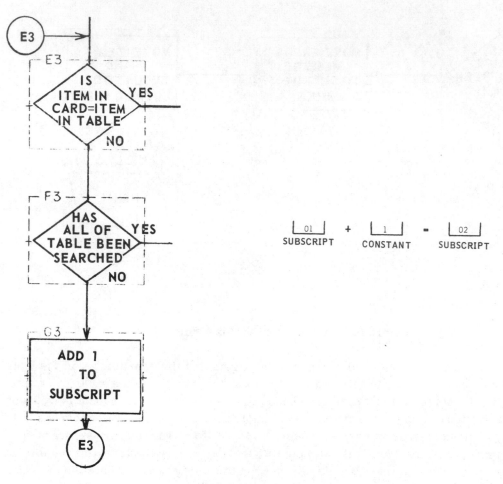

Figure 10-10 Subscript is Incremented by 1

In the example above it can be seen that the value "1" is added to the value in the subscript
field giving the value "2" in the subscript field. Thus, when the subscript is used to determine
which element in the table is to be used for comparison to the item number in the input card,
the second item will be compared.

Step 6: The second item number in the table is compared to the item number in the card.

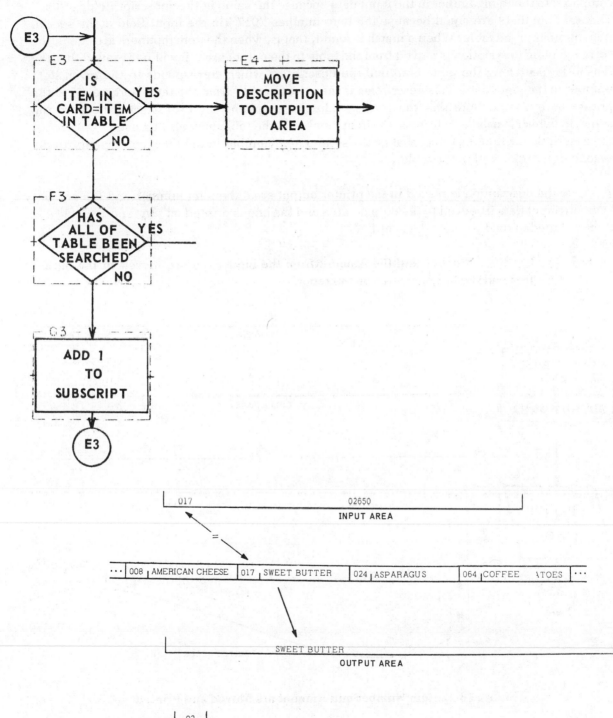

Figure 10-11 Item Number is Found and Description is Moved to Output Area

In the example in Figure 10-11 it can be seen that the second item number in the table is compared to the item number in the input data because the value in the subscript field is "02." The item numbers are equal because the item number "017" in the input field is the second item number in the table. When a match is found, that is, when the item numbers are equal, the corresponding description is moved from the table to the output area. It will be recalled that the reason for searching the table is to find the description which corresponds to the given item number in the input data. This description is then "extracted" from the table and moved to the printer output area. Note that the corresponding description may be extracted because the subscript which is used to reference the item number in the table may also be used to reference the description within the table, that is, the second item number in the table corresponds to the second description within the table.

After the description is placed in the printer output area, the item number and the amount from the input data is moved to the output   area and the line is printed on the report. Control is then returned to read the next data card.

Step 7:   **The Item Number and the Amount from the input area are moved to the output area and the line is printed on the report.**

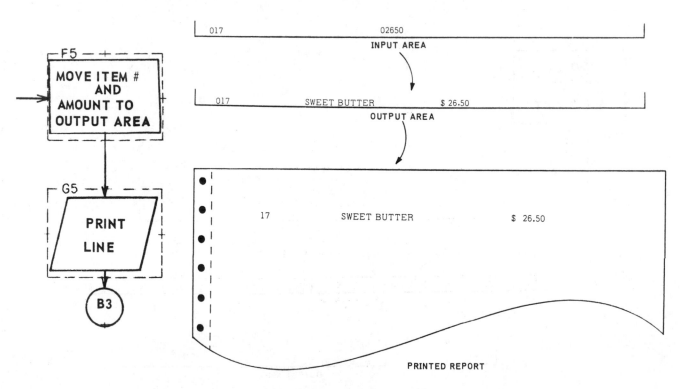

Figure 10-12 Item Number and Amount are Moved and Printed

Note from the example above that after the Item Number and the Amount are moved to the output area, they are written on the report. The description was already in the output area after it was moved in the example in Figure 10-11. After the line is printed on the report, control is passed to block B3, which reads the next input card.

Step 8: The next card is read and the subscript is initialized

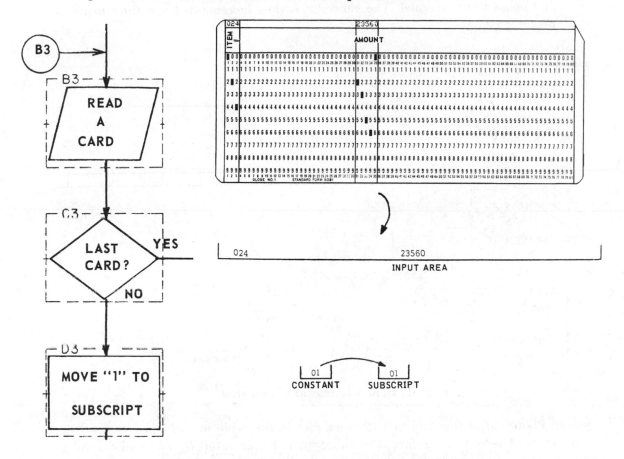

Figure 10-13 A Second Card is Read and the Subscript is Reset

In the example it can be seen that the second card is read into the input area and the value in the subscript is reset to "01." Note that, as a result of the processing of the previous card, the value in the subscript field was equal to "02." Whenever the table search is to begin for any particular item number, the subscript field must contain the value "01" so that the first entry in the table is examined. If the subscript field was not reset, the table search would begin with the second element in the table and the possibility exists that the item number in the input card would be for the first entry in the table. Again, prior to any searching of a table, the subscript field must be reset to reference the first entry within the table.

Step 9:   The Item Number in the input data is compared to the item number in the table and found to be unequal. The subscript is then incremented and the "loop" is processed again.

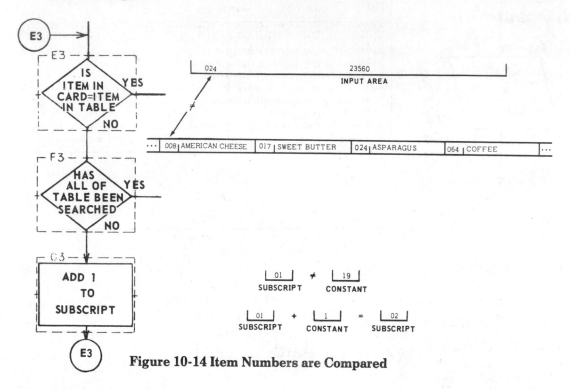

Figure 10-14 Item Numbers are Compared

Note from Figure 10-14 that the first item number in the table is not equal to the item number in the input record. Therefore, the subscript is incremented by one and control is returned to block E3 which will compare the item number in the card with the second item number in the table. This comparison will continue until an equal item number is found or until the subscript is equal to "19," which indicates that all of the entries within the table have been compared to the item number in the input data and none of them are equal. As can be seen from the example above, the item number in the input card, "024," is equal to the third item number in the table. Thus, when this equal condition is found, the corresponding description, "Asparagus," will be moved to the output area. The item number and the amount are then moved from the input area to the output area and the line is printed on the report. The report after the second input card has been processed is illustrated in Figure 10-15.

Report

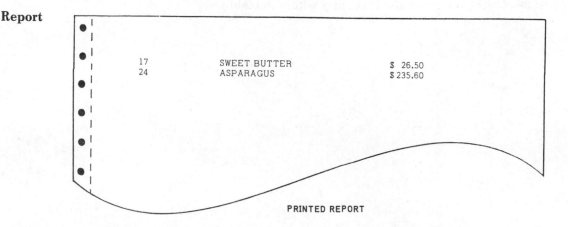

Figure 10-15 Report after Second Card Processed

Mitra Houshange
10-27-82

$125 / 1000

COMPANY GEE SELLS A PRODUCT FOR $125 PER THOUSAND. IF A CUSTOMER BUYS 10000 OR MORE, A 10% DISCOUNT IS ALLOWED. (a) MAKE A FLOWCHART THAT WILL SHOW HOW TO COMPUTE AND PRINT INVOICES (Bill) FOR THE CUSTOMERS OF COMPANY GEE IF THE CUSTOMER NAME AND NUMBER OF ITEMS PURCHASED IS GIVEN. (b) CODE IN BASIC FROM YOUR FLOWCHART. (c) USE SOME ARBITRARY DATA OF YOUR CHOICE TO MAKE A RUN AND PRINT OUT A COPY OF YOUR RESULTS.

VARIBLE NAME
Costumer Name = N$
D = discount
I = Invoice
Number of items = N

INPUT
N$, P1

20,000 × 125 $ × 10 × .1

10

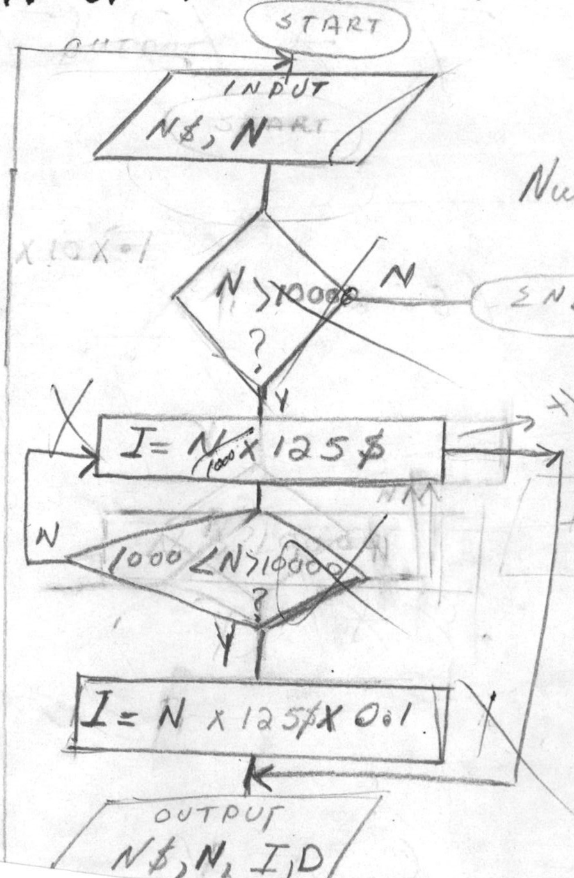

As noted previously, it is possible that the item number in the data card is not equal to any of the item numbers which are stored in the table. When this occurs, it is necessary to place a message on the report which indicates that the item number is not a part of the table. This is illustrated below.

Step 10: Invalid Item Number is processed.

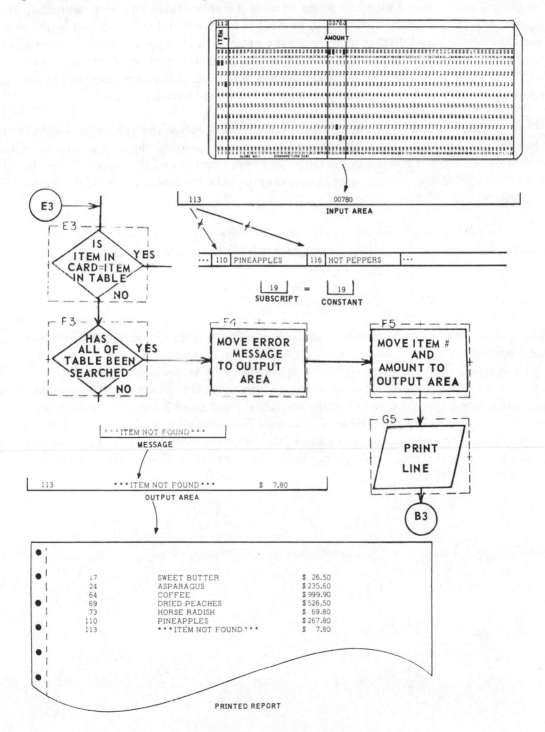

Figure 10-16 Processing of Invalid Item Number

Note from Figure 10-16 that the item number, 113, which is in the input data, is not contained in the table. Note that the example merely depicts the point in the table where the item number 113 would be placed if the table is organized in an ascending sequence, that is, each item number in the table is greater than the previous item number. When using the sequential search method illustrated in this chapter, it is not required that the table be in a sorted order. This is because each item number in the table is compared to the item number in the input card until either a match is found or until the entire table has been searched. Thus, the item number 008 could be the last item number in the table and still be found by the search routine. The method used to determine when the entire table has been searched is to compare the value in the subscript to a constant value which contains the number of elements within the table. When these two values are equal, it indicates that all of the item numbers in the table have been compared to the item number in the card and none have been equal.

When an item number is not found in the table, that is, when the subscript is equal to the number of elements within the table, an error message is moved to the output area to indicate that the item has not been found in the table. The item number and the amount from the input card are then moved to the output area also so that the card in error may be identified. The line is then printed and another card is read.

All of the cards in the input file will continue to be processed in a similar manner until the last data card is read. At that point, the program will be terminated.

MULTI-LEVEL TABLES

The table illustrated in the previous example is called a single-level or one-dimension table because each element in the table was an individual element and not dependent upon any of the other elements within the table. In some applications, it is desirable to be able to handle multi-level or multi-dimensional tables, that is, a form of table in which two reference points are required to locate a specific element within the table. Road maps frequently contain multi-level tables. On a typical road map, a table of distances between two cities is presented. To find the distance between any two cities, the names of the cities are located on the table and where the vertical and horizontal lines representing these cities intersect, the distance is given. This is illusrated in Figure 10-17.

Multi-Level Table

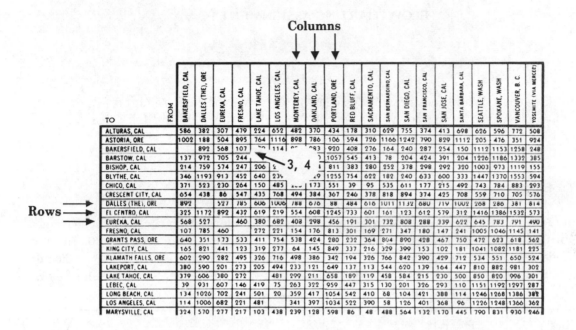

Figure 10-17 Example of Multi-Dimensional Table

In the example above it can be seen that the table of distances between cities is organized in terms of rows (horizontal) and columns (vertical). Thus, the distance between Bakersfield, California and Fresno, California is contained in row 3, column 4. In order to reference values within a multi-dimensional table, double subscripts are normally used. A double subscript is usually written in the general format (row, column), that is, the row in which the value is found is usually given first and then the desired column within the row is specified. Thus, in order to find the value for the distance between Bakersfield and Fresno, the subscript (3,4) would be used to indicate that the value may be found in row 3, column 4.

Multi-dimensional tables have many uses both in business and scientific programming problems.

CHAPTER 10

FLOWCHARTING ASSIGNMENT 1

INSTRUCTIONS

On a Flowchart Worksheet draw a flowchart to illustrate the logic required to produce a listing of employees of a company with a description of their Job Type and Job Class. The Job Type and Job Class is to be extracted from a table.

INPUT: Employee Cards

Input is to consist of Employee cards that contain the Employee Number, Employee Name, Job Type Code, and Job Class Code. The Job Type Code field will contain codes 01-30. The Job Class Code field will contain codes from 01-10. For example, a Job Type Code of "01" indicates an accountant, a Job Class Code of "01" indicates a Part-time employee. See the tables below.

OUTPUT: Employee Listing

Output is to consist of a listing of employees with a description of their Job Type, and Job Class. The descriptions are to be extracted from a table from the codes contained in the input name cards. Segments of the table and a portion of the report are illustrated below.

Tables:

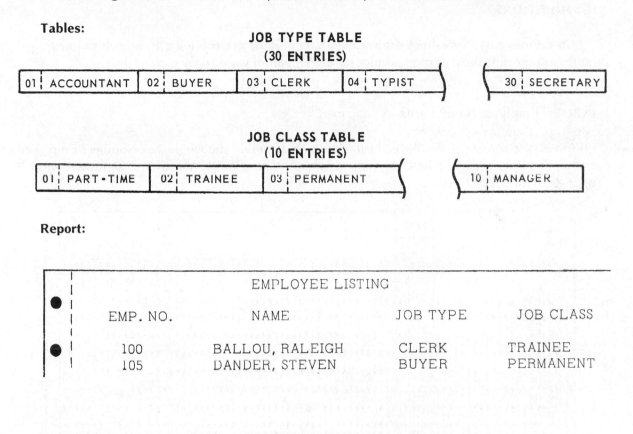

JOB TYPE TABLE
(30 ENTRIES)

| 01 | ACCOUNTANT | 02 | BUYER | 03 | CLERK | 04 | TYPIST | | 30 | SECRETARY |

JOB CLASS TABLE
(10 ENTRIES)

| 01 | PART-TIME | 02 | TRAINEE | 03 | PERMANENT | | 10 | MANAGER |

Report:

```
                         EMPLOYEE LISTING

    EMP. NO.          NAME              JOB TYPE          JOB CLASS

      100         BALLOU, RALEIGH        CLERK            TRAINEE
      105         DANDER, STEVEN         BUYER            PERMANENT
```

CHAPTER 10

FLOWCHARTING ASSIGNMENT 2

INSTRUCTIONS

On a Flowchart Worksheet draw a flowchart to illustrate the logic to search an insurance table to determine the cost of insurance for individuals of various ages.

INPUT: Employee Name Cards

Input is to consist of Employee Name cards that contain the Employee Number, Employee Name, and Date of Birth. The Date of Birth field contains a 2 digit Month, a 2 digit Day, and a 2 digit Year subfield.

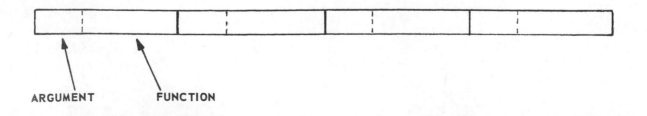

Design a table so that the programmer may perform a sequential search of the table to extract the Monthly cost of insurance. The specifications to be contained in the table are explained in the following paragraph.

''For individuals 1-20 years of age the insurance cost is $12.50 per month; for individuals 21-30 the insurance cost is $17.50 per month; for individuals 31-40 the insurance cost is $25.50 per month; and for individuals 41-50 the insurance cost is $42.50 per month. Insurance is not available for individuals over 50.'' Record the argument and functions of the table below.

TABLE

ARGUMENT   FUNCTION

CHAPTER 11

BINARY SEARCH TABLE LOOK-UP

INTRODUCTION

In the example in Chapter 10, the table was established in main storage and the table look-up took place in a sequential manner, that is, the first element in the table was compared to the desired item number and if they were not equal, the second element in the table was compared, etc. This method of table search is relatively efficient for a table with few elements or tables in which the argument within the table cannot be arranged in an ascending or decending sequence. If the table contains many elements and can be arranged in an ascending or descending sequence, however, a more efficient method of table search is the BINARY SEARCH technique.

A Binary Search of a sorted table is normally accomplished by comparing the middle item in the table with the desired value and then, depending upon whether the desired value is high or low, further dividing the table until the desired value is found. This basic concept of a binary search is illustrated in the following example.

EXAMPLE

Assume a table of 11 elements existed and the desired value to be found was 8.

1	7
2	8 - **Desired Value**
3	9
4	10
5	11
6	

Step 1: Examine the middle item, which is item 6. Item 6 is less than the desired item.

Step 2: Since item 6 is less than the desired item, examine the middle item between 6 and 11, which is 9. Item 9 is greater than the desired item.

Step 3: Since item 9 is greater than the desired item, examine the middle item between 6 and 9. As there is no middle item, the lower value, value 7, is examined. It is lower than the desired item, so examine the middle item between 7 and 9, which is item 8.

Note in the example that 4 comparisons to the table had to be made before the desired item was located. If a sequential table look-up were performed, eight comparisons would have been made. As can be seen, this is a 50% savings. In a larger table, however, much more savings in time can be realized. In a table with 1000 items, for example, the maximum number of comparisons which have to be made using a binary search is 10.

The example in this chapter will explain the technique used for a binary search in detail. The application will be the same as in Chapter 10, that is, the card input will contain an item number and an amount, and the output will be a report containing the item number, the description, and the amount. The description is to be extracted from a table. There are 19 items with related descriptions in this table. The card input and printer output are illustrated below.

INPUT

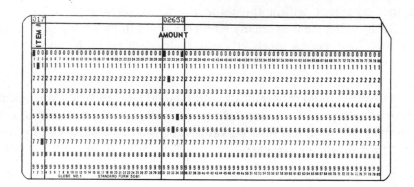

OUTPUT

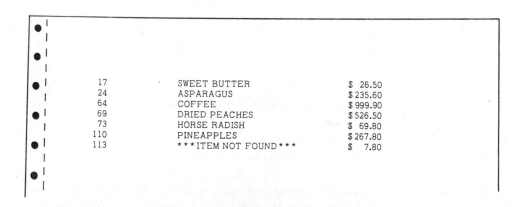

17	SWEET BUTTER	$ 26.50
24	ASPARAGUS	$235.60
64	COFFEE	$999.90
69	DRIED PEACHES	$526.50
73	HORSE RADISH	$ 69.80
110	PINEAPPLES	$267.80
113	* * * ITEM NOT FOUND * * *	$ 7.80

Figure 11-2 Program Input and Output

The flowchart for the binary search technique is illustrated in Figure 11-3.

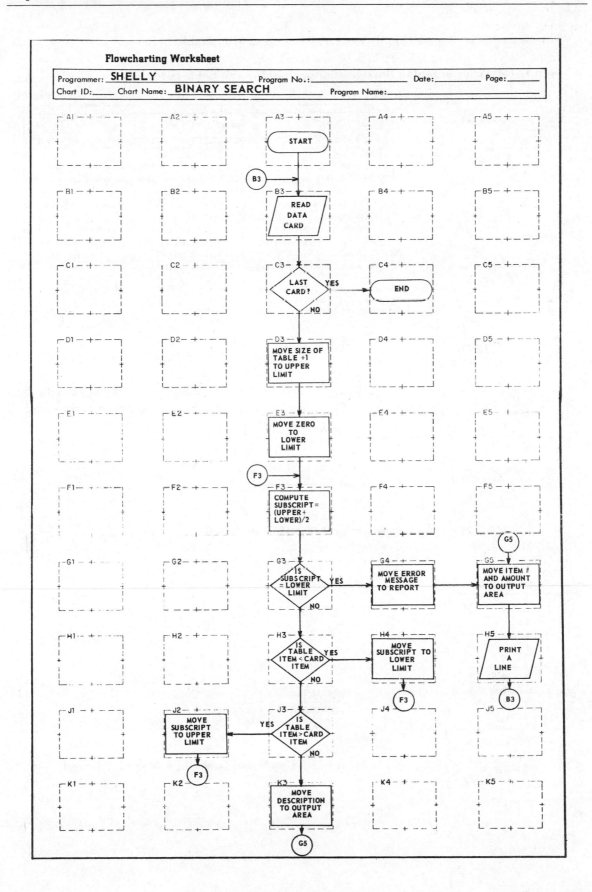

Figure 11-3 Flowchart

The steps involved in the binary search technique are illustrated below.

Step 1:   A card containing the item number and the amount is read.

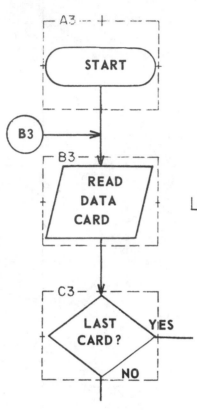

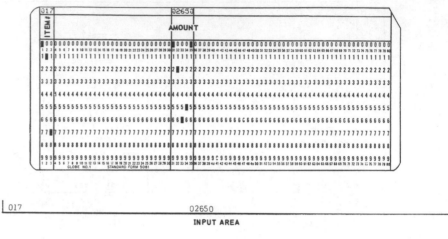

Figure 11-4 First Data Card is Read

As in the program in Chapter 10, the input data card is read and it contains the item number to be used to find the item description and an amount.

Step 2:   The Upper and Lower Limits of the table are initialized.

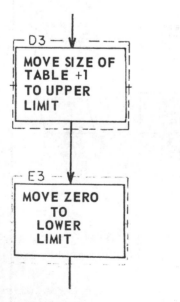

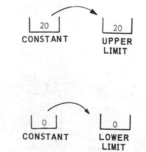

Figure 11-5 Upper and Lower Limits are Initialized

In the example in Figure 11-5, the value "20" is moved to the upper limit field and the value zero is moved to the lower limit field. The values in these fields are used in the calculation to determine which element in the table is to be compared to the item number in the card input data. It should be noted that the value "20" is one greater than the number of elements within the table. The reason that the entra one is moved to the upper limit is because of the possibility of remainders when the division by 2 takes place. This extra one will allow all elements in the table to be examined, if necessary. Thus, after the initialization of the limits, the entire table is being considered when searching for the desired value.

Step 3:   Compute the value to be used as the subscript in the table.

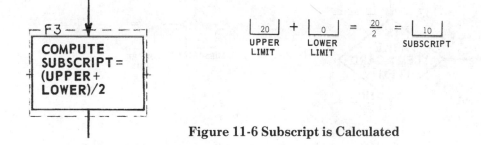

Figure 11-6 Subscript is Calculated

In the example above it can be seen that the subscript to be used to reference the element within the table is calculated by adding the value in the Upper limit area to the value in the Lower Limit area and dividing by 2. As noted in the example at the beginning of the chapter, the idea in a binary search is to divide the table in half each time a comparison is performed so that the area where the desired element is located is determined in an efficient manner. As can be seen from the example above, the result of the calculation, the value "10," is stored in the subscript field to be used as the subscript in determining which element within the table is compared to the item number in the card input. Thus, in this example the 10th item in the table will be examined.

Step 4:   The Lower Limit value is compared to the value in the subscript to determine if all of the elements in the table have been searched.

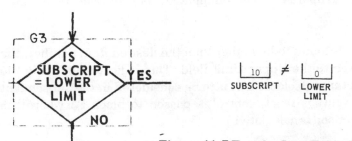

Figure 11-7 Test for Last Table Element

As was noted in Chapter 10, whenever a table search is to take place, the possibility always exists that the item number being searched for in the table will not be stored in the table and, if this occurs, an error message must be written. When a binary search is being performed, the entire table will have been searched when the value calculated for the subscript is equal to the value in the Lower Limit. Thus, a comparison must be performed to determine if this is the case. If so, an error message is written on the report. In the example above, it can be seen that they are not equal, so the table search will continue.

Step 5:   The Item in the card is compared with the Item Number in the table corresponding to the entry represented by the subscript value.

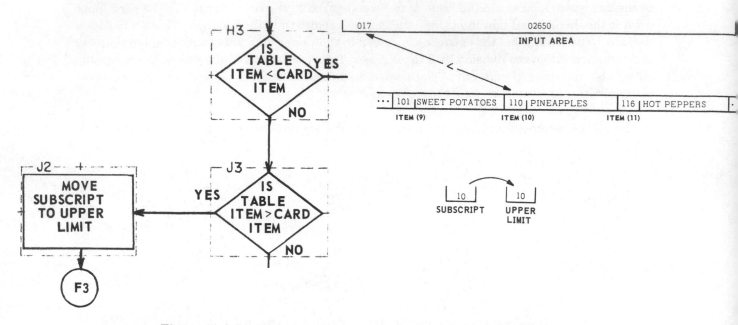

Figure 11-8 Card Item Number is Compared to Item Number (10)

In the example above, it can be seen that the value in the subscript field, "10," is used to determine that the tenth element in the table is to be the first compared to the item number in the card. The tenth item number in the table is Item Number 110, which is greater than the item number in the card, 017. Thus, the "no" path of the decision symbol in block H3 is taken and the "yes" path of the decision symbol in block J3 is taken. When the entry in the table is greater than the entry in the card, it means that all item numbers higher in the table than the one compared, that is, the item numbers in table elements 11-19, will also be higher than the desired item number in the card. Thus, the upper half of the table may be removed from consideration because it is known that the desired item number could not possibly be stored there. Thus, as desired, the first comparison has eliminated half of the table from consideration.

When the item number in the table is found to be higher than the desired item number, the computed subscript value (10) is moved to the Upper Limit field. This indicates that only the lower half of the table, from element 1 through element 9, is to be considered in the subsequent comparisons. After the Upper Limit value is reset, control is passed to block F3 where the subscript to be used for the next comparison is calculated.

Step 6:   The subscript is calculated for the second comparison.

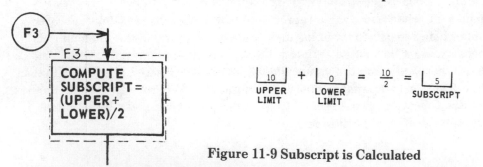

Figure 11-9 Subscript is Calculated

Note from Figure 11-9 that the same calculation is used to determine the second subscript as was used for the first subscript, that is, the value in the Upper Limit field is added to the value in the Lower Limit field and the sum is then divided by 2. As can be seen, the subscript to be used in the second comparison is "5," which is the answer obtained when 0 is added to 10 and divided by 2. Thus, the fifth element within the table will be compared to the desired item number in the input card. It should be noted that 5 is the midpoint between 0 and 10 and again, dependent upon the results of the comparisons, the table will be split in half for subsequent comparisons, if they are necessary.

Step 7:   **The test for the end of the table search is performed and then the comparisons with the item numbers take place.**

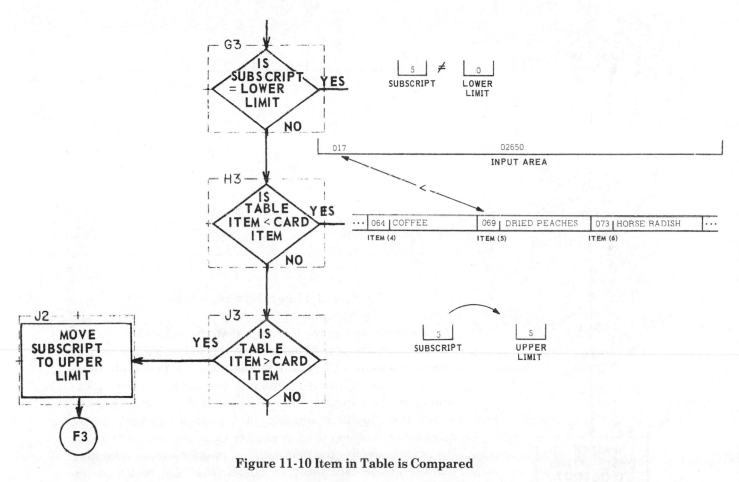

Figure 11-10 Item in Table is Compared

Note from the example above that the fifth item number in the table, 069, is compared to the item number in the card input data. The fifth item number is compared because the value in the subscript field is "5" and the subscript determines which table element is to be involved in the comparison. When the fifth item number is compared to the item number in the card, it is again found that the table item number is greater than the card item number. Thus, as was illustrated previously, the subscript is moved to the upper limit field. Thus, only the first through the fourth table elements will be considered in the subsequent comparisons. After the subscript is moved to the Upper Limit field, control is again passed to block F3 where the next subscript to be used will be calculated.

Step 8:   The subscript is calculated and the comparisons again take place.

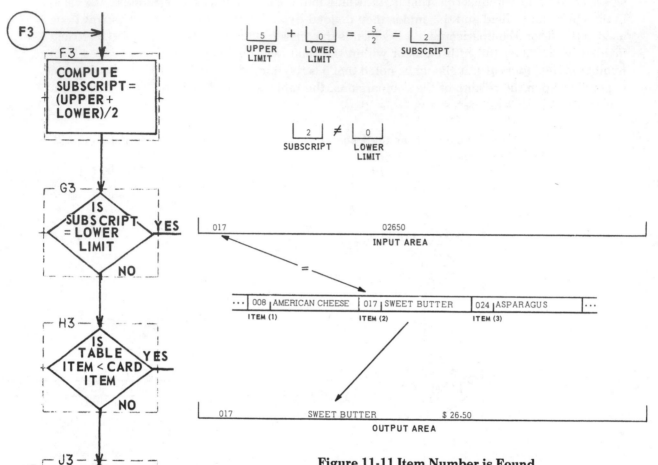

Figure 11-11 Item Number is Found

Note from the example above that the subscript value is calculated in the same manner as used previously. The answer to the division is "2," with a remainder of 1. Remainders are not considered when the subscript is calculated. When the comparisons are made in steps H3 and J3 of the flowchart, it is found that the item number in the table element being compared is not less than or greater than the item number in the card; therefore, the item number in the table and the item number in the card must be equal. This will result in the description from the table being moved to the output area (Step K3).

After the description is moved to the output area, control is passed to block G5 where the item number and the amount are moved to the output area and the line is printed.

Step 9: The item number and description are moved to the output area and the line is printed.

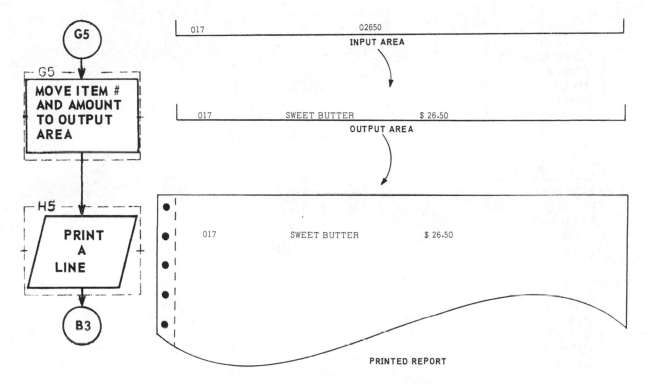

Figure 11-12 Line is Printed on the Report

After the description is moved from the table to the output area, the Item Number and the Amount are moved to the output area and the line is printed on the report. After the line is printed, control is returned to block B3 where the next data card is read.

Step 10: The second data card is read.

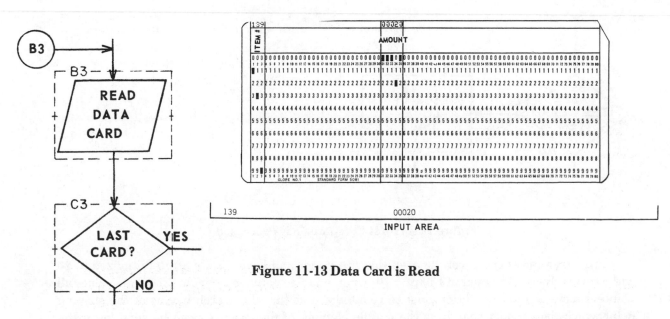

Figure 11-13 Data Card is Read

Step 11:   The Upper and Lower Limits are initialized and the comparisons are performed.

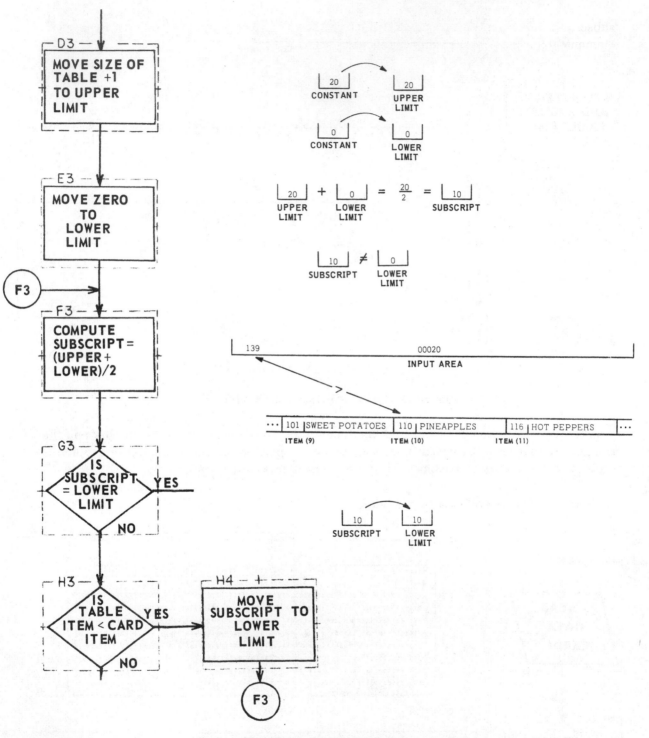

Figure 11-14 First Comparison is Processed

In the example above it can be seen that the upper and lower limits are reinitialized to 20 and 0 respectively. As noted in Chapter 10, when a table search is to begin for a new value, all pointers including the subscript must be reinitialized so that the search begins at the starting point which, in a binary search, is the middle element of the table. As can be seen, after the subscript is calculated, the tenth element in the table is compared to the item in the card and the item in the card is found to be higher than the item in the table.

When the item number in the card is higher than the item number in the table, it means that the desired item number must be in the upper half of the table, that is, the item number cannot be less than the middle item number in the table. Thus, the lower half of the table may be eliminated from consideration in searching for the desired item number. In order to do this, the subscript is moved to the lower limit field. This allows only the eleventh through the nineteenth elements to be considered in subsequent comparisons.

After the lower limit is established, control is passed to block F3 in order to recalculate the next subscript to be used in the comparisons.

Step 12:   The subscript is recalculated and the next comparison takes place.

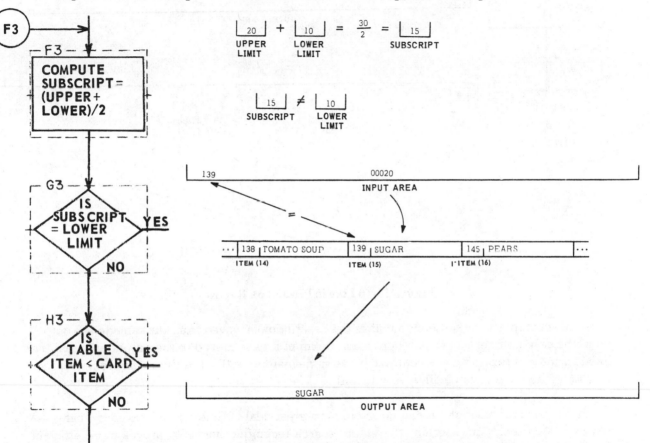

Figure 11-15 The Item Number is Found

Note in the example above that the subscript is calculated as "15," so the fifteenth element in the table is compared to the desired item number in the input card. As can be seen, the item number in the table is equal to the item number in the input card. Thus, since they are equal, the corresponding description is moved to the output area to be printed.

Step 13: The Item Number and the Amount is moved to the output area and the line is printed.

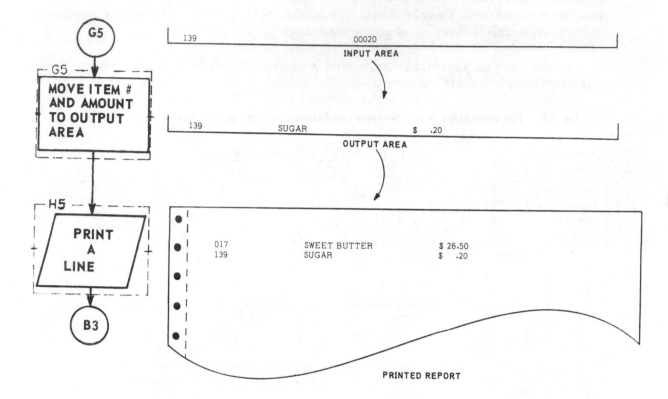

Figure 11-16 Line is Printed on Report

In the example it can be seen that after the description is moved from the table to the output area, the item number and the amount from the input area is moved to the output area and the line is printed. Processing will continue in the same manner until all of the cards are processed, at which time the program will be terminated.

In the previous example, it can be seen how a great deal of time may be saved by using the binary search technique. Again, the binary search technique normally proves more efficient than a sequential search when the table arguments may be placed in an ascending or descending sequence. If the table cannot be sorted, it is not possible to use the binary search technique.

CHAPTER 11

FLOWCHARTING ASSIGNMENT 1

INSTRUCTIONS

On a Flowchart Worksheet draw a flowchart to illustrate the logic to perform a binary search of a table containing 5000 item numbers and related unit costs of grocery products. In addition, a report is to be prepared to determine the gross profit of weekly sales.

INPUT: Sales Cards

Input is to consist of Sales Cards containing the Item Number, Description, Quantity Sold and Sales Amount of each product sold.

OUTPUT: Gross Profit Report

Output is to consist of a report reflecting the Gross Profit on sales for the week. Gross Profit is obtained by subtracting the Cost Amount of the Products sold from the Sales Amount. To determine the Cost Amount it is necessary to extract the Unit Cost of each item sold from a table and multiply the Unit Cost by the Quantity Sold field which is contained in the input data cards. A segment of the table and an illustration of the output report is contained below.

Table:

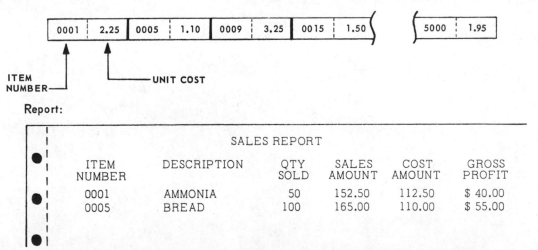

Report:

	SALES REPORT				
ITEM NUMBER	DESCRIPTION	QTY SOLD	SALES AMOUNT	COST AMOUNT	GROSS PROFIT
0001	AMMONIA	50	152.50	112.50	$ 40.00
0005	BREAD	100	165.00	110.00	$ 55.00

CHAPTER 11

FLOWCHARTING ASSIGNMENT 2

INSTRUCTIONS

On a Flowchart Worksheet draw a flowchart to illustrate the logic to search two tables to determine the Metal Cost, Shipping Weight, Shipping Charges, and Total Cost of specific metal types which have been ordered from a company.

INPUT: Sales Cards

Input is to consist of Sales Cards that contain the Part Number (which indicates a type of metal), and the size (length and width) of products ordered. The input cards are illustrated below.

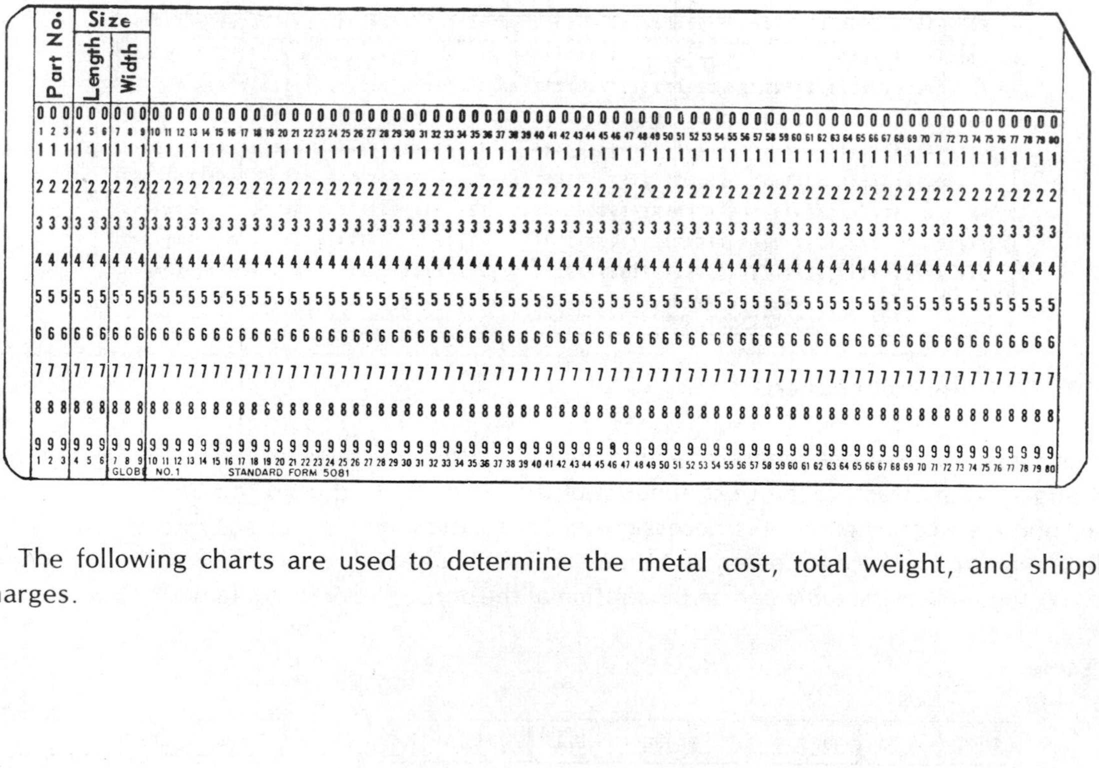

The following charts are used to determine the metal cost, total weight, and shipping charges.

CHART I

WEIGHT/COST PER SQUARE FOOT

PART NUMBER	DESCRIPTION	WEIGHT SQ/FT	COST SQ/FT
100	¼ Aluminum Alloy	3 lb.	1.25
101	½ Aluminum Alloy	2 lb.	2.00
102	¾ Aluminum Alloy	3 lb.	2.80
120	¼ Magnesium	1 lb.	3.75
121	½ Magnesium	2 lb.	7.00
122	¾ Magnesium	3 lb.	11.00

NOTE: Chart I Contains 500 Entries

CHART II

SHIPPING CHARGES
AREA 1

POUNDS	SHIPPING CHARGES
0-5	1.80
6-10	3.50
11-15	6.90
16-10	8.50
495-500	150.00

NOTE: Maximum Poundage 500 Lbs.

OUTPUT: Shipping Report

The output that is to be obtained is illustrated below. Note that the Metal Cost is obtained by: (1) determining the number of square feet of the metal type desired by multiplying the length field by the width field on the input data cards; (2) determining the Cost Per Square Foot from Chart I; (3) multiplying the number of square feet by the Cost Per Square Foot. For example, in the report below Part Number 100 is 2 feet in length and 2 feet in width for a total of 4 square feet. From Chart I it is determined that the Cost Per Square Foot is $1.25. By multiplying the number of square feet (4) by the Cost Per Square Foot ($1.25), the Metal Cost is obtained.

In addition the Shipping Weight and the Shipping Charges are to be determined from Charts I and II.

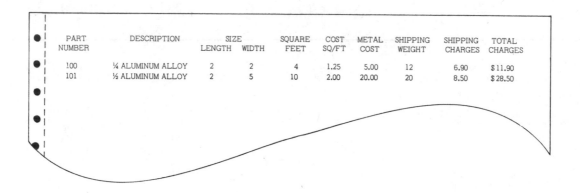

PART NUMBER	DESCRIPTION	SIZE LENGTH	WIDTH	SQUARE FEET	COST SQ/FT	METAL COST	SHIPPING WEIGHT	SHIPPING CHARGES	TOTAL CHARGES
100	¼ ALUMINUM ALLOY	2	2	4	1.25	5.00	12	6.90	$11.90
101	½ ALUMINUM ALLOY	2	5	10	2.00	20.00	20	8.50	$28.50

In the space below draw a diagram of the contents of the table or tables that are necessary to process the input data cards to produce the required report.

CHAPTER 12

INTERNAL SORT

INTRODUCTION

In Chapter 11 it was noted that the table which was searched using the binary search technique must be in ascending sequence based upon the item number. The methods used to ensure that the item numbers in the table are sorted are many. Perhaps the most common, especially with small tables with few elements, is to include the table as constants within the program. An alternative method is to load the table within the desired elements when the program is executed. The elements within the table are then sorted within the program and the binary search may then take place. The program in this chapter illustrates a technique which may be used to load the table into main storage from card input and then sort the table into the proper sequence to be used for the binary search.

The input to the program consists of cards which contain both the item number and the description. The format is illustrated below.

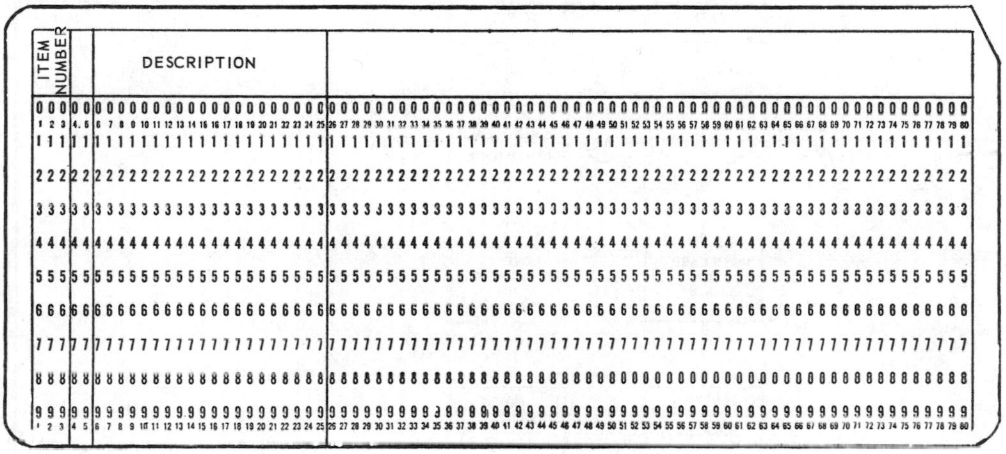

Figure 12-1 Card Format

Note from the card format illustrated above that the item number and the description are contained on each card. In the example which is to follow, the following data will be used.

024	Asparagus
017	Sweet Butter
008	American Cheese
069	Dried Peaches
064	Coffee

Note from the data illustrated that the item numbers are not in the ascending sequence required for a binary search operation. Thus, after they are loaded into the table, they will be sorted prior to beginning the binary search. The flowchart for the sort is illustrated below.

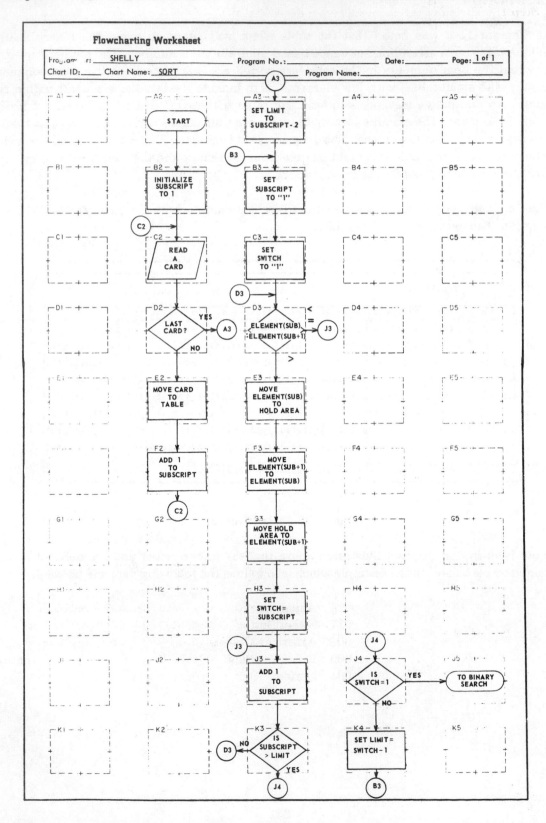

Figure 12-2 Flowchart

The steps involved in loading the table and then performing the sort operation are explained in detail on subsequent pages.

Step 1:   The subscript is initialized and a card is read.

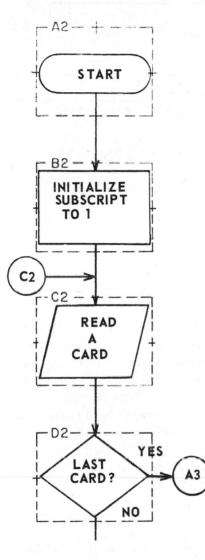

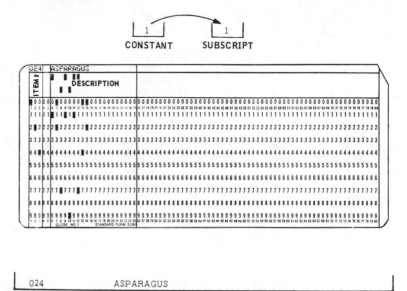

024   ASPARAGUS

INPUT AREA

Figure 12-3 Subscript is Initialized and a Card is Read

In the example above it can be seen that the value "1" is moved to the subscript area. As has been noted previously, whenever a reference is to be made to a table, the subscript should be initialized to the proper value prior to entering the routine which is to process the table. In this example, each card which is read is to be moved to an element within the table, beginning with the first element in the table. Thus, before the first card is read, the value in the subscript is set to "1" so that after the first card is read, it will be moved to the first element in the table.

A card is then read into the card input area. As with all previous input operations, a test must be performed to determine if the last input record has been read. In this example, of course, it has not so the "no" path on the decision symbol is taken.

Step 2:   The data in the card is moved to the table and the subscript is incremented by one.

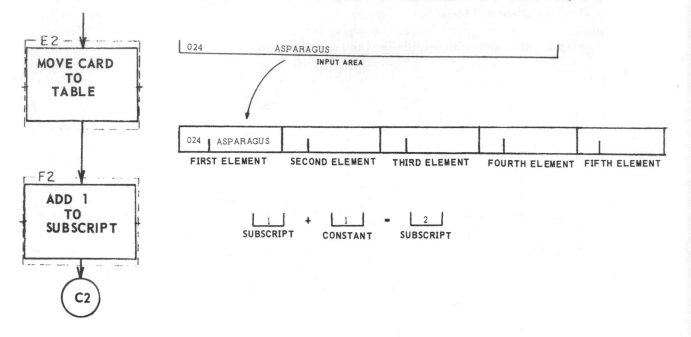

Figure 12-4 Data is Moved to Table and Subscript is Incremented

Note from the example above that the data which is read from the card and stored in the card input area is moved to the first element in the table. It is moved to the first element because the value in the subscript is "1," which indicates the first element is to be the one referenced. The remaining elements of the table do not contain any values because they are to be filled from the cards which are subsequently read. The value in the subscript field is then incremented by one so that the next card which is read will be moved into the second element of the table. Control is then passed to block C2 Where the next card will be read and processed.

In this example, five cards are to be read and placed in the table. After they are read, the table and the value in the subscript will appear as shown in Figure 12-5.

EXAMPLE

024 ASPARAGUS	017 SWEET BUTTER	008 AMERICAN CHEESE	069 DRIED PEACHES	064 COFFEE
FIRST ELEMENT	SECOND ELEMENT	THIRD ELEMENT	FOURTH ELEMENT	FIFTH ELEMENT

6
SUBSCRIPT

Figure 12-5 Table After Being Loaded

Note from Figure 12-5 that after the data has been read and processed, the table contains five elements which contain the values from the card input. Note also, however, that the item numbers are not in an ascending sequence as required for a binary search for the table. Therefore, the elements within the table must be sorted on the item number prior to being searched. Thus, when the last data card is read, the routine in block A3 is entered (see Figure 12-3).

Step 3: Values are initialized for the Sort routine.

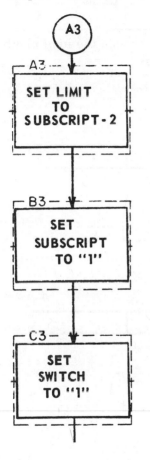

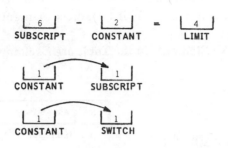

Figure 12-6 Values are Initialized

Note from Figure 12-6 that three values are initialized—a Limit value, the Subscript value, and a Switch value. The limit value is used to determine the number of "passes" which are required in order to sort the given data. It should always contain the number of items to be sorted less one. Since the subscript value which was generated when the table was loaded contains the number of elements plus 1 which were placed in the table, it is possible to subtract two from the value in order to obtain the value for the limit field. The subscript field will contain the subscript used to reference the table and it must be set to one prior to beginning the sort operation. The Switch field is used to determine when the sort has been completed. It should be initialized with the value one.

Step 4:   The first element in the table is compared to the second element in the table.

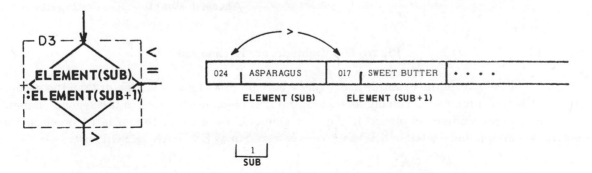

Figure 12-7 First Element is Compared to Second Element

Note from the example in Figure 12-7 that the item number in the first element is compared to the item number in the second element and that the first item number is greater than the second item number. Note also from the flowchart that the first item number is represented as ELEMENT(SUB) and the second item number is represented as ELEMENT(SUB+1). The "SUB" refers to the value which is stored in the subscript field. Thus, ELEMENT(SUB) refers to the first element or item number in the table and ELEMENT(SUB+1) refers to the second element or item number because the subscript field contains the value "1." As the sort progresses, the value in the subscript field will be increased by these references to the elements within the table will still be valid.

When the item number represented by ELEMENT(SUB) is greater than the item number represented by ELEMENT(SUB+1), these elements must be exchanged.

Step 5:   **The Elements in the Table are Exchanged.**

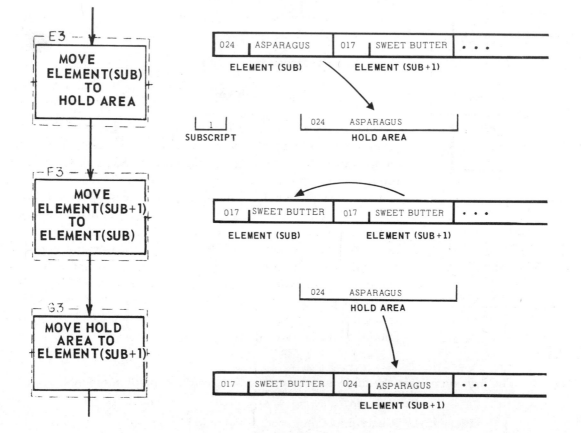
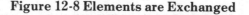

Figure 12-8 Elements are Exchanged

It can be seen from the example above that when the first element is greater than the second element, the elements are exchanged, that is, the first element is placed in the second element and the second element is placed in the first element. Because of this type of process, the sorting technique illustrated in this example is referred to as EXCHANGE SORTING.

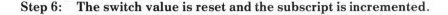

As can be seen from this first step in the sorting process, the element with the higher item number is placed in a higher position within the table. This is the basic job which must be accomplished with each pass of routine, that is, the element with the highest item number must be placed in the highest entry in the table.

Step 6:   The switch value is reset and the subscript is incremented.

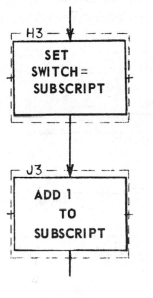

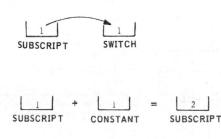

Figure 12-9 Switch and Subscript are Altered

As can be seen, the value in the subscript field is moved to the switch field. This is done so that it may be determined if the end of the sort has been reached, as will be illustrated. The subscript is then incremented by one so that the next elements in the table may be compared.

Step 7:   A check is made to determine if the first "pass" of the sort is complete.

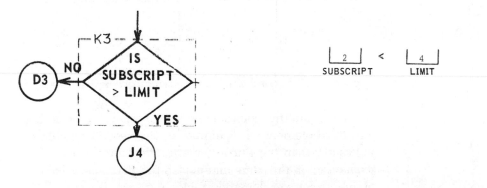

Figure 12-10 Subscript is Compared to Value in Limit Field

In the example above, the value in the incremented subscript field is compared to the value in the Limits field to determine if the first pass through the table has been completed. In most instances, it requires more than one pass through the table in order to place the elements within the table in the prescribed sequence. This test is performed to determine if a pass has been completed and if a test should be made to determine if the sort is complete. Since the value in the subscript field is less than the value in the limit field, a pass has not been completed and control is returned to block D3 where the next elements in the table are compared.

Step 8:   The second and third elements in the table are compared and processed.

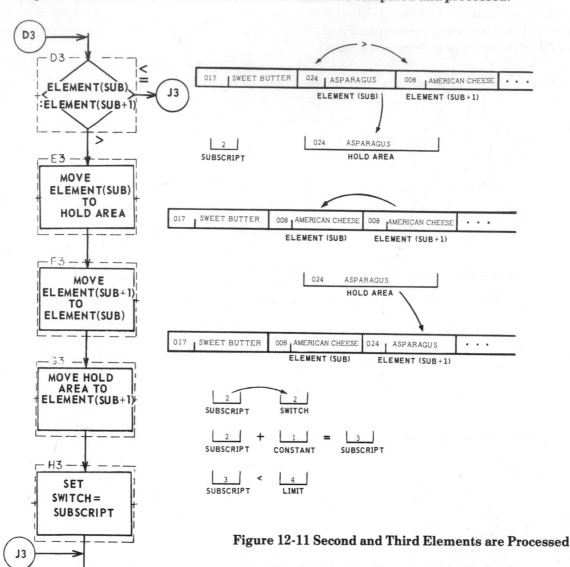

Figure 12-11 Second and Third Elements are Processed

Note from the example above that when the second and third elements are compared, the second element is greater than the third element. Therefore, they are exchanged in the same manner as the first and second elements were exchanged previously. Also, the value in the Switch field is changed to "2" and the subscript is incremented by 1. When the comparison between the subscript and the limit field takes place, it is found that the subscript is still less than the value in the limit field. Therefore, control is again returned to block D3 to process the third and fourth elements of the table.

Step 9: **The third and fourth elements of the table are compared and processed.**

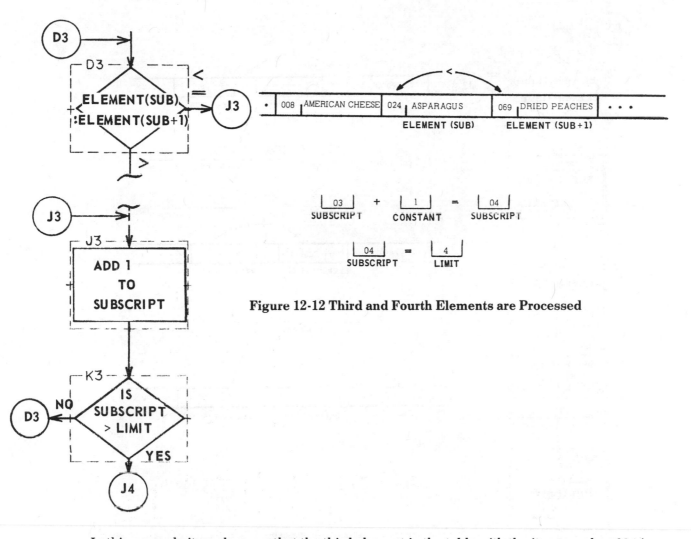

Figure 12-12 Third and Fourth Elements are Processed

In this example it can be seen that the third element in the table with the item number 024 is less than the fourth element with the item number 069. When the element being referenced with the value in the subscript field is less than the value being referenced by the value in the subscript field plus one, no exchange takes place. Thus, since 024 is less than 069, the two elements in the table will not be exchanged; rather, they will remain in the same sequence. The routine at block J3 is entered when this situation occurs and the subscript is incremented by 1. The comparison is then performed to determine if all of the table has been processed in the first pass. Since the subscript value is equal to the limit value, it indicates that there is still one element within the table to be processed before the entire table has been processed the first time. Thus, control is passed to block D3 in order to process the last element in the table.

Step 10:   The fourth and fifth elements of the table are compared and processed.

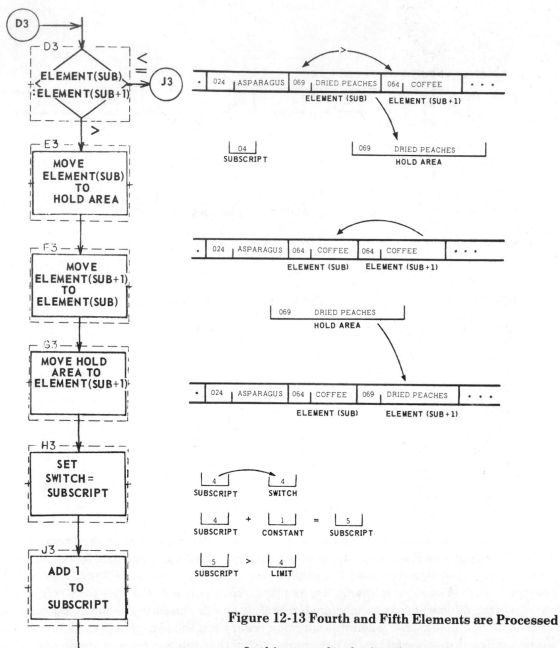

Figure 12-13 Fourth and Fifth Elements are Processed

In this example, the fourth element contains an item number that is less than the item number in the fifth element. Thus, as illustrated previously, the two elements must be exchanged in the table. When the subscript is compared to the limit value, it is found that the subscript is greater than the limit value. Because of this, the routine in block J4 is entered.

Step 11: When the first pass of the table is completed, a check is made to determine if the entire table is in the desired sequence.

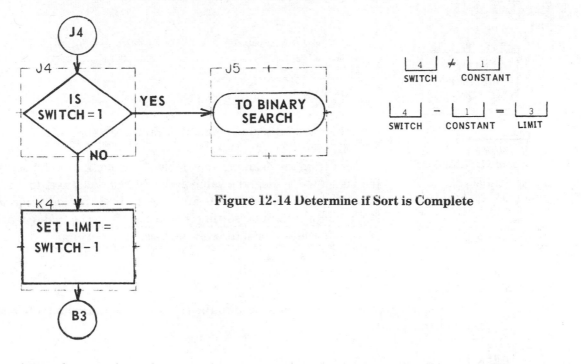

Figure 12-14 Determine if Sort is Complete

As can be seen from the example in Figure 12-14, the value in the Switch field is compared to the value "1." If they are equal, it indicates that the sort is complete. It should be recalled that, when this routine is entered, the value in Switch is equal to the value in the Subscript field from the last time an exchange of table elements was performed (see Figure 12-13). In addition, it can be seen from the results obtained in Figure 12-13 that after the first pass through the table, the table element with the highest item number has been placed in the right-most element of the table. Successive passes through the table will place the next highest item number to the left of the highest item number in the table. The sort will be complete when the only exchanges which take place in a sort pass is the exchange between the first element in the table and the second element in the table. When this happens, the value in switch will be equal to "1" at the end of the pass and the sort routine may exit to the Binary Search routine which may then perform the table search.

In the example, however, the value in Switch is not equal to "1." Therefore, the sort is not complete. As noted, however, the proper element has been placed in the right-most element of the table. Thus, it is no longer necessary to consider this element in the remaining sort passes. The elimination of this table element from consideration is accomplished by setting the Limit value to the value in the Switch less one. Thus, as can be seen from the example above, the value in the Limit field will be equal to "4 - 1" or "3." When the table is sorted on the next pass, only the first four elements within the table will be considered in the sort and the fifth element will be left as is.

After the value in the Limit field is set, control is passed to block B3 where the subscript is reinitialized and the second sort pass is begun.

Step 12: The Subscript field and the Switch field are reinitialized to begin the second pass of the sort processing.

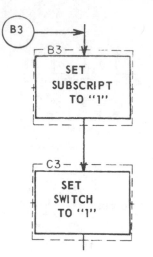

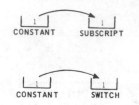

Figure 12-15 Subscript and Switch are Reinitialized

Note from the example above that the value in the Subscript field is set to "1" and the value in the Switch field is set to "1." These are the values which must be in these fields prior to beginning the actual sorting process. After the values are entered in these fields, the sort processing may begin.

Step 13: The first element in the table is compared to the second element in the table and they are processed.

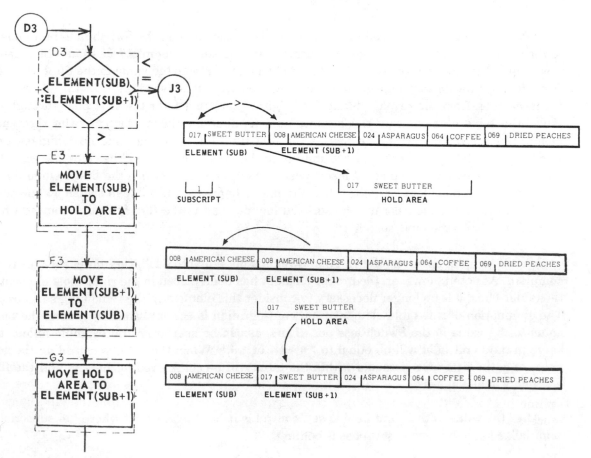

Figure 12-16 First and Second Elements are Processed

Note from Figure 12-16 that the first element of the table, which is referenced through the use of the value in the Subscript field, is greater than the value in the second element of the table, which is referenced by the value in the Subscript field plus one. Thus, these elements are exchanged as illustrated in previous examples. Whenever the element referenced by the value in the Subscript field is greater than the element referenced by the value in the Subscript field plus one, the elements are exchanged.

After the elements are exchanged, the value in the Switch field must be set and the subscript is updated.

Step 14:   The Switch field is reset, the subscript is incremented, and the test is performed to determine if the second pass is complete.

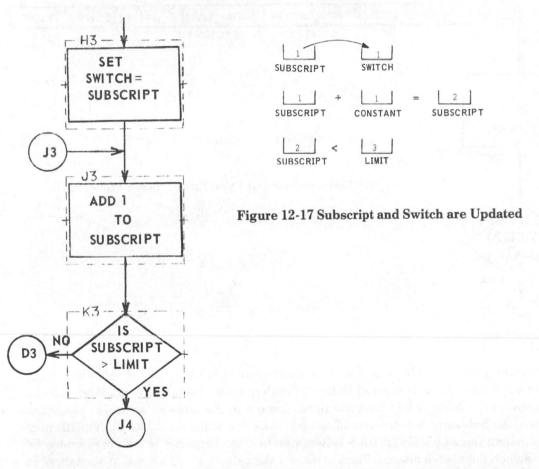

Figure 12-17 Subscript and Switch are Updated

In the example above it can be seen that the value in the subscript field is moved to the value in the Switch field. As noted previously, the value in the switch field indicates the elements which were exchanged. In this case, the first element was exchanged. The subscript is then incremented by one so that it can point to the next element in the table. When the subscript is compared to the value in the Limit field, it is found that the subscript is less; therefore, the routine in block D3 is entered so that the second and third elements within the table may be processed.

Step 15:   The second and third elements are processed.

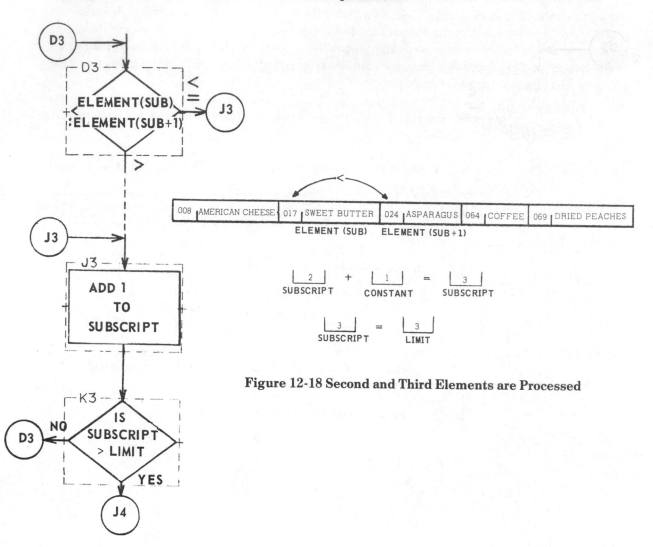

Figure 12-18 Second and Third Elements are Processed

In the example above it can be seen that the second element in the table, as specified by the value "2" in the Subscript, is compared to the third element in the table. It is found that the second element in the table is less than the third element in the table so control is passed to block J3 where the Subscript is incremented by one. Note that when the ELEMENT(SUB) item number is less than the ELEMENT(SUB+1) item number, the subscript is incremented by the value in the Switch field is not altered. Thus, it retains the value "1" which was placed there in Figure 12-17. This is important because the value in the Switch field is used to determine when the sort is complete.

When the subscript is compared to the value in the Limit field, they are found to be equal. Thus, control is returned to block D3 so that the third and fourth elements in the table may be processed.

Step 16:   The third and fourth elements are processed.

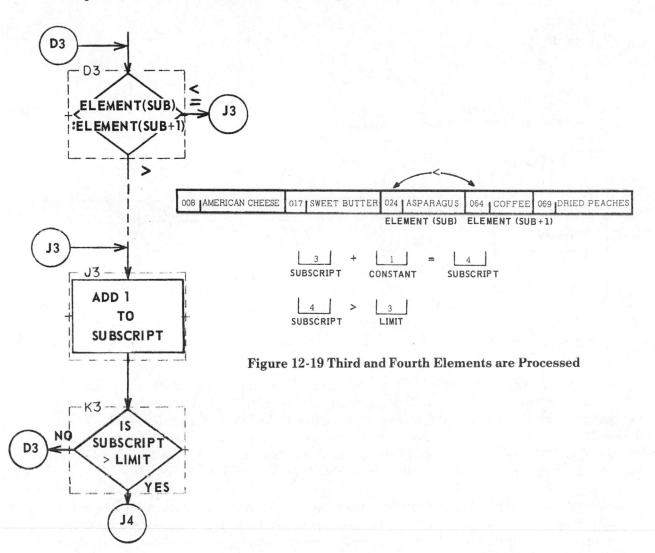

Figure 12-19 Third and Fourth Elements are Processed

Note from the example above that the item number in the third element of the table is less than the item number in the fourth element of the table. Thus, as in the example, the value in the Subscript field is greater than the value in the Limit field, thus indicating that the second pass of sort has been completed. Note that the fifth element in the table was not involved in the second pass of the sort. This is because it is known that the fifth element contains the highest item number in the table and thus need not be compared to any of the other item numbers in the table. When the subscript is greater than the value in the Limit field, the routine in block J4 is entered to determine if the sort is complete.

Step 17:   A check is made to determine if the sort is complete.

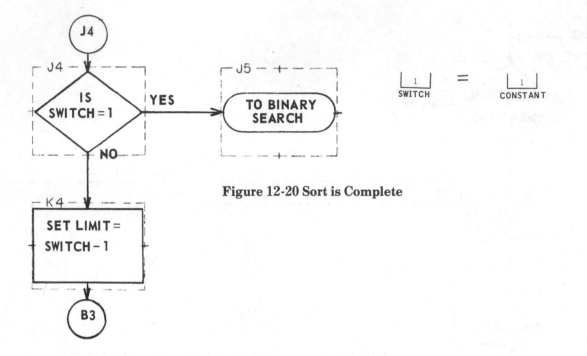

Figure 12-20 Sort is Complete

Note from Figure 12-20 that when the value in the Switch field is compared to a constant of "1," they are found to be equal. This indicates that the sort is complete because the only exchange which took place in the sort pass was between the first and second elements of the table. If an exchange had taken place at any higher element, the value in the Switch field would not be one. Thus, the sort is complete and, as illustrated in Figure 12-19, the entire table is in an ascending sequence based upon the item number in each element of the table.

As noted previously, when the sort is complete, that is, when the elements in the table are in ascending sequence, the binary search table look-up may then take place because the table is in the proper order. Thus, when the sort is complete, control may be passed to the routine which would perform the table look-up.

CHAPTER 12

FLOWCHARTING ASSIGNMENT 1

INSTRUCTIONS

Another sorting technique called the "shuttle-interchange" sort or the "pushdown and bubble" sort involves examining a list of numbers, finding a low value and inserting the low value in its proper location within the list.

For example if the following 5 numbers are to be sorted using a "pushdown and bubble" sort the following steps would take place:

Numbers To Be Sorted: 5 4 6 1 2

Step 1:

Before: 5 4 6 1 2

After: 4 5 6 1 2 - 5 is compared to 4, since 4 is lower the numbers are interchanged.

Step 2:

Before: 4 5 6 1 2

After: 4 5 6 1 2 - 5 is compared to 6, as 5 is less than 6 no interchange takes place.

Step 3:

Before: 4 5 6 1 2

After: 4 5 1 6 2 - 6 is compared to 1, since 1 is lower the two numbers are interchanged.

Step 4:

Before: 4 5 1 6 2

After: 4 1 5 6 2 - 5 is compared to 1, since 1 is lower the numbers are interchanged. Note that the proper location for the 1 is determined by stepping back through the list of numbers to be sorted.

Step 5:

Before: 4 1 5 6 2

After: 1 4 5 6 2 -   4 is compared to 1, since 1 is lower the numbers are interchanged. Note that the proper location for 1 has been found so comparison can proceed with the highest number that has been found thus far in the list which in the example is the number 6.

Step 6:

Before: 1 4 5 6 2

After: 1 4 5 2 6 -   6 is compared to 2, since 2 is lower the numbers are interchanged.

Step 7:

Before: 1 4 5 2 6

After: 1 4 2 5 6 -   5 is compared to 2, since 2 is lower the numbers are interchanged.

Step 8:

Before: 1 4 2 5 6

After: 1 2 4 5 6 -   4 is compared to 2, since 2 is lower the numbers are interchanged.

Step 9:

Before: 1 2 4 5 6

After: 1 2 4 5 6 -   1 is compared to 2, since 1 is less than 2 no interchange takes place.

Step 10:   The comparison should again proceed with the highest number that has been found, thus far in the list which in the example is 6, since there are no more numbers in the list to be compared to 6, the sort is complete.